Just a Girl and a

Bike

An Unexpected Adventure

in Finding Myself

Kerri,
Always follow ♡
your dreams

Julie Minn

Just a Girl and a Bike

An Unexpected Adventure in Finding Myself

Julie Hiner

Just a Girl and a Bike © 2016 Julie Hiner

Printed in the USA

First Printing 2016

Publisher: Julie Hiner: **powerpuffjd@gmail.com**
Editing by: Elyssa Gutbrod: Elyssa: **elyssa.gutbrod@gmail.com**

Photos of the Paris Roubaix finish and Brugge taken by Gregg Germer: **info@thechainstay.com, www.chainstay.com**

All other photos by Julie and James Hiner

Cover design by Julie Hiner

Visit the author's website at **JustAGirlAndABike.com**

First Edition

I dedicate this book to my husband, James. Without him, I would not have met my bike, climbed mountains, and faced my fears. He has created so many adventures that have changed my life, and that have changed me. He has always been there to tell me that I can, and has always believed in me even when I did not.

CONTENTS

Just a Girl and a Bike

INTRODUCTION

'Try and fail, but never fail to try.' – Jared Leto -
Contributed by Diane Bowles

Something strange happens when you describe your dreams to other people, especially when you talk about those dreams coming true. When dreams come up in conversation, people spout things like, "nice pipe dream," or some other platitude. It makes you stop to wonder why. Why can't dreams become reality?

Dreams can, in fact, come true. Don't ever let someone else convince you that you can't or won't be able to accomplish something. Don't ever let someone else take away your dreams. You, and only you, hold the power to make your future whatever you want it to be. You absolutely must follow your deepest passion and find the thing that makes your heart ache with longing, the thing that truly makes you tick. Follow your dreams, and you and your life will absolutely change for the better. You will be better at every other aspect of your life because of it.

It's okay to not know what your passion is. You can find it. Personally, I had no idea what my dreams were when I started out on the journey that I describe in this book. I had no idea that my dreams would start with a bike – a Trek 2000 Women's Special Design, to be exact. The person I once was had no idea what was coming.

I was a studious individual dedicated to higher learning and a respectable career. Given my young age, I was far too serious and boring. I can't regret who I was when I reflect back on my past, but I am grateful for the person I have become thanks to three key things:

My husband James, who became my cycling partner, coach, and navigator

My Trek 2000 bike

A famous mountain in the French Alps known as Alpe d'Huez

These components were the cornerstones of my transformation into someone new who can identify her passions in a heartbeat. When I say passions, I refer to those things that one cannot live without, that make one's soul tick. I wholeheartedly believe that the road to happiness and finding one's true self can only be traveled once you learn where your passion lies.

This book is the story of how I found my biggest passion with the help and guidance of my true love and best friend. My passion for cycling is endless. When I feel like I can't go on, it is my passion that makes me dig deep and find another gear within myself. There are times when cycling leaves me feeling absolutely broken, yet I am always left wanting more.

My journey has taken many twists and turns along the way, each of which have left their mark on me with important life lessons and some of my dearest memories. I have found my inner athlete, discovered a mental toughness that I would have never dreamed I possessed, and learned that there is a whole world filled with rich culture out there. Traveling by bike has led me to new places that I would have never found otherwise. It has lead me to new friendships that would have gone undiscovered if I had travelled any other way.

When I am cycling, I have the most fun I have had in my life. It makes me feel strong. It makes me feel free. It humbles me. For me, it is the most satisfying and rewarding experience I've ever had and I can't imagine a life without it.

GIRL MEETS BIKE

'Life is short, live fast!' – Contributed by Ronald Ronald

Growing up, I was never an athletic person. I was the child that hated gym class, hiding from the ball and hoping to avoid being singled out by the teacher for my lack of participation. Despite my effort to become invisible during gym class, one teacher in particular seemed to love calling me out. The worst part was that he couldn't even remember my name, which embarrassed me terribly and made me even more self-conscious about my inadequacies than I already was.

One of my worst memories is of the annual fitness test where I had to prove how many sit ups and pull ups I could do. I could never conceive of a situation in which I might actually need to pull my entire body weight up with my arms. The whole thing was painful and pointless in my mind, and the more I grew to believe that, the less interested I was in participating in that fitness test, or indeed in sports of any kind.

Physical activity seemed more like a form of torture than an enjoyable pastime when I was younger. At the time, I was completely uncomfortable with my physical being, and unaware of its potential power. I was absolutely a bookworm, prone to losing myself in an author's world instead of getting outside and experiencing my own reality. In addition to my tendency to withdraw into books, my short, chunky stature was also not on my side when it came to physical activities. While my fellow classmates received patches in bronze, silver, and gold for their jackets for their physical achievements, I was lucky to earn paper participation cards. I would have preferred to read a book.

When I graduated from high school and moved on to the world of post-secondary education, it became possible to completely avoid the whole realm of physical activity. I was in heaven. This was fine for a while, until the junk food and lack of activity caught up with my 4 foot 10 inch frame in a big way! Before I knew it, I had blown up up like a blowfish.

Not being a fan of diets or quick fixes, I consulted with my doctor to find a healthy way to lose weight. I was soon following a regular regiment of well-balanced eating according to Canada's food guide, coupled with regular visits to the gym. Over time, my success with this routine fluctuated. The truth is, I like to eat, and I don't do well with restrictions in the long term. I also find that going to the gym is fine when I have a weight loss goal, but without that motivation I don't stick with it. My weight fluctuated like a sine wave, falling when I felt the urge to diet and exercise, and then rising when I inevitably stopped. I had no real reason to make a diet and exercise regimen a regular part of my life, and thus had no lasting motivation to put forth the effort required to keep up with it.

My love affair with my bike actually has its origins in another love, and only began after my longtime boyfriend, James, proposed. Both of us wanted a different, healthier lifestyle together in the long term, and the wedding date was a tangible goal that we could use as motivation to make an ambitious change. I rose to the challenge, eating well and exercising regularly. My routine became a comfortable one, filled with visits to the gym and familiar jogging paths, and it felt good, almost like an old sweater. Knowing that this effort would leave me looking incredible on my wedding day kept me going, even when I felt the urge to stop.

While I frequented the gym, James chose to revisit an old passion of his own: cycling. I gradually learned that James used to do a fair amount of road cycling when he was younger. In order to get back into that groove, he purchased a low-end mountain bike. As the weather improved over the course of spring in Calgary, he spent an increasing amount of time going for rides. It soon became obvious that if I wanted to spend much time with my husband-to-be, I would need to see if I could share his interest in cycling.

Now that I knew what I had to do, I dug my old clunker of a bike out of the closet and started hitting the road with him. Prior to my first outing with James, my idea of a bike ride was to cycle casually on the bike paths for an hour or so. I quickly learned that James's idea of a bike ride was completely different. The first time we set out, I had to maintain what I perceived as an unreasonable pace in order to stand any chance at all of not losing sight of him. He was always so far ahead of me that I was afraid I might lose him. The ride seemed to go on forever.

That first ride set the pace for every one of our early outings. I am not sure how much I really enjoyed those rides, but I struggled through them the best I could. At the time, I was still hitting the gym for my predictable exercise routine and only rode with him occasionally. I was still at a point in my life where I lacked a real sense of adventure. I liked having a plan, I liked knowing what I was getting into, and I liked having control over every possible detail.

By the deadline of our wedding at end of the summer, we had both succeeded in getting into reasonable shape. I felt great about myself and wonderful in general, a sentiment that continued through our fantastic honeymoon and beyond. The cycling routine did not end here, however. After we had been back to reality for a couple of months post-honeymoon, my husband bought me a real road bike.

We wandered into a local higher end bike shop one November day, which turned out to be a bit of serendipity since the staff was clearing out old stock for the new year's models. As we browsed through the different bikes, we came upon the one that spoke to me in a way that none of the others did. There it was, the Trek 2000 women's special design, in my size, and a nice colour. We pulled it down so that I could try it out, and it fit. It was absolutely gorgeous! According to James, this beauty was a good bike for a reasonable price. I was ready to commit, and soon I was suited up with shoes, pedals, and tight-fitting clothing.

I left the store with my new treasures, a big smile, and absolutely no idea what I was getting myself into.

When we arrived home, James set up my new bike in our basement suite on an indoor trainer. The November weather wasn't conducive to outdoor cycling on a lightweight bike with thin tires, so the idea was that I would ride the bike indoors until the weather became more cooperative. My workout routine over the winter transformed into a daily spin session on the indoor trainer. Although I was constantly sore at first, my body gradually became used to the bike and accustomed to the seat. I enjoyed the morning spin sessions as an invigorating way to start the day, and it was very convenient to exercise without the commute to a gym.

Once winter once again transformed into spring and the weather outside became bearable, it was time for my first ride outdoors. I discovered right away that riding with clipless pedals is a totally different experience than what I had become accustomed to over the winter. I seemed unable to remember that my shoes were actually clipped into the pedals, so I would constantly come to a stop, panic, and fall over. Really, people walking by must have wondered what was wrong with me! I had to come up with a series of instructions that I would repeat to myself as I approached a stop: slow down, foot out, stop, foot down. It took a while, but functioning with clipless pedals did eventually become second nature even if I felt rather asinine at the time.

On our first trip out of the neighbourhood, I couldn't believe how nicely the bike rode. It was so light. Going up what I used to classify as hills felt so easy! This was the first time in my life that I had ever enjoyed a physical activity that I would consider a sport, and it felt amazing. My doubts seemed to melt away. I was having fun! I felt fast! I felt good!

It wasn't long before James inquired whether I was interested in going on a cycling trip. I think that in my mind a cycling trip involved leisurely rides through flat fields of flowers and long picnic lunches. It all sounded nice to me, so I agreed.

James planned a two week trip for us that would involve cycling through the French Alps. As he outlined his itinerary to me, I realized that he was quite keen on doing some of the famous climbs of the Tour de France. Great! I would get to go to Europe, get some fresh air, and eat! I didn't see a downside to this plan.

In retrospect, I don't think that either of us really knew what we were getting ourselves into when we naively booked the trip, although I do believe that James may have had a better idea than I did. In an effort to start helping me prepare, he started taking me out for rides that were longer and harder. Our cycling trips became less fun and more stressful. The more time we spent on our bikes, the more I grew to realize that I was much slower than James. I constantly felt like I was holding him back, and that he was always waiting for me. Instead of telling him this, I internalized my concerns and tried to push through it. The result was that I became more stressed and thus didn't have a chance to truly enjoy the rides or to perform to my greatest potential.

Eventually, my frustrations came out in an explosion of feelings right in the middle of a ride. There is something to be said about hard physical activity and the way it heightens your emotional state. What you are feeling is worn on your sleeve when you are physically exhausted. To my surprise, after hearing out my outpouring of emotions James made it clear to me that he wanted me out there with him and that he didn't care if he had to wait for me at times. We actually talked about solutions now that he knew there was a problem, and settled on arranging meeting points on our rides. We started seeking out routes with extra hills that he could do instead of waiting on me, which gave him the chance to bike more without my worrying that I was slowing him down. I started to once again enjoy our rides more, and to worry less.

Now that we had worked out a routine that allowed us to mutually enjoy cycling together, the next major step towards preparing for Europe was completing my first 100 km day, also known as a metric century ride. When James proposed the idea, all I could think was that 100 km sounded like a lot. I was right: it was.

On the day of our first century ride, we drove our bikes to the community of Westhills, which is near one of the major highways outside of Calgary. This community turned out to be one the prime spots for accessing the good cycling routes, and would eventually become our home. We parked the car, got set up on our bikes, and away we went towards the town of Bragg Creek.

The route was fairly flat since the primary goal of this outing was to cycle 100 km. We made it to Bragg Creek okay, but on the way back, I had my first real experience with a strong headwind. I was tired. My legs ached. The wind was strong. I wanted to stop.

For the first time in my life, I found myself in a situation in which stopping was not an option. We were biking alongside a highway with no way to get home but to continue on. Knowing this, I kept pedalling even though I was in agony. Eventually, we made it back on the edge of town. The end was in sight. I was so relieved that we were almost at the car.

My dreams of getting to the car and going home weren't quite ready to be realized, though. James informed me before we made it back to Westhills that we would not make our 100 km goal if we returned to the car quite yet. I couldn't believe my ears!

I can't say that I was graceful in my disagreement as I begrudgingly followed him into a neighbourhood where we continued to cycle until we reached our goal. I had never felt so physically spent in my life, but as we made our weary way back to the car I realized that I had also never felt so proud of my physical abilities. That was an incredible realization, and I have to admit that I wanted more.

I was so excited about this achievement that I told everyone at work the following Monday. I think the only one who really understood what an accomplishment this was for me was my co-worker Wade. Wade raced competitively as a road cyclist, and therefore had a true appreciation for the meaningfulness of a cyclist's first century ride. Being able to boast about a physical achievement that someone like Wade could relate to was a first for me. I hadn't exactly hung out in the circles that included the jocks in high school.

I had come a long way in a few months. I could ride a real road bike with clipless pedals. I had completed my first century ride. Looking forward to our Europe trip, I felt nothing but optimism. How hard could these French Alps be? No problem, right?

My First Cycling Trip

'If you think you can or think you can't, you're right.' -
Henry Ford - Contributed by Mark Doerksen

The Bavarian Forest

Our first cycling trip was two weeks long and divided into three parts. The first four days were to be spent in Germany, cycling through the Bavarian forest, followed by another three days in a small German town attending a wedding. Our final week would be spent cycling some of the famous mountains of the French Alps and then resting before heading home.

After a long flight followed by a train ride, we arrived in Munich with our backpacks in tow. I had never traveled so light in my life, let alone tried to live out of a backpack before this trip. To make things even more interesting, the contents of my backpack included cycling shoes, pedals, and a dress for the wedding in addition to my normal clothes. I was absolutely amazed to realize how little I actually need in my life.

Exhausted and disoriented, we groggily found the hotel we were to stay in for the night and quickly fell into a very deep sleep. The morning came much too quickly. Jetlagged and in a fog, I really just wanted to roll over and go back to sleep. My dear traveling companion, however, was eager to be on his way, so up I got. Once we made our way to the common room, I was delighted by the breakfast spread. This was my first real exposure to the European style breakfast that was customarily included with many hotel stays. Pastries, jams, cheeses, and of course, Nutella, were spread out beautifully on a long table. How delightful! Topping everything off was the wonderful, dark, strong European style coffee. I ate, and I ate, and I ate.

The next step was to walk over to the bike rental place that James had contacted prior to our trip. While he hadn't been able to procure road bikes for us, he had been able to find reasonable mountain style bikes that would do the trick. Cycling gear on, backpacks in tow, and pedals installed on the rental bikes, away we went.

The plan was simple: We would cycle through the lovely Bavarian forest and find places to stay along the way. All we had were our backpacks, our bikes, and a map that James had retrieved from a library book before we arrived. At this point in my life, I was still quite unadventurous and I still liked to have a plan to stick to. I didn't see myself as the kind of free spirit to go off gallivanting through Germany on a bicycle. Thank goodness that I had James at this time to push me beyond my comfort zone. Looking back, this excursion through the Bavarian forest may have been one of the key experiences of my life.

We rode, and we rode, and we rode. We biked along paths through vast fields, on paths with a ceiling of tree branches, on paths along the lake, and on open paths in the middle of the countryside. At one point we found ourselves in a big open field, surrounded by brilliant yellow mustard flowers. I looked around me, breathed in the air, and felt completely free. There was no detailed plan, no pressing timeline to stick with. It was just me, James, our bikes, and nature. We stopped for lunch at an Italian café in Starnberg to fuel up on pasta. I couldn't believe how hungry I was considering the amount of breakfast I had eaten, but every bite of food that was set before me seemed to disappear.

Once we were on our way again, the day went on, and on, and on. The afternoon started to fade, and evening began to descend. I felt like we had been cycling at this slow pace forever, and that the path we were traveling on might never end. As I struggled along, a couple of cyclists breezed by us on their road bikes. I looked at the woman with envy, and I thought to myself how I wished I could be that effortless, that smooth, that quick.

We stopped for a break in Percha and sat together by a lake. Against the backdrop of this scenic view, James put on his coaching hat and explained that we needed to pick up the pace if we wanted to make it to our goal before sundown. In return, I told him how tired I was and how hard this was for me. He was very understanding of my position, and urged me on in such a gentle way that I knew I had to try.

We climbed back on our bikes and pressed on. In my mind the journey seemed endless, but eventually we arrived at our destination town, Murnau. It was the most beautiful place I have ever seen. It literally looked like a postcard had come alive! Perfect little rows of shops and restaurants lined a cobblestone street, and there was not a speck of dirt or the tiniest piece of trash to be seen. Everything sparkled.

We cycled around looking for a place to stay. Our goal was to find a zimmer, which is a reasonably priced bed and breakfast establishment. We were so wrapped up in looking for the perfect place to spend the night that we didn't even realize we were on our way out of town. It was only when the buildings vanished and the countryside seemed to materialize again out of nowhere that we realized that we had lost our way, and that we had somehow lost the town. How could this be? We were just there!

I was completely depleted, desperate to find a way back to town, and so very hungry that I could barely think. Thank goodness I had an energy bar with me to gobble down. While I was eating my snack, James calmed me and put things into perspective. Even though we couldn't see the town, it couldn't be very far away. Once I had some food in me, I realized the logic of his words. We retraced our steps, found the town again, and thankfully secured a place to stay.

As soon as we made it to our room, we laid down on the bed side by side in utter exhaustion as we chatted about how hard this was. Hearing my seemingly-indefatigable husband admit that this wasn't easy and knowing that we were in this together was a balm to my weary soul.

After finding the motivation to get off the bed and make ourselves presentable, we walked through the town to find some dinner. As we took in our surroundings, our fatigue seemed to vanish. Murnau is a gem of a place. We were entranced by the beauty that we saw everywhere as we walked down the main street and gravitated towards the only place with people spilling out of it. There was an empty table on the outdoor patio under the stars, the perfect place to enjoy a well-deserved meal. James and I don't speak German, but our waiter in this little rural town spoke enough English to help us order. Soon we were eating delectable Greek-style food and enjoying German beer while reliving the highlights of the day. As we reminisced, I found myself amazed by everything that I had accomplished in a single day. There had been so much hard work, so much emotion, and so many new memories that our conversation seemed to flow from an endless well. Best of all, I came to the realization that my husband had now officially become my cycling partner and my navigator.

As the night cooled, everyone packed into the tiny restaurant and the servers brought out shooters infused with sparkles. To this day I don't know what the mysterious, sparkly drink was, but I remember vividly how magical that night felt. It didn't matter that we were strangers or that there was a language barrier that kept us from fully communicating; we were simply included in the joyful gathering of people around us.

The next morning came all too soon. We both were sore, tired, and wondering how we would get through another day of cycling. When our alarm went off, we both groaned as we rolled over and attempted to sit up. Everything hurt. As James attempted to put his contact lenses in, he exclaimed that his eyes were on fire. Just then, from the little radio on the nightstand, we heard Johnny Cash singing to us about a burning ring of fire. My husband began to sing, "burning, burning, burning, eyes of fire," and we both dissolved into laughter. To this day we both giggle when one of us sings that line.

That moment of levity was just what we needed to get moving. We geared up, fuelled up on another wonderful breakfast, and then stopped in town for some snacks to take on the road. As I waited with the bikes, I watched as people poured into the main street from the side streets. It was like a scene of a small town had been plucked right out of a movie. It was perfect.

Soon we were on our way once again. I can't explain how or why, but as we cycled along through the lovely countryside with the fresh air filling our souls, we forgot all about our pain and fatigue. All I remember is how beautiful the ride was, and how free and very alive I felt.

This was the first time I can ever recall truly experiencing my surroundings while traveling by bicycle. This isn't a feeling that could ever be achieved by taking the exact same route by car. When you're out in the open and surrounded by nature, every little beautiful detail stands out. It's more than just a feast for the eyes. The lovely scents of the wilderness around you float through the air until you can almost taste them as they infuse your being. The gentle sounds of nature aren't dampened by car windows or obliterated by the sound of a motor. You are literally engulfed in your surroundings as your body moves in tandem with the bike. Instead of moving through your surroundings in a bubble as you might with a car, you are fully exposed. You feel every pedal stroke, and your entire being is engaged every step of the way. Arriving at a destination is a reward that you earn only at the conclusion of a journey that is never forgotten.

THE SIX PEAKS

After leaving the magical little town of Murnau, we made our way towards Oberammergau where we enjoyed a delicious lunch. The plan for the remainder of the day was that we would continue on through the Bavarian Forest to the famous Disney Enchanted Castle.

We weren't supposed to climb six peaks. It wasn't in our itinerary for the day, but sometimes the unexpected turns into a great adventure. Looking back, the events that unfolded that afternoon seem quite absurd and even insane. At the time, however, we did what we thought was the best course of action given the information that we had.

I am not quite sure how we got off track, but not long after leaving Oberammergau we did. We realized our mistake quickly enough. Our bikes were heavier mountain bikes instead of lighter road bikes, so when we found ourselves on a gravel road it wasn't a big deal. When the road started to incline sharply and my bike tires were spinning in the loose rocks, however, I began to find it difficult to climb. There were sections where I had to walk my bike, but we kept pushing on. James was quite sure that we would find the path that we were looking for very soon. Time passed, the path remained elusive. We could see the road that we were pretty sure we were supposed to be on, but it was on the other side of a ravine. There wasn't anywhere in sight where we might be able to get across.

Given that we were cycling on a reasonably formed path, we decided to continue on for a while to see if we could connect with the road on the other side. Once we committed to that course of action, we kept on going for a long time. We traveled upwards, riding when we could and pushing our bikes when we couldn't ride because of steep terrain or loose gravel.

Eventually, we took a break and sat down. We were getting tired, and our frustration with seeing the road we wanted to be on but not being able to get there was growing. As we looked around us, though, something happened. We each took a deep breath of the fresh air and felt ourselves become calm. Surrounded by the glorious beauty of nature, we allowed ourselves to be soothed by the warm sun and the magnificent view. Sure, we were lost in the middle of nowhere, but we simply could not be upset. We saw a group of sheep, including a little lamb frolicking as its ears flapped up and down. At that moment, it felt like time absolutely stood still and that nothing in the world could possibly matter than being right here. I don't think we could have possibly felt more connected with the natural world.

After some contemplation, we realized that if we went back down the mountainside then we were unlikely to make it to our destination for the evening. We decided to take the risk of continuing on our current path since there was still a chance that we might be able to hook up with the road across the ravine at some point farther along. Our decision made, we climbed back onto our bikes. Onwards and upwards we went. It was hard work making our slow trek up the mountainside, but any time I started to feel negative I would simply look around and reconnect with my surroundings.

Eventually, the ravine closed in and we were able to cross over to the other side just as we had hoped. A new challenge immediately presented itself, however, as we found ourselves looking straight up a steep, grassy combination of a hill and a cliff. The road we wanted to be on was at the top of that cliff.

James started scaling up the steep incline, literally dragging his bike alongside him. I watched him for a few moments, and then decided that we hadn't come this far to quit now and tried to follow suit. It was absolutely gruelling work. I sweated profusely, and puffed and groaned in agony as I worked to drag my bike up the very steep stretch. Much to my relief, as soon as James made it to the top with his bike, he came back for mine. I made a rather less than elegant summit to the road, and took possession of my bike once again so that we could keep pushing forward.

Surrounded by lush, green trees and fresh, woodsy scent, I found it surprisingly easy to look past my fatigue as I admired the beauty around me. We cycled on for what was starting to feel like forever when we finally saw something in the distance. It looked like the very top of the climb that we had been making all day. As we got closer, we could see that there was some sort of building up there. Maybe it was a restaurant. I started to dream of cold drinks and delicious food.

There was still a lot of road between us and the building, though. As we got closer to our goal, we encountered an extremely steep stretch that looked like it would take us to the summit. We were stopped on the side of the road discussing who in their right mind would be able to bike up this stretch, when out of nowhere a man on a road bike whizzed right past us on and up the seemingly-impossible stretch. He disappeared around the corner as we exchanged a look of shock. I guess if you live in the mountains in the Bavarian Forest and you ride your bike every day, perhaps cycling up such an intimidating incline might be an everyday occurrence!

Encouraged by the cyclist that had gone before us, we decided to go ahead and give it a try. I didn't make it very far up the incline before I had to dismount and walk my bike the rest of the way. When we did reach the top, we were ecstatic to find that the building was indeed a little establishment that served food and beverages. We eagerly drank cold water and wolfed down soft pretzels. It was getting late in the day, though, and while we would have liked to linger we knew that we needed to get moving.

We wandered to the other side of the peak to look for a path down the other side. We couldn't find one, but we could see down to the bottom of this castle in the sky. My navigator pointed to the valley below, and exclaimed that we were looking at the town that we wanted to be in. In my depleted, fatigued state, I suggested that maybe we could just try to scale down the slope and take the direct route. James looked at me like I was crazy, and retorted in a very sarcastic tone that we were not scaling down the side of an extremely high mountain!

Unfortunately, he had brought up a valid point. As disappointing as it was, we realized that we simply were not going to make it to our destination this late in the day. The only logical thing to do was to go back down the way we had come and to make our way along the road all the way to the bottom again. There, we could find a town where we could rest and decide what to do tomorrow.

Feeling defeat every step of the way, we walked our bikes down the extremely steep bit of road we had just climbed and attempted to start backtracking. I soon found out that biking downhill wasn't as easy as I had hoped it would be. Even though the road in front of me was less steep than the road behind me, it was still quite intimidating. The combination of the road's sharp incline and the looseness of the gravel left me terrified. I had never cycled down something so threatening in my life. I was so afraid that I simply could not bring myself to let the wheels begin to turn, nor even think about clipping either of my cycling shoes into the pedals.

Finally, James came back to see what was going on with me and to have a discussion about where to go from here. The facts were that the sun was slowly setting, and that we simply had to make it to the bottom of this beast of a mountain in a reasonable amount of time if we didn't want to be left cycling in the dark in an unfamiliar place with lots of wild animals. When James put it that way, I realized that I didn't have any choice but to pick up the pace.

In spite of my good intentions, going down the steep slope at anything faster than a crawl was easier said than done. I had to forcefully will myself to let my bike start moving on its own. I took it easy, I didn't clip both feet in, and I went nice and slow so that I wouldn't spin out if I had to apply the brakes. After a little while, my heartbeat slowed and my nerves started to calm. I felt myself relaxing and focusing more and more on letting my bike and gravity do most of the work. The further down we got, the less worried I became.

Eventually, we found ourselves back at the very bottom on the road that we had started on that morning. It felt like a lifetime ago! We ended up returning to the town where we had eaten lunch and found a lovely place to spend the night. At this point, we were so tired and hungry that all we cared about was having some sort of food and a bed to sleep on. As we cleaned up our weary bodies to make ourselves presentable for dinner, I came to the realization that I stunk. I don't think I had ever smelled as much like a barnyard animal as I did at that moment. Every part of me hurt. I had wounds in places that I don't even want to talk about. All of the time in the saddle and the actions of pushing my bike and even pulling it up the side of a cliff had the combined result of me being able to feel muscles that I didn't even know I had.

Our pace slow and weary, we walked through the town until we found a place to eat. Soon we were seated on a lovely patio poring over a menu on which everything looked fantastic. I wanted to eat it all! We each ordered a delicious pasta dinner and a soothing beverage, and then took our time enjoying our food while we relaxed underneath a blanket of stars. We talked about the day that we had, and I couldn't help but giggle uncontrollably at how ridiculous it all seemed now that it was over. We had both been so convinced that we were going to find a connecting road to take us to where we wanted to be that neither of us had actually stopped to consider the logic of the situation. Who would have thought that we could have such a crazy adventure as a result of missing a single turn on the way to our destination?

With a big sigh, we decided to let it all go so that we could devote our remaining energy to enjoying the lovely evening before us. Sometimes things do not go as planned. It had never been more apparent to me than it was that evening that when you don't end up where you thought you would, the best thing that you can do is drink in whatever alternative has presented itself. This may not have been the death knell for my cautious, unadventurous side, but it was definitely the beginning of the end for the part of me that had to have every part of my life planned out.

THE LONGEST DAY OF MY LIFE

When I completed my first century ride, I thought that cycling 100 km was a very long distance. Little did I know that 100 km would pale in comparison to what was ahead of me.

Thanks to getting off track on our second day of cycling in the Bavarian Forest, we knew that we would no longer be able to follow the original route that we had planned for this section of our trip. On the morning of our third day of cycling, we decided that the better alternative was to start heading back to Munich. We needed to budget time to get from Munich to the small town where the wedding that had precipitated this trip would be held, which left us with no flexibility to make up for lost time on this leg of our journey.

We embarked on our third day of riding. I actually think that my body was starting to get used to consecutive long days on my bike. It was either that, or my mind and body were so numb at this point that it was simply an illusion that I was adjusting.

As the day progressed, we gradually began to leave the mountains behind. When we reached the nice little town of Seeshaupt, we stopped for lunch on a patio. As I looked out at the lake, I felt my whole body and soul start to relax as the peacefulness of the town seeped into me. I wondered if perhaps we might be able to call it quits and stay there for the evening. James disagreed. We were close enough to Munich by this point that he thought we should push on so that we could give ourselves a little breathing room in getting to the town where the wedding was.

I trusted my navigator's judgement so, despite my exhaustion I agreed to keep going. I think my attitude was starting to deteriorate by this point. After three days of long rides, my inner strength was stretched very thin despite the moments of peace that I had begun to find in my surroundings. I had a few moments where I had to stop and let my frustration out instead of bucking up and continuing to hold it in. During one of those moments I found myself standing there out in the open, feeling like I physically couldn't go on and that time was standing still while everything around me was a haze. Thankfully, James was there to encourage me to get back on my bike and continue pedalling so that we could stay on track.

It is really funny how the mind can actually control the body. Even though I was at the end of my endurance, I remember coming upon another cyclist who was actually moving slower than I was. As I approached him, my motivation to cycle grew, my adrenaline surged, and my speed increased. It didn't matter how tired I was; there were always more energy reserves there somewhere. The trick was finding it and tapping into it.

We finally reached the train station that would take us to Munich. I was so relieved, but that feeling didn't last long. A few minutes after boarding the train with our bikes, we were told to get off again. Apparently, bikes are only allowed on the train during certain times, meaning that we would have to wait for another 20 minutes. There wasn't anything we could do about the demand to get off the train, although we were surprised that this rule was enforced since the car we were in was empty.

Back on the platform, I sat down to wait the 20 minutes. James, of course, had another plan: Since we were so close to Munich, we should just cycle the rest of the way instead of waiting. I agreed reluctantly, and on we went.

By this point, I felt completely numb both physically and mentally. I don't really know how I made it through this last part of the day. I just know that I put one foot in front of the other and kept on going. By the time we reached Munich, we had cycled 200 km that day. 200 km! This was twice the distance that I had cycled when I completed my first century ride. I never would have thought in a million years that I would be able to bike for 200 km in one day. Somehow, though, I had done it.

After returning our bikes to the rental shop and finding a place to stay, we went to our room and crashed. It was time for us to take full advantage of the rest that we had earned. We slept for a very long time, and took our time in getting up the next day. All in all, we enjoyed a lovely time in Munich, drinking in our beautiful surroundings and taking in the indescribable culture before embarking on a long train ride to our next destination. I relished in the leisurely feeling of not having to be anywhere at any specific time.

I imagine that my time in Munich would have been special even without the days of cycling that led up to our arrival. Arriving after days of pushing myself past my limits even when I wanted to quit made Munich seem downright magical. Those days of cycling through the countryside had helped me to discover a side of myself that I hadn't known existed. I had been forced to embrace the unexpected and to dive headfirst into the challenges that come along with an adventure. Following those days of physical exhaustion and self-discovery up with a day of rest and relaxation in Munich felt like the biggest treat in the world.

A FAIRY TALE WEDDING

After our restful time in Munich, we headed to the Northern part of Germany by train. Our destination was the sleepy little town of Grietz, a place that you would only visit if you knew someone who lived there. In our case, we were heading to Grietz for the wedding of my husband's university buddy and former roommate. Although James's friend wasn't German, his bride was, and they were getting married in her hometown.

As we relaxed and looked out the windows, taking in an entirely different landscape than the one we had just left behind, James suddenly exclaimed that we had to get off the train. I was confused, but I went along with it. It turned out that he had just remembered that the bride-to-be had told him that the hotel in Grietz only accepted a special European card and cash. We couldn't use our credit cards, and we were dangerously low on cash.

As soon as we exited the train, James dashed around the strange town in which we had disembarked in search of a bank while I followed him in a frantic chase to keep up. It was late on a Friday afternoon, and we thought that we might be out of luck. Fortunately, we were able to find a bank machine that allowed us to take out a limited amount of cash. It wasn't enough, but it was better than nothing. Back onto the train we went en route to our final destination.

When we arrived in Grietz, we got off the train and walked through the train station to the main entrance. As we exited the station, we paused and looked around. I am surprised we didn't hear crickets chirping. The town appeared to be deserted. There wasn't a soul in sight, and there wasn't a sound to be heard.

Undeterred by this turn of events, James decided to attempt to use the pay phone to contact the bride as she had provided us with a cell phone number. He had already tried to get in touch with her several times during the day without any success, but still he tried again. The number wasn't going through, and we just couldn't figure out why. We weren't familiar with the area code system in Germany, and we were obviously doing something wrong. James attempted to use the help system, but alas, the operators only spoke in German. It was clear that we were on our own. It seemed that our only option was to walk to the hotel, so, we set off on our way.

There we were, two Canadians in a deserted town in Northern Germany, walking along in search of a hotel full of wedding guests. After a little while our path took us out of the main part of town and towards a hill. I think that at this point it must have become apparent to James that the hotel may be further away than we had thought.

To some, our situation may have seemed bleak. To others such as James, the situation was simply a problem that needed to be solved. Early on in this European adventure I had realized that when James was in navigator mode he liked to work through problems in his head without too much chatter. Thus, I remained fairly quiet as we walked and only offered the occasional comment or suggestion - not that there were many options to suggest. We ended up turning around and making our way through the town again, looking for any sign of life. By the time we arrived back at the train station, we hadn't seen a single soul.

I cannot for the life of me explain what happened next. There, in front of the train station, stood a little taxi stand. I looked at it and thought how useless it was as it was bound to be empty. James, on the other hand, never lost hope. He marched straight up to the taxi stand and knocked on the door. To my complete disbelief, it opened and a man peeked out. I couldn't believe my eyes! Was I dreaming?

Undeterred by his inability to speak German, James found a way to communicate the man, and next thing you knew we were in the back of a taxi being driven to our hotel. The whole thing was nothing less than incredible! The hotel turned out to be a fair ways outside of the town, up on the top of the hill that we had started climbing prior to turning around. We arrived at the hotel, and into the warm, welcoming arms of our hosts.

There were about 30 people from many different places around the world staying at the hotel for the wedding. We were quickly settled into our room, and found ourselves swept into the excitement around us in the hotel lobby. The bride's side was German, the groom's side was French Canadian, and the friends of the bride and the groom were mostly Europeans who spoke a multitude of languages. Lucky for us, many of the Europeans spoke at least a little bit of English.

While we had been able to acquire some cash earlier in the day, it wasn't very much. James had determined that we had just enough to cover the room that we would be staying in. We had a place to stay, but there wasn't any money left for anything else, including food. We were making progress, but our problems weren't solved yet.

I was able to do a bit of information gathering by chatting with some of the European wedding guests, and soon learned that as I had suspected and hoped the hotel provided breakfast with the room. That revelation helped to ease our concerns quite a bit. We had enough money for the room, we would be provided breakfast, and at some point during the wedding celebration there was bound to be food. Since we were only staying for two nights and then leaving the morning after the wedding, it seemed that as long as we were careful our food situation wouldn't be as dire as we had previously feared.

We eventually went back to our room for the evening, where we feasted on the stale bread and old cheese that we had in our backpacks. It was the dinner of champions! Nestled in the warm, cozy bed in this tiny town hidden away in Germany, we soon enjoyed a quiet, peaceful sleep.

When I woke up the next morning, I was starving! My belly had become accustomed to eating big spreads of food every morning, then replenishing on entire pizzas for lunch after a hard morning of riding, and of course, eating a several course meal after making it to the destination town for the evening. The other people attending the wedding must have wondered what was wrong with me as I stuffed myself on eggs, pastries, jams, and coffee. Not knowing when we would next eat, I put my pride aside and dove right in.

After breakfast, we were herded off to a castle where the wedding ceremony would be held. When I had learned that the we would be going to a castle, I had assumed that it would be some sort of new build knockoff, but this place was the real deal. While we waited for the ceremony, we walked through the winding staircases and explored dark passageways of the incredibly old, still intact, castle.

As the time for the ceremony approached, we were all lined up along the street just outside the castle's chapel so that the bride and groom could walk up the pathway and into the chapel together. It was a sight right out of a child's fairytale book. There they were, walking up the path, hand in hand. She looked like an angel, the intricate white patterns of beautiful fabric embracing her body, and her long, red hair glimmering in the sunlight and flowing down her back. Her smile couldn't have been wider.

Into the chapel they went, and we all followed. The chapel was small, but we all packed in tightly and somehow managed to fit. The ceremony was conducted in German and French. Although I couldn't understand a word of it, it was the most beautiful ceremony I have ever been to. The sun was streaming through the tiny stained glass windows, and the bride and groom were both beaming with joy.

After the ceremony, everyone jubilantly exited the chapel and we were all given a balloon. Each balloon had a note inside, and we were asked to release them into the air all at the same time. It was such a romantic scene as the blue sky was filled with white and red balloons floating away to places unknown. We were then herded over to a lovely, quaint, brick building beside a pond where the festivities would continue. We all chatted excitedly about the beautiful ceremony. Just when I thought I had experienced more than enough romance to last me a lifetime, we looked up to see the bride and groom perched in a small boat that was being rowed across the shimmering pond to join the party. I had never seen anything like this gorgeous entrance before.

As the newlyweds arrived, we all streamed into the small building. Embraced by old bricks with open windows looking out over the pond, the groom cut a large, heart shaped cake made of red jello and garnished with whipped cream while we all looked on. All of these romantic traditions were so very different than the ones we had back home. James and I were completely entranced!

The afternoon faded into evening, and the festivities continued with food, wine, and warm company. As night descended, we heard some sounds from outside and learned that the evening was to end with a magnificent display of homemade fireworks. It brought back memories of a time when the bride was visiting us back home in Canada on New Year's Eve. She hadn't been able to believe that we didn't share her tradition of setting off fireworks in the streets to ring in the new year, and had been so persistent about it that we had actually lit a few fireworks off on one of the main city streets. Setting off fireworks like that is illegal in Canada, and at the time I was terrified that we would be caught. To her, however, it was a tradition that must be followed.

As we drank in our surroundings and admired the ad hoc fireworks display, we truly felt that we were now a part of this beautiful new set of customs and traditions. It was quite literally the experience of my life being submersed in what can only be described as a fairy tale happy ending.

CYCLING WITH THE PROS

The morning after the wedding, we took a train from Germany to France. When we arrived at our destination we met up with Bruno, the tour guide that James had arranged prior to our trip. Road bikes, accommodations, luggage transport, and cycling routes had all been organized for us. All we had to do was ride our bicycles when the time came.

When Bruno picked us up, he drove us through the French Alps. Soon, we were ascending the famous Alpe d'Huez. Before this, I had never seen a real switchback in my life. I mean, I had seen switchbacks before, but not like this: A perfect curve, steep on the inside, a little more forgiving on the outer edge, and daunting to both driver and to cyclist. As we made our way up each of the 21 switchbacks, I became unnerved by the steepness of the turns. Bruno was quick to reassure me that it wasn't so bad, but I didn't buy it. My stomach churned, I felt a strange tingling sensation, and I began to sweat. I was nervous. I was uncomfortable. I was afraid of the unknown. How would it feel to be on a road bike climbing this beast? I had no idea. I could not comprehend what was before me.

We reached the top of Alpe d'Huez and enjoyed a pleasant lunch of fresh tomatoes, cheese, and bread. James and Bruno worked out the final logistics as we ate. They behaved as if everything was normal, as if there wasn't this daunting and treacherous task before us that I could not even begin to wrap my head around. Despite our lovely surroundings, I just could not relax.

After satisfying himself that we would be all right, Bruno left us. James was filled with excitement. He babbled on about the various professional riders that he had spotted training on the very mountain that we sat on top of. He wanted to spend the afternoon riding, so onto the bikes we climbed and down the 21 switchbacks we went.

I had never been so terrified in my life. My nerves teetered near a breaking point as I maneuvered my way down the mountain inch by inch, gripping the brakes so tightly that my forearms cried out in pain. Each tight turn was gut wrenching, and each stretch between felt to me like walking on a tightrope. In my mind's eye I could see myself plummeting off of the edge and down the cliff to my doom. I had to stop numerous times to ease the strain in my forearms, to take a few breaths, and to make a vain attempt at calming myself.

Somehow I made it to the bottom. I was so unnerved that I wanted to vomit. I couldn't control my nerves any longer, and the next thing I knew I began to sob. As soon as the tears started flowing, all of my anxiety came pouring out. I looked at James, and I told him to go ahead without me, that I would meet him at the top. I needed to somehow figure this thing out, and I didn't want to slow him down while I tried to pull myself together. He knew me better than to argue with me, so he hopped on his bike and off he went.

Now that I was on my own, I took stock of my situation. There was only one way to get back to our hotel room, and that way was up. As I saw it, my choices were to attempt the daunting ascent in front of me, or to lie down in the ditch and give up. After weighing those options, I reluctantly started to climb the long, steep stretch of road in front of me.

Up I went. I grunted, I sweated, and somehow I used brute force to make it up the first long, steep switchback. As I hung my head over the front of the handle bars and gasped for air, all I could think of were the 20 switchbacks that still lay ahead of me. How in the world was I going to get to the top? I couldn't even picture myself making it.

It took a few minutes, but I finally caught my breath and decided to take on switchback number two as my options hadn't really changed at all since the last time I had taken stock of the situation. The only real difference now was that I didn't have a ditch to lie down in. I repeated this performance one agonizing pedal stroke at a time, slowly conquering one switchback after another. It took time, but I settled into a rhythm of sorts. Each time I approached one of the tight little turns, I would stop and regroup. Then I would make my way through the turn and force myself up the long stretch of road, rest, and repeat. I continued with this strategy until I reached the halfway point. When I looked up, James was standing there waiting for me. I am sure that he was wondering if he was going to be divorced by the time this trip was over, but whatever was going through his mind he didn't share it with me. Instead, we took a break and shared a snack.

The rest turned out to be exactly what I needed. I can't quite explain what happened while we were sitting together on the side of the road, but something switched in my brain. My train of thought changed from "how am I going to make it to the top" to a much more positive "I am going to make it to the top." I knew in that moment that I didn't care how long it took me, and

I didn't care how graceful my ascent was: I was simply determined to get there.

Our break over, we pushed on. As we neared the top, the switchbacks became shallower and shorter, but I still couldn't do more than a few at a time. This may have been a physical challenge, but I realized that the biggest challenge was all in my mind. Using mind over matter, I willed myself on until I couldn't go any further. Then I took a break, caught my breath, and continued. I felt the burn of every single pedal stroke. My whole being was completely immersed in the moment as I poured every physical and mental resource I had into simply continuing on.

We were nearing the top when I heard something behind me. I looked to my left, and saw the most amazing thing I have ever seen. Smooth as silk and exerting what appeared to be no effort at all, Ivan Basso, a famous Tour de France contender, cycled passed me with a couple of his teammates. This was the year that Alpe d'Huez was to be a time trial for the Tour de France, and Ivan was there training for it. His support car soon passed me, and the fellow in the passenger seat hung his head out of the window and shouted, "Allez, Allez!" at me. The whole moment felt surreal, like a hazy dream.

It took a long time, but I somehow finally made it to the home stretch and found myself staring at the sign for the very last switchback. We stopped and took pictures, and I kept waiting for it to sink in that I was done. Soon, I could see the hotel in the distance. All I wanted was to teleport myself there. Everything is a bit fuzzy from that point on. The next thing I remember is sitting in my warm wool sweater at a dinner table, looking out of a window at the 21 switchbacks up the side of the mountain that I had just climbed. Nothing felt quite real, and a part of me wondered if I was dreaming. The lady at the table next to ours commented that she had seen us on her drive up. She asked if we had biked to the top, and I replied, "Yes, we did." I could barely believe it myself.

Alpe d'Huez: 13.8 km, 8.1% average gradient, 13% maximum gradient, 1071 m ascent.

Of all of the things that I had accomplished to this point in my life, none of them had resulted in the euphoria that I was experiencing at this moment. It was a heady mix of disbelief, awe, amazement, excitement, celebration, thankfulness, and absolute satisfaction. There had been so many times in my life that I had put forth plenty of effort to achieve something, but had been left feeling unsatisfied with the results. Never before had I found something that both embraced and required the fiery passion that I was made of. I knew at that moment that I was completely in love with cycling, even though I still had yet to realize how perfect it was for me.

TAKING ON EVEN MORE

It turned out that Alpe d'Huez wasn't enough for me and James. The next day, we once again descended down the 21 switchbacks. This time, we continued on instead of going right back up. We rode through the little town of Bourg d'Oisans, and onto the base of Croix de la Fer.

Up until that point in my life, Alpe d'Huez was the most difficult physical challenge that I had ever undertaken. It was a beast, but it was an approachable beast to tackle since you could see exactly what you were getting into from the very start. Croix de la Fer is a different sort of monster. There is no place where you can see the entirety of the mountain before getting started. For the first chunk of riding, you can only see a little ways ahead of you. The path forward isn't laid out symmetrically in 21 switchbacks winding back and forth; instead, it is sneaky with long stretches of elevating gradient that wind in many directions and hide themselves from the cyclist's eye.

We started our ascent. It very quickly became apparent to me that if I was going to survive this day, I would have to take the climb one tiny piece at a time. I would literally grind away at each pedal stroke until my body was physically spent and I had to stop for a brief recovery. I repeated this over and over and over, ascending the mountain one small stretch at a time. I was only able to focus on my immediate surroundings, so I had absolutely no idea what the terrain was like any distance ahead of me or how long this climb would take. All I could do was look as far ahead as possible and then will myself to make it as close to that spot as possible before I was gasping for air and in need of another break.

After brute forcing my way up Alpe d'Huez, I didn't question the outcome of this second climbing attempt at all. I just focused on finishing each little stretch before putting my mental resources towards the next bit of road. I found this strategy to be very successful at helping me to keep going without becoming discouraged.

It took a lot of repetitive effort hammering out my grinding and resting cycle to make it about of a third of the way up the mountain. At this point, the view just opened up and it was breathtaking. Ahead of us was a valley ringed by beautiful white-capped mountain peaks. The road we were on led us past a small gathering of buildings that were set against this scenic backdrop, but nothing was open thus on we went to tackle the next chunk of the mountain.

In this section we found ourselves cycling up long stretches of open road. I am not sure if this openness made things easier or more difficult. On one hand, we could see farther into the distance to gain a better idea of what was coming up next. On the other hand, the distance simply revealed endless long stretches of road that made it obvious that we still had a long way to go. At least the long stretches of road gave me a good goal as I continued to repeat my grinding and resting cycle.

Eventually, we came upon a series of switchbacks. Smooth, steep and daunting, these switchbacks were anything but easy. I tackled them with the same determination that I had put into every moment of the ride so far, and was pleased to make it to the top without any panic attacks. My reward upon reaching the top was yet another long stretch of road. When viewed from the side, I could tell that this section of road was really steep, but there was James already making his way forward. He was standing up on his pedals and leaning over the front of the handlebars to keep the bike grounded against the steep incline as he worked his way upwards. I gulped, and then I took a deep breath and started up after him.

If I had learned anything over the last couple of days, it was that the best option in the face of a seemingly-impossible challenge was to simply keep going. I couldn't believe how steep this road was. I had thought that I was grinding before, but I definitely had a new definition of grinding now. I hadn't thought I could bike any slower, but here I was going forward at a snail's pace.

It took some time, but we both made it up the ridiculous stretch of road. I am not even really sure what we were thinking at that point. We were just two nuts cycling up a steep ridge on the side of a mountain in the middle of nowhere. I have to admit, though, that despite being drenched in sweat and smelling like a farm animal, despite my constant battle to keep pedalling against my physical depletion, and despite having no idea how long this was going to go on, I was having fun. Where else would I rather be, anyways? I was in one of the most scenic places in the world on the side of a famous cycling mountain in France!

We continued on for a while longer, but unfortunately for us it eventually became apparent that the few restaurants along the roadside weren't open. At this point in our adventures, we were still very green and really didn't have any idea how to eat to support our biking habit or what to carry with us while we were on the road. We were about two thirds of the way up this beast when we stopped for another break. We ate our few remaining morsels of power bars, and then laid down in the grass in exhaustion.

As we lay there, we compared notes and quickly realized that we were both spent, our bodies depleted and in need of food. It was obvious to us that the best and safest choice for us at this moment was to turn around and descend towards the town at the foot of the mountain where we could get some proper lunch.

It was a decision based in logic, yet it was a very difficult one to make. After feeling the victory of reaching the peak of Alpe d'Huez, we had had our hearts set on achieving the same thing on this mountain so that we could look out from the highest point around and revel in the sheer accomplishment of being there. It wasn't to be, though. We were both getting fuzzy, and we were concerned about descending safely. Turning back now was the right choice.

We agreed that even though we were leaving for another town the next morning and wouldn't have another chance on this trip to attempt to summit Croix de la Fer again, we would perhaps have another chance to do so in the future. Disappointed and exhausted, we turned our bikes around and began our descent. I could feel my heart sink more the further we went. I was committed to our decision, I knew it was for the best, and I didn't doubt that we would make it back here someday, but turning away from this challenge still felt like admitting defeat.

As we continued descending, my disappointment gradually turned into awe of how much climbing we had done. As I went down every steep stretch, and curved around every switchback, it became apparent to me that we had accomplished a lot. We just kept descending and descending until we finally reached the bottom. I simply could not believe how much my little legs has climbed!

The day does not end here. We made the descent safely, but we still had to cycle back to the town. We were both extremely spent and in need of food by this point, which made the short ride back feel like it took forever. This was my first experience finding myself in a situation in which I was completely depleted, but where stopping wasn't an option. I had to dig really, really deep in order to continue as we were not back at the town yet. All I could do was put my head down and keep my legs moving.

We did eventually make it back to the town, where we found some lunch and then basked in the afternoon sunshine to try to recover a bit of energy. I wasn't really sure how to ask James about how we were going to get back to the top of Alpe d'Huez and to our hotel room. I knew that there was absolutely no way that my body could possibly ride a bike up 21 switchbacks after what I had put it through the last couple of days.

It turns out that I shouldn't have worried because James brought up the topic of getting back to the hotel room on his own. Apparently, he had seen a bus stop a little ways back at the beginning of the town, and I agreed to go with him to check it out. I have to admit that at this point I had my doubts about the existence of this magical bus that was apparently going to appear in this tiny little town and take us and our bikes to the top of a mountain to our hotel, but I should have known better than to assume the worst.

There was no bus out front when we found the bus stop, but James wasn't ready to give up. He left me with the bikes and went inside the little bus depot, and then emerged victorious a few minutes later. Apparently, there *was* a bus that went up Alpe d'Huez for just €2,50 each, and it would be here in a few minutes. We were especially lucky because we were just in time for the last bus of the day. The lesson here is to *never* doubt that there is such thing as magic!

A few minutes later, the bus pulled up and the friendly driver loaded our bikes into the luggage compartment. The bus was empty besides us two stinky cyclists that looked ready to fall over. Up the mountain we went. As we ascended, my gratitude for this bus ride grew with each tight turn. I could not believe that we had found this bus. My relief that I did not have to somehow attempt to bike up this mountain again after what we had already done today was almost overwhelming. The bus stopped at the top of Alpe d'Huez, but a little ways from our hotel. We got off the bus and mounted our bikes. My mind and body were both completely numb, and I don't really know how I made it to the hotel but eventually we arrived.

We had an absolutely lovely evening. The hotel we were staying in was completely focused on providing amenities that are attractive to cyclists. We had safe places to stow our bikes, and the meals were incredible. In fact, many of the pros, including the ones that we had seen on Alpe d'Huez, stay there while training. The hotel was run by a tiny French woman in her eighties with an incredible amount of energy. Actually, this woman ran two hotels. She would get things in order in our hotel, and then hop in her SUV and drive through the mountains to check on things at her other hotel. I always wondered how many of the real pros she had met over the years. The way she ran around with that boundless energy was so inspiring.

Thanks in large part to the efforts of this wonderful French woman, we rested deeply and prepared for our journey to a new town the next day.

Croix de la Fer: 31.5 km, 5.75% average gradient, stretches in excess of 11% gradient, 1522 m ascent.

THE FINISH LINE, LILIES AND SPARKLING FRUIT WINE

We had already cycled for several days in the French Alps. We had conquered Alpe d'Huez, and we had attempted Croix de Fer. Our easiest day thus far had been the 60 km ride from Bourg d'Oisans to La Mure. Now it was time to embark on our final day of cycling through these amazing mountains.

Our terminal destination would be the lovely town of Villard de Lans. Feeling a bit like super heroes after taking on the nemeses of the previous days, we looked at the profile for the ride ahead of us and didn't think that the climbing was going to be all that bad. We were so naïve; we had no understanding of the cumulative effect of consecutive days of strenuous physical activity on our bodies, and somehow believed that flatter days through the French Alps would actually involve some level terrain. We had a lot to learn.

Col d'Ornon was our first challenge of the day. It was the perfect warmup, giving us a nice little climb that allowed us both to get into a reasonable flow. As lunchtime approached, we had covered some reasonable ground. We were feeling pretty good about ourselves, and we didn't think we had that much further to go. Why not indulge in a little early day celebration of a nice, cold beer to accompany that delicious thin crust pizza we were about to devour? What a lovely lunch we had, sitting there like two peacocks on a sunny patio in a tiny town in the French Alps. Oh yeah, we were all that *and* a bag of chips!

After basking in the sun for a while, we decided to roll on out. The next thing we knew, we were climbing again, and I mean *really climbing*. I soon stopped to consult with James. He revisited the map and riding profile, and then declared in a surprised tone that we had a 15 km climb ahead of us. I couldn't believe my ears. I had believed we were done the climbing for the day and just had a nice, easy coast into our destination town ahead of us. No, it turned out that we had to climb Saint Nizier before we would arrive at our place of rest.

Now that the bombshell had been dropped, I just wanted to get going. We didn't waste any more time talking about it before hopping on our bikes and starting forward once again. This type of snap decision making was becoming really common between me and James now. Honestly, it was much easier to simply get on with it then to deliberate or argue against the inevitable. There was only one reasonable path to take, after all.

We started climbing. James was up ahead as usual, and there I was, grinding away, feeling a bit tipsy from the hot sun and the beer, and just wondering how much longer it was going to be. That was when it started raining. I contemplated pulling over to put on my pants and maybe my jacket, but the rain wasn't that cold. By the time I had decided that maybe I should pull over and avoid getting drenched, the rain had let up and so I kept pushing on.

Onward and upward we went. We were tired and we wanted to be finished, but the reality was that this climb stood between us and the rest we craved. We climbed, and we climbed. The funny thing is, looking back I know now that I wouldn't have wanted it any other way. I wanted to get to our destination town, and I wanted to enjoy the sense of accomplishment that comes from cycling the distance that we had set out to achieve despite any challenges that got in our way. Of course, I also wanted to enjoy the fruits of my labor with a lovely dinner in a little French town.

The climb seemed to go on forever. Fifteen kilometres feels like a lot when you must exert yourself for every single pedal stroke. We stopped part way up to take a little break and to regroup. I was getting a bit emotional at this point. I was just so depleted from the consecutive days of going up against such grand mountains. Always my grounding force, James was quick to offer encouragement. He promised me that we would have a big ice cream at the top. It turns out that I can be bought with sweet treats. I was ready to get back on my bike again if it meant getting to the ice cream faster!

Just as we were about to start pedaling again, a beat up looking Volkswagon van pulled over and a lady stuck her head out of the window. She asked us if we knew how much further it was. We replied that we didn't. I am not sure if there was some sort of weird thing going on and our voices were being eaten up by the air, but she acted as if she hadn't heard us. She asked us again if we knew how much further it was to the top. We again replied that we didn't. This went on for a few minutes until she finally gave up and the van pulled away. As we watched the van disappear around the next switchback, we laughed at the situation. How bizarre. Maybe this van didn't even exist. Maybe it was all in our minds, and was simply a distraction to provide us with some sort of comic relief. Whatever purpose the van served, it was over now. On we went.

At the time it really did feel like the journey took forever, but I remember so much about that mountain. I remember the curves in the road, the trees lining the edges, and the spectacular view of the French countryside. The air was fresh with a light misty coat of moisture hanging on from the rain. My physical discomfort aside, I was enchanted by the picturesque views.

We eventually did make it to the top, but there wasn't any ice cream. To this day, I look at James with scepticism anytime he promises me a specific treat in return for finishing something that I am struggling with. I did, however, thoroughly enjoy a gooey chocolate bar filled with caramel. We chatted with a couple of bikers who were travelling on beautiful machines of their own. It is really interesting how cyclists and bikers seem to be looking for the same things. In this case, we were all in search of a beautiful mountain nestled in the European countryside that offers a journey to the top via a series of smooth switchbacks along its side.

Thankfully, the way down the mountain was easier. We coasted down the other side, and into the town that would be our home for the next few days. The town of Villard de Lans is exactly what you would want a little town in the French mountains to be. It was like a fairytale town where everyone was always happy. There were separate little shops where one could buy delectable fresh bread baked that morning, and types of cheese that I had never heard of.

As I settled into our little dwelling, James ventured out and brought back celebratory items for me. He presented me with beautiful pink lilies, sparkling fruit wine, and of course, chocolate. We celebrated what we had accomplished throughout the week. We had survived our first real cycling trip, we had learned a lot about ourselves, we had learned how to communicate better in situations when the day was getting long and we were getting hungry, and most of all, we had learned that we had no idea what we were capable of accomplishing.

The next day, we found ourselves on the little balcony attached to our room enjoying the sun. We ate the freshest bread we had ever tasted and the most delicious cheese that we have had to this day. We drank little beers from the local grocery, and we shared our thoughts, our feelings, and our triumphs of the past few days. We concluded that we should continue to reach for the stars.

Col d'Ornon (from the North): 11.1 km, 5.8% average gradient, 643 m ascent

Saint Nizier (from Grenoble): 14.6 km, 6.5% average gradient, 9.2% maximum gradient, 953 m ascent

BACK TO LIFE, BACK TO REALITY

Something strange happened after we returned to the reality of home. We arrived back at our house and settled in. I went to work very early the following day since my internal clock hadn't yet readjusted. The building was quiet when I arrived and sat down at the computer, and by the time I became aware that the rest of my coworkers had trickled in I was well on my way to destroying my 'to do' list like some sort of superwoman. I was on fire.

I was confused at first about this newfound productivity, but then I realized that everything I was doing was just so much easier than climbing a French mountain on a road bike.

Throughout my trip, I had gotten a small taste of my true potential. My expectations for myself were now higher, and things in life that may have seemed like a challenge before were accomplished smoother and easier now. My whole perspective had been changed.

I had been changed.

LEARNING TO TRAIN

'Always fall asleep with a dream and wake up with a purpose.' – Source unknown

CYCLING TO NOWHERE

If there was one thing I had learned while I was in Europe, it was that I was irrevocably in love with road cycling. I had discovered that I possessed the mental toughness and motivation to battle through difficult rides, which was a step in the right direction. Unfortunately, I was also now aware that my physical fitness was not at the level required for me to gracefully complete the types of rides that I was interested in doing.

The summer following our cycling trip through the French Alps, we moved into our first real home as a married couple. Although we hadn't realized it at the time, we had successfully found the perfect little place for us right in the middle of a prime cycling location. In fact, our new house was located very close to the starting point of my first century ride.

After the epic rides we had done in France, I found that I was quite laid back about cycling now that I was back at home. I did enjoy riding on the smaller highways to visit the towns surrounding Calgary. James and I would often ride out to the more scenic areas and enjoy picnic lunches surrounded by trees and softly bubbling streams.

The summer soon turned into fall, and the air became cool and crisp. The short cycling season that we enjoy in Calgary was over, and I couldn't help but wonder what we would do now. What does someone who used to be an average gym rat do in the off season of the sport that they have just discovered and fallen madly in love with? As always, James was there with the answer: We would train, of course! That sounded great, and I agreed with plenty of enthusiasm! I had no idea what the concept of training actually meant.

In addition to his roles as my cycling buddy, navigator, and trip planner, James now became my coach. He was well read in many cycling related matters, and he was way ahead of me with regards to knowing how to approach this whole training thing. He was the one that explained to me that if we wanted to do more cycling, and perhaps another cycling trip, then we needed to condition our bodies to be better prepared. Thinking back to how much I had struggled in the French Alps and acknowledging how badly I wanted to do more, I knew that this made perfect sense. Besides, I had made it up those crazy mountains. How hard could it be to train indoors?

We transformed one of our bedrooms into a training room by setting our bikes up side by side on indoor trainers, hooking up a sound system and a TV, and decorating the walls with eye-catching photos of the professional cyclists of the past riding on famous stretches of the Tour de France. James also purchased a bike computer for each of us so that we could monitor all sorts of things including our heart rate and cadence. Once everything was ready, we commenced our first training session.

According to James, I was to monitor my heart rate while I was on my bike. I needed to work hard enough to keep my heart rate above the fat burning zone and in the endurance building zone. This all sounded quite foreign to me. None of it had any real meaning until I tried it. Decked out in training attire, water bottles at hand, I climbed onto my bike and I started pedaling.

As I warmed up, I checked out my heart rate and realized that I would have to work a little harder than this if I was going reach the desired zone. I pushed harder, but saw that I still had a ways to go. I pushed harder yet. This continued for a while. Once I was finally able to get my heart rate high enough, I could only sustain my pace for a few minutes. I eased up, and with an exasperated tone asked James how anyone could sustain such a high level of physical exertion. I looked over at him, and was shocked to see him pedaling along, sweat pouring down his face. He was completely into his training and as far as I could tell he was having no trouble at all.

Knowing that I was going to have to find a way to do this, I took a few moments to contemplate my options and then decided to try the same approach that I had used while confronting those daunting switchbacks. I tackled my goal of reaching and staying in that endurance building zone one small piece at a time. First, I committed to a specific duration for a spinning session. During that session I attempted to spend as much time as I could in the proper heart rate zone in spite of my discomfort. Initially this meant spending small amounts of time in that uncomfortable zone and repeating it over and over in an interval-style workout.

While this type of workout was effective at increasing my endurance, it was very tedious and monotonous. I had to come up with ways to distract my thoughts. Listening to music worked well for me, while James preferred the approach of watching stages of the Tour de France that he had recorded. This was how I spent time most days during the long winter: in a room surrounded by four walls, pedaling hard and going nowhere while finding motivation in the voices of the gods of grunge and rock. Beside me, James raced up French mountains with Armstrong, Basso, and Ullrich. It seems a bit ridiculous.

Years later when I saw the movie *You, Me and Dupree,* I recall being the only one in the theatre laughing hysterically at a particular scene where Dupree has bought an old road bike and is attempting to get into shape. In this particular scene he is chatting on the phone and spinning away on his bike, which is mounted on an indoor trainer just like the one I had become accustomed to. He is watching coverage from the tenth stage of the 2001 Tour de France when a very famous scene known as

"The Look" takes place. Lance Armstrong passes Jan Ullrich on the famous Alpe d'Huez, and as he whizzes by Lance slows down and gives Jan a good five-second look. This wasn't just any look; this was *the* look that says, "Yeah, this is happening." At this point in the movie, Dupree declares to his friend that he has to go because he has to beat Lance! This scene depicted my new reality so perfectly that I found it downright hilarious.

Just like that scene from *You, Me and Dupree* depicted, it soon became habit for me to spend the majority of my time in the little training room pedaling away and dreaming of the mountains. This new pastime led directly to another lesson that I had to learn. Years ago in order to reverse the blowfish effect of my weight gain, I had started to follow the Canadian food guide. I had learned about proper portion sizes and balancing the foods I eat. I had not, however, learned about eating to fuel the body for high-intensity physical activities.

It turns out that eating to lose weight and eating to fuel the body are two entirely different things. The continuous stream of spin sessions soon caught up to my inability to provide the appropriate nutritional requirements to fuel said sessions. This problem was compounded by my blood sugar being naturally on the low side. I was already aware that I function most effectively when I eat very regularly, but soon I observed that my ability to perform to my satisfaction during a spinning session was highly correlated with my food intake for the day. This included both the quantity and quality of food.

Now I had acknowledged that there was a problem, but I was at a loss for what to do about it. James advised that we try keeping a nutritional spreadsheet to track the amount and quality of calories we were eating. I found the prospect daunting. Fortunately, in addition to his multitude of other talents, James was also a spreadsheet wizard. He could miraculously whip up the most complex and amazing spreadsheets in no time at all, which he proceeded to do in this case. With this nutritional spreadsheet, we were able to monitor and analyze what we were eating and the impact our food had on our cycling performance. Since I had very little understanding of the new nutritional requirements that my body had developed, I was happy to go with the flow.

Soon I was suited up with my own personal nutritional spreadsheet. Every day I would come home and input my food intake for the day. This was more than just a simple entry of what I had eaten; it also required that I add entries to an ever-growing database of the nutritional makeup of my food. These database entries included calories, fat, protein, and carbohydrates since apparently the percentage intake of each of these things has an impact on the body's ability to perform.

I had gone into this training with a positive mindset, but things were quickly getting out of hand. Confining myself for hours every week in a small room where I pedaled madly on a bike that wasn't going anywhere had been a necessary evil. Now I had the added commitment of spending time entering detailed information about everything I ate into a spreadsheet after a long day at work. I had to keep reminding myself that I really wanted this.

Soon, the toll of the constant effort of the workouts and the nutritional spreadsheet began to catch up with me. I was already working full time at a professional career with the associated commute twice a day, taking care of a home, and attempting to spend time with friends and family. I really, really wanted to become a real cyclist on top of these commitments, but it was a lot of hard work. Even more discouraging, I felt like we had only begun to scratch the surface of the level of effort that I would need to put in to make this dream a reality.

I pushed on despite my misgivings, continuing with my real life and then coming home to immerse myself in this other life of pedaling to nowhere and analyzing every morsel that went into my mouth. Every day we pedaled side by side. I worked my way through album after album, trying to lose myself in the delightfully intense voices of rock. Meanwhile, James continued to conquer the greats as he climbed the most famous peaks of the Tour de France.

I kept going with this routine, but there is a limit to my endurance and one day I finally reached it. It was a training session just like all of the ones before it when, physically and mentally depleted, I cried out that this was taking over my life and proclaimed that I couldn't do this anymore. I stormed out of the training room.

James knew me well enough to take my outburst in stride. He continued with his session, and after a few minutes of time out and calming down I realized that there was only one choice for me. I made my way back into the training room, climbed back onto my bike, and finished the session. This was the path I had chosen, and I knew that at the end of the day it would lead me to the place I wanted to go. Perhaps I simply needed a bit of a break once in a while, but at the end of the day I knew that all of this effort would be worth it. It had to be!

It was a relief when winter began to turn into spring. You cannot imagine the glory of breaking free from the training room and being able to ride my bike outside where it was intended to be ridden! This was what I had been craving!

It quickly became apparent that all of the effort I had put forth throughout the long winter had been more than worth it. My cardiovascular abilities were far beyond what they had ever been. I felt like I was flying on my little Trek 2000. My bicycle had now become a complete extension of my body as I glided up hills that had once felt like mountains. Best of all, I now knew what to eat to fuel my body for the rides that I longed for. It seemed that I was well on my way towards becoming the type of cyclist that I dreamed of being.

Little did I know, however, that my difficult lessons weren't quite over for the season.

WIND AND HILLS

Wind can be a blessing and a curse for the road cyclist. A tailwind can push you along nicely and is a real treat. A headwind, on the other hand, is a force to be contended with, and can make you feel like a salmon swimming upstream.

My hometown of Calgary is a very windy place. Warm summer breezes can turn to unexpected high speed gusts without warning. The cold of winter is frequently soothed by warm winds known as Chinooks that sweep in with a high cloud arch. It's fair to say that in Calgary, you come to expect the unexpected.

I have actually been on a bike ride on the outskirts of Calgary while cycling into a headwind for at least an hour until we reached our turnaround point. After a lunch break, we expected a tailwind when we turned back in the opposite direction. Imagine our surprise when we once again found ourselves up against a headwind! Incredibly, that sneaky wind had actually completely shifted during our short stop. That's Calgary for you.

Headwinds can be difficult to deal with, but the worst type of wind for the cyclist, in my opinion, is the sidewind. With a headwind, at least you can find a place of strength and focus within yourself so that you can battle through it. A sidewind, however, will sneak up on you out of nowhere and can actually knock you right off of your bike. You really have to watch openings in the treeline, especially when you are descending at high speed.

During a ride through the prairies that James and I did one summer, we were up against sustained high winds that were gusting up to 100 km an hour. Such high winds hadn't been in the forecast, and we were out in the middle of the wheat fields by the time things got bad. With no choice but to carry on, we had to find a way to battle through this. Biking into a headwind was at least an achievable goal, but trying to beat this sidewind was another story. I had to walk my bike for a while as the wind was pushing me right over.

Anyone living in Calgary or a similarly unpredictable area must learn to bike into the wind. The first time I attempted to bike into a decent headwind, my first instinct was to stop. I couldn't figure out why we would bike right now if we didn't have to. This was early in my training, and my naivety and short term thinking prevented me from realizing that a cyclist could be caught in the middle of a beautiful ride when the wind unexpectedly picked up. I hadn't yet fully experienced the unpredictability of the weather until this particular ride.

James would have none of this quitting attitude. We were already on the road, and we were finishing this ride. Off he went, leaving me to find a way to bike into the wind or get left in the dust. The decision turned out to be an easy one since, upon contemplation, I realized that I didn't have many options: I could either wait here on the side of the road as my husband disappeared into the distance, or I could quit being a wimp and try to keep up.

Like many of the other things I had learned to do on my bike, this new challenge really was a matter of focus and willpower. Cycling can be a very lonely sport. There I was, choosing a focal point a ways ahead, concentrating on getting my legs moving in a reasonable flow, and digging a bit deeper to find the strength to take on this wind. Once I got started, it actually wasn't that bad. I would later be very, very grateful to James for once again helping me make the decision to try rather than to give up. The more I learned about cycling, the less inclined I was to shy away from challenges that I faced.

Now, I am not suggesting that the cyclist knowingly put themselves into winds that are gusting at unsafe speeds. In fact, it had become habit for James and I to check a weather website that posted data from a site nearby our stomping grounds in close to real time before we ventured out. Once you got onto those open roads, though, the wind situation could be entirely different than what you might observe while poking your nose out the back door. What I am suggesting is that the cyclist could be a fair distance out when they find themselves in a windy situation, and that it is important to be able to get into a reasonable flow despite adverse conditions.

As the training season came to an end, I had successfully increased my cardio ability and learned the whole concept of heart rate. I had improved my skills at biking into the wind, and I had achieved some basic hill-climbing skills. All of these new accomplishments would soon be put to the test.

THE GOLDEN TRIANGLE

James enrolled us in our first Golden Triangle at the end of my first real training season. The Golden Triangle is a three-day cycling event in the Rocky Mountains. Each of the three days consists of approximately 100 km of riding, with a reasonable amount of climbing on the first and third days and a slightly easier day of flat and slightly descending roads in between. It is truly one of the best events in which I have ever taken part. It is very well organized and relies completely on a wonderful group of very dedicated volunteers. This event would be a true test of all the training I had put myself through and all of the lessons I had learned until this point.

We drove out to the meeting point that morning. When we arrived, we loaded our bags onto the truck that would cart them to our first overnight stop and signed in. Soon, we were off.

The first climb comes fairly quickly after the starting point, and I will never forget how it felt. After all of the training I had done with James, this climb felt absolutely fantastic to me, like I was just floating uphill. It was invigorating.

I was beyond excited about the rest of the day after how well I had just climbed up this hill, and it turned out that my excitement was justified. The rest of the day was very enjoyable. The event is held on a weekend in May, which is a time of year when the weather can be very unpredictable in the mountains. The first day went off smoothly, though, and we were fortunate enough to find ourselves basking in the sun at the rest stop before the day's final climb, which felt just as incredible as the day's first climb. I was hot from the sun, and I was motivated to make it to the town. I did have to dig a little to find some energy after cycling all day, but this was one time when it wasn't too hard.

After reaching the summit, we coasted down a long descent and into the town of Radium. We found the park where we would be setting up our tents for the night, and proceeded to get settled. After a relaxing dip in one of the area's famous hot pools, we joined the group of other cyclists for dinner. This was our first real experience with the comradery that naturally occurs as a result of a long day of cycling. You find yourselves forming connections with people that you may not have had the opportunity to meet otherwise.

Unfortunately, after dinner I didn't feel quite right. I left my husband to enjoy a beer in a local pub with our new friends so that I could go back to the tent and call it a night. During the night, I awoke multiple times. I knew something just wasn't right. Something I had eaten at dinner wasn't agreeing with me.

Each time I awoke, I walked over to the facilities thinking that something bad was going to happen, but each time my insides would settle just a bit. This was probably due to the fresh air. When the inevitable "something" did finally happen, it was probably a good thing. Sometimes a little explosion is all that is needed. Whatever I had eaten that didn't agree with me was finally gone and I was finally able to get some sleep.

Unfortunately, relief had come too late. By the time I fell asleep, the morning was already peaking around the corner. Much to my dismay, it was soon time to get up, pack up the tent, and get ready for the long ride ahead of us. We joined the group for breakfast, and I attempted to at least eat a bit of food. I was groggy and weak, and all I could think was that it was a good thing that this was the easier day without any real climbing. Even knowing that it was an easier day than yesterday, I was worried about making it to our destination.

It was at this point in time that James realized he didn't know where his wedding ring was. When he admitted this to me, I looked at him and I told him that right now all I cared about was getting through this 100 km ride. Now, you must understand that to me a ring is a ring. We understood what we were to each other regardless of whether he had a ring on his finger. I am not saying that I didn't care at all; I am saying that it wasn't the most important thing to me at the time. Besides, James had had a hard time picking his ring out and had never really liked the one he chose. James losing his wedding ring was far from a disaster, and I didn't have the mental resources to work myself up by worrying over it.

My focus was completely on the day. I needed to breathe, I needed to relax, and I needed to gently get my body through this challenge. This is precisely what I ended up doing. I took it easy, found a flow that I could handle, and just kept going. My dear sweet husband came back frequently to make sure that I was ok.

He had made a new cycling friend, and the two of them would cycle ahead for a while, then circle around and come back to check on me. I ended up having a pretty good time in spite of the way I felt.

When we rolled into the town of Golden, I was relieved that the day's work was over. Once the tent was set up and I was freshened up, I tucked myself into my sleeping bag and I had the best nap ever. Once I woke up, I felt like a new woman. We strolled into town and enjoyed some food and drinks during what turned out to be a great evening hanging out with our new cycling friends. Our tent was located right next to the train tracks, but in spite of this I had the deepest sleep of my life that evening. The fatigue from the night before, the long day of riding, and the clean fresh air filling my lungs all combined to put me into a state of total relaxation.

The third and final day of riding the Golden Triangle was definitely my favourite. We kicked things off by climbing our way through the beautiful, white capped mountains out of Golden. I had found my legs, which felt fantastic. I put my whole heart into it as I climbed. At the rest stop at the top of the climb, I once again looked forward to the rest of the day with excitement. This part of the route, which took us through a winding route nestled between two mountains, was absolutely breathtaking. It wasn't the type of road that I would recommend riding on alone, but the opportunity to ride it safely with hundreds of other cyclists was amazing.

By the end of the day I was definitely tired. At the final rest stop, we eagerly gobbled down the offered treats, looked at each other, and declared that it was time to finish this thing. On we went to tackle the final stretch, which took us over smaller, less travelled roads. It was quiet and peaceful, and we were surrounded by beautiful forest. It was such a lovely way to end the three days. I could feel the strain of cycling in my entire being and my legs were sore, but I felt so peaceful.

I knew then that I was no longer that young girl uncomfortable with her physical being and afraid of being adventurous. I was now a real cyclist, and completing a three-day event with hundreds of other cyclists was just something that I did with my husband on a long weekend. Whatever I had been in the past was now gone and was replaced with something much stronger.

MY FAVOURITE JEANS

Most of my experiences with jean shopping have not been happy ones. Very few of my attempts have even been slightly successful, which makes sense since I had spent my life being generally uncomfortable with my physical appearance. The only fashion sense I had, if you could even call it that, was in my mind.

All of this changed at the conclusion of my first training season. I was still a beginner in the world of cycling, but there was more to the benefits of training than the amazing physical abilities I had discovered. I soon learned that most of my clothes were too big. I *needed* to go shopping.

I love jeans, and I knew about a little hidden gem of a store in a trendy area where with a little bit of patience and effort a girl could get designer brands for a great price. This type of store was not well organized and didn't have stellar service, but there were treasures to be had.

On this particular shopping trip, I walked in and went to work. I picked out a few pairs that were in line with what I would have bought in the past. As I tried each pair on, I was pleasantly surprised. They were all too big! I went out again to grab a size smaller, but the results were the same. As I went down size after size, my disbelief grew. I was astonished. I knew that I had been working hard, but I had been so focused on the performance results that I had not taken a good look at the physical results.

My new waist size was strangely liberating. I tried on styles that I wouldn't have dared to try on in the past. I had started to develop a shape that was rather becoming to the most critical eyes in the room: my own. I was starting to see a cycling butt, a strong core, and toned arms. I could get used to this!

This shopping thing had become fun! After trying on a little bit of everything that I could find, I finally settled on a style that accentuated my new assets and that made me feel absolutely wonderful. Little did I know at the time that these jeans would become my favorite pair ever, and that they would travel with me on many cycling trips through the mountains of Europe. I was also unaware that I had just unleashed a side of myself that would eventually become more adventurous in developing that unique style that I can only call my own. The bottom line is that we only live once, so it's important to let ourselves be who we truly are.

THE FRENCH PYRENEES

'The good Lord gave you a body that can withstand almost anything, it's your mind that you have to convince.' -Vince Lombardi

THE TREK 2000 MEETS THE SWITCHBACK

Following my first training season, my shiny little Trek 2000 that had been there every step of the way finally got to stretch its wings on some real mountains. Tucked away in a travelling case, it flew with us to Gatwick and then on to Toulouse. This was my first experience traveling with a bike. The case itself isn't heavy, but it is bulky for a little girl who stands all of four foot ten. It can be challenging to haul a bike case through airports and train stations, especially in places where the only option is a set of stairs.

After wrangling our cases onto a train and finding an awkward place to wedge them at the back, we headed to the little French town of Pau. Upon arrival, pre-arranged transportation was waiting to take us to our destination for the day. We piled our cases into the back of the van and chatted excitedly with our driver about the French mountains that we would visit. Our destination was in the Pyrenees. We were staying at Hotel Relais Aspois on the outskirts of the tiny town of Gurmencon. We were dropped off in front of the hotel with our bike cases in tow, and in we went.

It appeared that the hotel was not open yet, which left us wondering if we were going to have to simply sit there for a while. Luckily, we were able to find someone who was willing to let us into our room early. After settling in, we quickly realized that we were both hungry. Since there wasn't anything to eat in our room, off we went on foot. We probably walked for a good hour until we finally came upon some civilization and a grocery store. By the time we sat down for our picnic lunch, we were famished.

After lunch, we made our way back to the hotel where James began going through the materials that had been provided by our driver to guide us on the rides that we would be taking on over the next week. To his astonishment, he quickly saw that we had not been given much more than a basic map. To this day, it amazes me how James has been able to guide us on amazing rides in foreign countries through places that he had never been, often with a shockingly small amount of information at his disposal. I recall how much work he had to do that day as he prepared to navigate us through the lovely Pyrenees. Once again, he took a disappointing situation and spun it into a problem to be solved.

That night, I was absolutely floored by the amount of traffic that I could hear through the open window. We were way off the beaten path in a hotel in the middle of the mountains! I couldn't fathom where all these people were coming from, or where they were going to. It simply astonished me to realize how many people live in the heart of these mountains.

The next morning, we embarked on our first ride in the French Pyrenees. Our route covered about 77.5 km, and included the lovely little mountain of Col Marie Blanque. Being on my own bike that was perfectly fitted to me was an incredible difference-maker. As we embarked upon the winding switchbacks of Col Marie Blanque, I was stunned to find out how well I could climb in comparison to my attempts at the French Alps the year before. I didn't know everything, and I knew that I had a lot more to learn, but all the times that I wanted to quit a training session and still chose to continue had paid off. I only stopped twice as we rode up this mountain. I was able to do multiple switchbacks in one swoop. I was elated at the evidence that all of my hard training had paid off so wonderfully.

At the peak, we found ourselves in a mist of cloud with a chorus of cowbells serenading us. This is when I learned that the fans at the professional races such as the Tour de France, often rang cowbells as encouragement to the riders. This was symbolic of the surrounding areas that were highly populated with cows. At that moment, having smoothly ascended this mountain peak as a result of my dedication and hard work through the winter months, the chorus of bells ringing through the air made me feel like my own champion.

The rest of the day was fantastic. We cycled through little towns lined with old buildings that looked as though they had been there forever. We saw herds of brightly-colored ewes. Their shaggy coats came in a rainbow of colors, including pink and blue, and electrified the lush pastures. I would later learn that these colors were a way for shepherds to mark their herds.

What a very different and lovely world I had found myself in.

Col Marie Blanque: 9.5 km, 7.5 % average gradient, 15 % maximum gradient, 715 m ascent

THE BIONIC WOMAN

Do you remember that cheesy 80s TV show called *The Bionic Man,* or the spin-off show, *The Bionic Woman*? The man or woman would literally become bionic, a process which was signaled to the viewer by a technical, space-aged sound effect when the super bionic powers were about to take hold. The man or woman would take advantage of their powers of speed and strength to accomplish with ease whatever strenuous physical task they had taken on. On the day that James and I tackled Col d'Abisque, I mistook myself for the bionic woman.

Col d'Abisque is a rather impressive mountain in the French Pyrenees. We had been cycling for a few days in this lovely mountain range, and had tackled a few smaller mountains with ease. Since I had just completed a portion of my life during which I had physically trained for the first time ever, I was feeling quite strong. I was amazed at my cardiovascular ability, and astounded at how I could gracefully fly up multiple switchbacks without having to pull over and gasp for breath. In my mind, a higher mountain would simply mean that I would have to climb for longer. I could do that!

Before we got started for the day, James determined that we should change up our originally planned route a bit. When we made our way to the bottom of the mountain, there was a sign that distinctly outlined the average gradient of each kilometer. It was color coded to provide a visual indication of the easiest and toughest sections. I recall taking in the information provided with a rather light and haughty air.

As we looked around to get our bearings and figure out which turn in the road to take in order to begin our ascent, a scene that I swear was pulled directly from one of Peter Seller's *Pink Panther* movies began to unfold. Out of nowhere, a small, three-wheeled motorized vehicle pulled up beside us. These vehicles are quite common in certain European mountain ranges. They are often loaded up with all sorts of items that the driver is hauling through mountain passes, and we always wondered how these things make it up such steep climbs on so little power.

We both stopped to stare as this particular vehicle putted along towards us. It screeched to a halt, and an old man with a bushy beard and overalls who looked like he had definitely spent some time in the mountains poked his head out of the window. He wanted to know whether we needed some help finding our way. I thought for a crazy moment that I was speaking to Peter himself, all decked out in one of his disguises and on his way to attempt to catch the Pink Panther who was hiding out in his French villa nestled in the mountains. James showed the mountain man his map and pointed to where we were attempting to go. The mountain man pointed us in the right direction, and soon we were on our way. Little did I know the agony that was waiting around the corner.

Onward and upward we went. We had just started cycling when we passed a fenced-in area with two little donkeys peering out at us. We joked that this would soon be us, just two jackasses on the side of the mountain. Looking back at how I had shrugged off the daunting gradients of the switchbacks that we were about to encounter, I would have to say that even when we passed the donkeys there was already at least one jackass on a bike present.

Soon we started to climb, and it felt great. I could have sworn that I heard a series of technical space-aged sounds to signal the onset of my bionic abilities. Sure enough, my bionic cardiovascular ability kicked in, and I flew up multiple switchbacks in a single swoop. The steeper turns definitely slowed me down, but I was still in a good solid flow and I was still making it up these stretches without a second thought. On we went for a while. My cycling partner was a little ways ahead. The day was glorious. The fresh air was fantastic. I was on top of the world.

Somewhere along the way, I started to feel a bit hungry, but I decided to just ignore it for the time being. I kept egging myself on and cajoling myself to keep going for a while until, bam! I bonked.

Although I had heard other cyclists use the term "bonking" in the past, I believe this may have been the first time that I had fully experienced this sensation. I had understood the phrase to mean the loss of one's energy, but I hadn't realized that the energy loss was so severe and so fast that it was akin to the feeling of running into a brick wall. It came on very quickly, and I suddenly found myself unable to continue.

As soon as I felt myself crashing I stopped and ate a snack, but it was already too late. When one bonks, it takes a while to recover. The food takes a while to enter the bloodstream and then replenish the body's glycogen stores, so it takes the body some time to respond. Worse, if the person continues to engage in an intense level of physical exertion such as climbing a famous French mountain during this process, their body is provided little opportunity to recover.

Still, I was in the middle of a mountain and stopping where I was wasn't an option. I continued on meekly, and soon found James taking a break in a beautiful little shaded spot under a tree. I stopped to join him and continued to attempt to refuel my engine with more food energy. To my despair, I wasn't feeling much better. The combination of waiting too long to eat and of living some delusional dream that I was bionic and could exert my body beyond its comfort level for hours at a time without fading, had caught up to me.

All too soon it was time to continue trekking on. Turn after turn, daunting gradient after daunting gradient, I kept pushing forward. Each switchback seemed to look down at me and let out a deep, dark laugh as I approached in my bedraggled state. Somehow, I dug deep, deep within myself and found the motivation and will to get my body and my bike up each stretch. I told myself in the midst of every switchback that we must be nearing the end.

Eventually I found myself cycling along a long ridge with a cliff to my left. I looked out over the ridge and took in the view as I putted along. I thought to myself, what do we think we are doing up here? I could hardly believe that we were so high up. I cycled along this long, straight stretch of road, which appeared to simply end at what looked like a little restaurant. It seemed that if I could just reach the restaurant, then I would be at the end of the climb! Oh, how I hoped that my eyes weren't deceiving me. Was I really seeing this, or was it a mirage?

As I approached, I felt jubilant that I had finally reached the end of this leg of my trek. James was already there waiting for me near the entrance to the building, but as I neared the end of this road, I realized that it continued on past the mystery building. I turned my head to the right and saw that the road flowed into another switchback that would continue to take me up to a peak that I could not yet see. It was now apparent to me that before I could rest my weary body I would have to make it up one last switchback, at the very least. I was stunned and frozen with fear. I simply didn't know how I was going to push through this final obstacle. Stopped and staring at the incline, I reminded myself once again that my options were to continue or to stay out here on the side of a mountain for the evening. On I went.

At this point, I don't really know how much time we had already spent climbing. My brain was fuzzy, making it difficult to recall all of the details. What I do remember is that time and space just seemed to blur into one big fuzzy haze. I remember being numb all over. I remember crying out in my head in a desperate plea for the whole thing to end. I remember looking at the side of the road and seriously considering climbing off of my bike and laying down in the dirt, simply because I wanted so badly for the suffering to stop.

Instead of giving in to the urge to quit, I pushed forward. I stopped frequently. My whole body was at the end of its endurance, and I was completely and utterly depleted. In fact, I felt so beyond exhaustion that continuing on at all was a huge undertaking. Each time I stopped, I hung my head over my handlebars, took a deep breath and somehow dug deep again to find a way to continue. On I went, tackling one little stretch at a time. I had stopped trying to convince myself that the end of the line was just around the corner, and had defaulted to pure survival mode. Time no longer had any meaning.

I don't know how long it took, but I somehow made it to the last stretch. There was the peak of this mountain, right in front of me in all its glory! Right there at the top, of course, was James standing there wearing a triumphant expression. I had made it! I had overcome the odds and made it! I don't know if I could ever find the words that would fully describe how I felt at that moment. To have completed something that seemed so far out of my reach and so beyond my abilities left me with a feeling of overwhelming accomplishment. There are few things in life that result in such a powerful outpouring of emotion.

We hung around at the top of the mountain for a while, taking some pictures and chatting with other cyclists. We quickly noticed that the bulk of the cyclists appeared to be coming up the other side of the mountain. As we conversed with a couple of guys from Australia that had made the trek up from this other side, they inquired about our ascent. At one point, one of the Australians said with a bit of shock in his voice, "Oh, you mean to say that you came up *that* side?" It turns out that we had made our ascent up the difficult side. My feeling of accomplishment swelled even bigger.

We made our way to a little restaurant and attempted to replenish our weary selves with cheese and bread. At this point, the food was nothing more than a side consideration. I was just so completely relieved that I had made it to the top that I didn't have room for any other concerns or thoughts.

Our descent down the other side was quite fun. We quickly realized how much easier this side was as we observed the much lower gradient on many of the switchbacks. It was beautiful. The long, open switchbacks were laid out before us and lined with trees. We felt ourselves suffused with joy as we coasted all the way into the valley and towards the hotel that we would call home for the night.

Our destination was the tiny town of Aucun. Once we arrived, I realized that I was voraciously hungry. We found a restaurant and had an absolutely wonderful meal. It astounded me how much I could eat and still not feel full. After our delightful dinner, I eagerly ordered a dessert. The moment the waiter rounded the corner carrying my confection, my eyes locked on to the treat: a gigantic ice cream sundae complete with whipped cream, cherry, and colorful, sparkly topper all piled high in a tall dessert glass. I ate every bite with zest. My soul was filled with celebration. I was so proud of both of us for persevering and completing what we set out to do.

After dinner, we drank wine and chattered excitedly about all of the details of the day. The moment left our hearts overflowing with the joy of our accomplishments. When we left the restaurant, we strolled around the tiny town nestled in the mountains and admired the quaint little dwellings and lush little gardens surrounding us. It was like a dream.

My adventure on Col d'Abisque taught me many important lessons. Perhaps most importantly, I learned that attempting something that seems entirely beyond my ability and that creates a little fear within me can result in a most unexpected experience and a significant amount of personal growth. Anything easy is probably not worth doing. You can always learn something from a difficult experience, even one that might have seemed like a failure. In this case, I learned the critical concept of pacing on long rides. I also learned that celebration is an important part of life that is often forgotten. It must be done with zest, and it must be done immediately after the event that merited it.

*Col d'Abisque: 30.1 km, 7.2% average gradient, 13% maximum
gradient, 1247 m ascent*

ASCENDING WITH GRACE

After our evening in Aucun, we cycled about 50 km the
following day to the sleepy town of Aste. We stayed in a lovely
little family-run hotel located very close to the base of our next
mountain challenge. Known for its carrots, Aste was replete with
various offerings that used carrots as a surprising main
ingredient. That evening, we feasted on carrot tart at the hotel.
The rest of the spread was equally amazing, and consisted of
trout with bilberries, rich cheese, and decadent chocolate
mousse.

The hotel was very obviously the domain of the mother, who ran a tight ship. She was keen to please her guests, and she knew exactly how to accomplish that. We were completely enchanted by this place in the middle of nowhere, surrounded by mountains and blanketed by a feeling of peace.

Rays of sunshine peeked through the window and dried our cycling attire, readying our clothes for their next adventure. The calm of our surroundings resulted in a long, deep sleep to the soundtrack of the river and croaking frogs. The fantastic home cooking infused with fresh ingredients from the local farms refueled and satisfied our bodies. We were ready to take on the next mountain. That night, I wrote, "I would like to grow tomorrow" in my journal as I tried to summarize the peace I currently felt and my preparedness to work hard as we resumed our journey.

The next morning we set off towards the famous Tourmalet. A longtime part of the Tour de France, this mountain is widely known, talked about, and traversed. As we pedaled toward the magnificent mountain, the lessons that I had learned a few days prior from Col d'Abisque filled my head. I thought about how I had so naively mistaken myself for the bionic woman, and about how my zest and excitement had taken over and contributed to my demise on the mountainside. I thought about what I could, and should do to make this next feat a different, better experience.

One idea occurred to me when I looked at the computer mounted onto my handlebars. Among many things, it displayed my current heart rate in real time. I didn't know a lot about cycling at this point in my life, but I did know from my recent training sessions back home that I could comfortably cycle for long periods of time when my heartrate was in the low 150s. Once I reached the 160s my exertion became unsustainable. I decided that my strategy would be to attempt to find a pace that would keep my heartrate in a place that I could sustain for several hours without reaching system overload.

On the surface, my plan seemed simple enough but I was far from calm. My stomach churned, and I felt tingles of anxiety. I really, really, really wanted to be able to complete this ascent gracefully and without repeating the experience of bonking. This was my focus, my one goal. As we got closer to the beginning of the climb, my nervousness grew. Take a deep breath, I told myself. Try and relax, try and focus. I began to climb.

The ascent up Tourmalet is absolutely breathtaking. The smoothness of the switchbacks and the surrounding countryside are beautiful. I felt my pedal strokes, I monitored my heart rate, and I tried to remember to breathe. As I conscientiously forced my legs into a smooth cadence, I could feel my physical and mental selves working together, and my soul and my surroundings merging into a place of complete cooperation. I found a flow like I have never found before. Everything around me and everything within me combined to create a single, powerful being. My mind was clear. The fresh air filled my nose and infused my body. I was alive in a way that I had never been before.

I worked hard, but I respected my body, and in return my body performed beautifully. As we reached an area of restaurants and homes about halfway up, we stopped and took a break. While we were resting, we enjoyed the company of some donkeys that were wandering around. Years later I would learn about the tranquility of donkeys, and I would look back and realize how fitting it was that at the same time that I found a flow with natural surroundings, I would also encounter a creature that had such wisdom on this topic.

On we went. As the day progressed, my confidence drastically increased and I found a very relaxed state. My strategy was working, so I focused on sticking to it. I listened to the bleating of the ewes that filled the grassy hillside. I looked ahead of me and saw a herd of cows crossing the road. I realized that cows would not be a threat, but it is rather intimidating to approach and cycle right through an entire herd. When I was surrounded by the mooing animals, I looked ahead to see James snapping photos. I giggled and continued on.

The closer and closer I got to the top of Tourmalet, the more excited I became. I had paced myself and kept my body fueled in an effort to respect my physical being. Now I could taste the victory. As I continued to climb, I soon came upon another cyclist, a French man, standing in the side of the ditch yelling out French words that were probably not so nice and throwing his bike down. I knew exactly how this man felt, and while I sympathized deeply with him I also felt a great sense of validation. It sure was wonderful to see that I was not the only one who had struggled with this difficult sport.

I will never forget that last stretch of road leading up to the summit. There he was, James, standing there with his camera and a victorious expression. We had done it, and what's more we had done it gracefully! The area was filled with other cyclists, all triumphant. We chatted excitedly and had our photos taken together beside a magnificent statue of a cyclist. After the excitement died down a little, we found our way to a sun soaked table on a patio and enjoyed a beer. Yes, the celebration had begun, but our small elation up on the summit would have to be enough until we had safely descended.

The climb had taken me about two and three quarters of an hour. The descent took another hour. That evening, James brought real French champagne back to our little cozy room nestled in the mountains and we enjoyed a quiet celebration with just the two of us.

The day of Col d'Abisque had taught me a lot. The day of Tourmalet provided the opportunity for me to apply what I had learned, and to grow as both a cyclist and a person. I had found a way to harness my inner fire, to control it a little, and to unleash it slowly so that it would last all the way to the top of a mountain.

I was just a girl who had climbed a mountain on her Trek 2000.

Tourmalet: 19 km, 7.4% average gradient, 10.2% maximum gradient, 1404 m ascent

FLAT TIRES, FRENCH FRIES, AND FANTA

The day was getting long. Most of the morning had been consumed by a small ascent up Col d'Apsin, followed by about thirty kilometers of cycling. It was well past noon, and the sun beat down on us with unrelenting heat. The air was still and stifling, without even the slightest hint of a breeze to relieve the suffocating warmth. Coupled with the high humidity, it was the type of day that could drain the life out of even the most determined soul.

We approached the famous Peyresourde, a beautiful brute of a mountain that formed a magnificent wall between us and our destination, and we started climbing. As I grunted my way up each switchback, sweat pouring down my face and stinging my eyes, heart beating hard against my chest, I couldn't help but look around me. Despite the heat, the beauty of the mountainside simply could not be ignored. As we climbed on and on, I dreamed of reaching the top and coasting down to our resting place. This was one journey, however, that would stretch out for far longer than I could have imagined.

The first challenge appeared in the form of a flat tire. Lucky for me, James was on hand to play the part of mechanic. It is not that I couldn't have changed my own tire; I knew the logistics of doing so and had practiced in the training room back home a number of times. It was simply that James was much more knowledgeable regarding the mechanics of a bicycle, and much quicker than I was at changing a tire. As he worked away on replacing the deflated tube, I looked around and tried to regroup a little. I was quite tired and overheated, and I wondered how long this climb would drag on. I wasn't used to doing two climbs in a single day, and I definitely wasn't conditioned for this moist heat clinging to my body.

Tire changed, we were soon on our way. We just kept on digging away, one pedal stroke at a time, one switchback at a time. It continued to get hotter. We were starting to run low on water, and I was definitely feeling the cumulative effects of prolonged fatigue. Then, out of nowhere, I got another flat tire! One flat tire isn't terribly unusual, but two in one day is definitely out of the ordinary. I could see James just ahead, and as I approached I realized that he was changing his own flat tire. This climb was just turning into a comedy of errors.

As James worked away at fixing our bikes, it sunk in how tired, hot, and thirsty I was. I was feeling quite depleted, and I knew intellectually that I was probably hungry as well even if my body was too hot and uncomfortable to feel it. A few tears pushed their way out and trickled down my face. I exclaimed that I just didn't know how much longer I could go on. We both looked at each other, and of course we both knew that despite my frustration I would go on for however long it took us to get to the top and down the other side to our home for the evening. James gave me a wonderful little pep talk, there in the soothing shade of the one tree that we could find. I listened to him, let my emotion pour out, and then really regrouped. I could do this.

Once the tires were changed and inflated, we were off once again. I dug deep and concentrated on focusing on the road a little ways ahead to give myself small, attainable goals that I could reach. We kept at it, and slowly crawled up the side of the mountain. I gradually became lost in my thoughts, dreaming of an ice cold glass of water and a shady spot to rest, only to be jolted out of that happy place when there was a commotion behind me.

Soon, a group of cyclists were passing me, calling out joyfully to each other and then to me. They were having an absolute blast cycling up this mountainside! Their energy infused the air, infused me. It was contagious. I simply could not complain about my situation. At this moment, I had to enjoy what was around me.

As if the cyclists themselves weren't encouragement enough, their support van soon passed me by and more cheers, coming from the passengers inside, filled the air. It was like this second round of cheers was just the magic that I needed to find my own salvation, because all of a sudden I could see the top! A little restaurant was nestled right on the peak. I just had to keep on going a little further.

Reaching the top was a true victory. Climbing two peaks in one day was an accomplishment in and of itself, but to complete the second climb in the middle of the hot, humid afternoon was an amazing feat. My exhaustion, my thirst, and my readiness to quit had all snowballed into a barrier that I had had to chip away at and mentally break down in my mind. I had needed to convince myself to keep going, and I had done just that. It felt fantastic to be at the top of this mountain!

James and I took some pictures and enjoyed the jovial shouts of the group that had passed us on the way up. Then, we found a spot on the little restaurant's patio. A small, very happy man, approached us and asked what we would like. We immediately asked for cold Fanta. I saw some very fresh and delicious looking french fries at a table next to us, and I pointed and said that I would love some of those. The man rushed off to get our order. It may have been the circumstances, but that Fanta was the coldest, most delicious drink I had ever had, and those fries were freshly made, crispy on the outside, soft on the inside, and exactly what my body wanted. It was one of the most enjoyable afternoon snacks I can remember.

Col d'Aspin: 12.8 km, 6.5% average gradient, 10% maximum gradient, 779 m ascent

Peyresourde: 15.27 km, 6.1% average gradient, 9% maximum gradient, 939 m ascent

As we sat there looking around and taking in the view, I wondered how long this man had run this restaurant. How many times had he seen the famous riders of the Tour de France pass over this mountain? How many people had he served during such an exciting time when it must be absolutely packed up here on this peak, full of crowds eagerly awaiting a chance to catch a glimpse of such an epic race and cheering on each rider as he passes by? The anticipation of the arrival of the first rider, the ones that follow, and the main peloton must be incredible. The frisson in the air as they pass by, muscles bulging, faces dripping with sweat, must be outstanding. I wondered how many times the happy restaurant owner had been swept up in such excitement.

THE 10 FOOT BURNING CARROT

I believe that I fell madly in love with cycling because it is a very individual and all-in activity. It requires a fairly high level of personal motivation, and the more you put into it the more you get out. For me, it was the first thing that I had ever done that gave back everything and more than I put in, even during my hardest training sessions. Perseverance always paid off, and my personal growth never stopped.

Cycling also opens up completely new worlds for me, both culturally and in terms of the relationships that I make along the way. When you travel by bike, a secret doorway is opened and you find yourself in completely new worlds where you can meet other people that you would have otherwise never had the opportunity to talk to. You make immediate, strong connections with others who share your experiences and goals.

In addition to meeting new people, you also discover new places. Cycling allows you to experience remote and hidden gems that may remain undiscovered when traveling in any other form. There is just something about being on a bike and earning your way to your destination that is utterly satisfying, and that creates a special bond between the cyclist and the earth. Every turn, every nook, every tree, every animal, every peak, all become such a vivid part of one's experience. Every town that you find yourself in for an evening of recovery becomes a permanent picture inside of your head.

After completing a very difficult week of cycling through the French Pyrenees and multiple ascents up famous French mountains, we found a permanent home for the second half of our trip in the French town of Luchon. Our stay was during the month of June, and therefore it was hot and *very* humid, especially for a girl from the prairie city of Calgary. Compared to what I was used to, Luchon was a totally different world.

Luchon has one main street lined on either side with little shops and restaurants, and with a perfect row of trees down the middle. The mornings are sleepy, and nothing really wakes up and gets going until at least nine or perhaps ten. Siesta is strictly adhered to, so everything shuts down by one or two in the afternoon and stays closed until at least seven. Dinner doesn't start until eight or nine. The simple Canadian, uneducated on the protocol of a little town nestled in the French mountains that observes siesta, might find herself hungry and with nothing to eat. Once the simple Canadian becomes a little more educated and adjusts her normal routine to the workings around her, however, she can quickly become enchanted.

I soon found myself completely entranced by the slow, sleepy mornings and the plethora of sweet pastries and smooth, foamy lattes for breakfast. What was left of the morning was spent strolling leisurely down the main street. There were multiple stops to acquire fresh bread baked that very morning, varieties of cheese that I had never heard of, and other delectable items for our afternoon lunch. The afternoon, of course, was spent picnicking on the delicious items we had found and submerging ourselves in the siesta.

We quickly understood why the siesta was so strictly followed. Between the heat, humidity, and complete lack of any breeze of any sort, it was easy to succumb to a state of stillness. We would find ourselves full of pastry, bread, and cheese, lying like beached whales on the bed in our quaint little hotel room. We would open the windows, but it wouldn't matter. The air did not move for hours.

Eventually, the hot, stiff air would give way to the delicious, soothing evening breeze. In this tiny mountain town, it cooled down significantly in the evenings. What a relief this was after the stifling heat of the afternoon! The evenings were so peaceful. We would lay in complete relaxation with the windows open and the cool, crisp air soothing our bodies. I recall one evening when we were engulfed in the cool air, fast asleep, and were awoken by the most beautiful sound we had ever heard. We both stirred and our ears pricked up, taking in the beautiful sound and trying to identify the source. It was the sound of voices. It was an entire chorus of voices singing in unison with perfect harmony. The sound rose up into the air and drifted into our little room.

Following an afternoon of resting in the heat, a typical evening would unfold and the town would slowly awaken from its slumber. The shops and restaurants would come alive, and soon the main street was lined with twinkling lights and filled with chatter and laughter. The earlier part of the evening was time for drinks and socializing. Here, people did not stay in their homes watching their televisions and ignoring each other. Instead, everyone in the town came out, sat on patios, breathed in the fresh evening air, and engaged in conversations with their friends and family.

Eventually after several hours of social time, the restaurants would start serving dinner. Regardless of whether you were enjoying a drink or a full meal, the server would not bring your check until you asked for it. Back home this may have been irritating, but here people placed so much emphasis on socializing and taking their time that the Western way of quickly herding people in and out of restaurants would have seemed rude.

In fact, everything about this town operated with an entirely different style than what I was used to. We had come from a Monday-to-Friday hectic routine with crammed weekends that did not allow for much relaxation. Here, we found ourselves pulled into a slow, calm rhythm. After a week of cycling aggressively up mountains, it was quite easy to succumb to this new lifestyle and forget all about how things worked at home. It might have been one of the first times that I had actually felt my entire being slow down and exist in the moment. Day by day, we were slowly pulled into the Luchon lifestyle. By the end of the week, we were completely submersed and I felt that I could have stayed there forever.

One afternoon as we slowly emerged from our deep siesta, we strolled down the main street looking for a place to hang out and socialize. Later on, we found ourselves in a small Italian-style bistro nestled in a small, rustic basement where we enjoyed a long, leisurely dinner of wine and thin crust wood-fired pizza. Bellies full, we made our way back to ground level and strolled around, enjoying the evening.

We soon observed a crowd of people milling around in front of the town center, which was unusual since there aren't often crowds in such a small, quiet town. Curious, we joined the others and waited around to see what was going to happen. There was a wooden structure, taller than the town hall and very narrow with paper roughage sprouting off the top, in the center of the crowd. The structure had been built during the week, and although we had noticed the activity we hadn't been able to figure out what it was for. Now that it was completed, it seemed to be the focal point of whatever event was about to unfold.

The crowd continued to grow, and we could feel the excitement mounting around us. All of a sudden, a live band started playing. Before our eyes, the band led an entire parade with all kinds of people in various costumes to march their way into the town center. They surrounded the mystery structure, and somehow it all came together and dawned on us that this was the festival of the carrot. Yes, that's right, the festival of the carrot. You see, we were in another area that was famous for its carrots. We could attest to how good the carrots were as we had enjoyed them enormously in a multitude of forms over the past week.

As the parade circled what now became apparent to us as the ten-foot wooden carrot, my dear sweet husband declared out loud, "They are going to set this thing on fire!" My first reaction was that there was no way that was the plan. It was taller than the town hall, there wasn't any fence around it, and there were children running everywhere. The simple Canadian inside of me could only think how uncontrolled and ridiculous it would be to burn the carrot.

We weren't in Canada, however, but in a small French town nestled in the mountains, and it turned out that James was right. Next thing you know, the giant wooden carrot was on fire. The crowd went wild. We all stood around, watching chunks of flaming debris falling to the ground to narrowly miss the children running around the base of the flaming carrot and wondering which way it was going to fall!

Eventually, the burning carrot did fall without hitting anyone. The whole event was over, and nothing tragic had occurred. The crowd of contented people starting making their way to their little homes nestled in the mountains. What an evening, and the perfect example of the undiscovered places and cultures that I wouldn't know anything about if I hadn't fallen madly in love with cycling.

ONE LAST CLIMB

The two weeks of our French cycling trip had flown by. It was hard to believe it, but we were nearing the end of this wonderful experience, and would soon be heading home. I had had the amazing opportunity to put my first training season to the test on some of the most challenging mountains of the Tour de France. My physical and mental abilities had been completely put to the test. Spinning on a bike going nowhere day after day within the confines of four walls had paid off.

I had been amazed at how smoothly I was able to ascend the smaller climbs such as Col Marie Blanque. That I was able to take on multiple switchbacks in one fell swoop and only stop a couple of times on a climb absolutely blew my mind. Completing multiple climbs not only in one day, but after consecutive days of cycling these towering beasts was something that I hadn't even thought of doing before this adventure.

Climbing the French mountains also showed me that I was still very green as a cyclist, and that I had lot to learn. There is nothing more humbling than being physically and mentally broken on the side of a mountain. There is also nothing more rewarding than finding the gusto to grind through it and make it to the summit. Hitting my physical and mental bottom as I crawled my way up Col d'Abisque will always remain one of the most vivid and compelling memories of my life. There were moments on the side of that mountain in which making it to the top seemed incomprehensible. Knowing that I was able to dig so very deep inside of myself and find the physical ability and mental focus to finish it will always remain one of the most rewarding moments of my life. My ability to brush myself off, reflect on the day, and apply what I had learned on the Tourmalet will forever be one of my greatest cycling successes. To this day, I can vividly picture in my mind many parts of Tourmalet and the thoughts and feelings that I had at those moments.

Memories of the moments of celebration and those of complete surrender to our serene surroundings still dance around in my head. I can picture my celebratory dessert topped with a sparkly splash. I can feel the fresh mountain air infusing my soul as we strolled through the tiny town of Aucun inspecting all the perfectly manicured gardens. I can hear the sonorous sounds of chorus echoing through the night in Luchon.

Despite the gruelling effort it had been at times to haul a bike case up flights of stairs and onto trains, it had been an absolute blessing to have my Trek 2000 there with me every pedal stroke of the way. As soon I started pedalling on our first ride, it just felt completely right that my bike and I were together in one of the most amazing cycling places in the world. My bond with this little bike had grown bounds by the end this cycling adventure. It wasn't really that different than sharing blood, sweat, and tears with another human being. I literally felt that my relationship with this bike was now deeply grounded within my soul.

After spending several days resting in the lovely little French town of Luchon, we had reached our final day before heading home. We decided to use this last day to cycle up one more mountain. This ascent was the lovely little nine km climb of Portillon.

In order to beat the day's heat, we got started in the morning while there was still a much-welcomed cloud cover. It was invigorating and wonderful to simply get up and climb a mountain. Cycling like this had quickly become a normal part of my routine, and I loved it! It amazed me to think that this was becoming ordinary for me. It amazed me even more to think of a nine km climb as short. After the climbs that I had accomplished the week before, my perspective on what I could achieve had been changed.

This particular peak was a real treat. The air was still fresh as the stifling and still heat had not yet descended upon us. The switchbacks were smooth and beautifully laid out before us. We were surrounded by lush greenery. I had not a care in the world. As I began the ascent, I completely sank into the moment and enjoyed every pedal stroke. Reaching the summit was another small victory. This one was special because it came at the end of a short two week journey that had taught me more than I had learned in years. The summit is right on the border between France and Spain, and the views are breathtaking. You could literally put one foot in each country at the same time, which I proceeded to do as a small, silly reward to myself.

It was really hard to head home and leave my beloved mountains behind, but it was time to go. The only thing that made leaving easier was that I knew that I would be back.

Col du Portillon: 10.2 km, 6.5% average gradient, 663 m ascent

THE ITALIAN CHAPTER

'Don't Ever Give Up.' - Contributed by Ania Bergmann

FANCY BIKES, FOOD AND FRIENDS

When James signed us up for a two-week cycling tour of Italy, I had no idea what an absolutely amazing and life-changing experience it would be. Now that I had a couple of cycling trips under my belt, I was aware of how difficult our upcoming tour could be. On the other hand, I was also much more aware of and confident in my own physical abilities than I had ever been.

This had not been my most hardcore offseason in terms of commitment to a physical and nutritional regimen, but at least I had been reasonably consistent with my exercise routine and with healthy eating. Looking back, it was actually a fairly well-balanced approach. As soon as the weather warmed up, I was outside most days on my bike even if just for a short one-hour ride. I made sure to insert as many hill repeat days days as possible into my routine. As for eating, I didn't restrict anything completely but I did try to focus on a healthy balance most of the time. I think the key thing that I did was to not overdo it.

Bikes loaded into travelling cases and backpacks filled with strategically chosen items so that we could comfortably live for two weeks with very little luggage, we were ready to go. The flight was long, but we were greeted by our tour guides at the airport in Verona so there was never any point that we were alone once we landed. They whisked us off through the lovely Italian countryside to the cycling hotel where we would be staying for the first part of our adventure.

After a good sleep, we indulged in a true Italian breakfast on a little patio. Delicious pastries and rich, strong coffee perked us up out of our jetlag. Soon we felt up to exploring the grounds. We quickly realized how perfect this spot was, surrounded by breathtaking views of vineyards and a plethora of great riding routes. In fact, James and I were in total agreement that the hotel was fantastic. The food and service were outstanding. There was no shortage of fuel for the motivated cyclist wishing to conquer the great mountains. The hotel even boasted a separate room in which you could store and prep your fancy ride and the case that it travelled in.

Later that morning, we met the group for our first ride. I was nervous. It was only going to be a short ride to stretch our legs a little and to get accustomed to riding in the area, but this was my first real group ride with people that I didn't know. I didn't know much at all about riding in groups. I was sure there was secret cycling protocol that I hadn't been exposed to yet.

Despite my misgivings, we were soon off. Almost immediately, my concerns melted away. I loved it! This was awesome! There I was, prancing along on the pedals, feeling the sunshine on my face, and taking in the beauty around me. It felt pretty fantastic to be cycling through the vineyards of Italy on a Monday morning instead of being stuck behind a computer all day. It was glorious.

Best of all, riding with the group was fun. They were really positive people, and it was very motivating to be in their midst. When we reached a long, straight stretch, the guys took off. I took it easy, sitting up a little to take in the scenery and to enjoy the whole experience. I knew there would lots of opportunity to challenge myself, and I wanted to take the time to let the beauty of my surroundings really sink in and suffuse my soul.

20% GRADIENT

It was our second day of riding on our two-week cycling tour of Italy. I was already completely acclimated to the routines and the culture. I thoroughly enjoyed the breakfast buffets that included pastries, Nutella, and delicious frothy lattes. I loved the huge feasts and wine in the evenings with the company of our newfound cycling friends. There were eight of us in total including our tour guides, and although we had all just met I felt like we were in the company of old friends. The group's synergy was outstanding.

After gearing up and regrouping in the cycling room, we were off. It was another picture-perfect day. We rode through a fairly flat, straight stretch alongside Lake Garda for a while, and then eventually we started a climb. Of course! You simply cannot ride in Italy without climbing. It was a short, yet hefty climb. I could feel the fire of the physical activity burning in my belly, and I was off. I felt good. I felt strong. My legs were on my side.

We regrouped at a plateau. The guys planned to continue on and tackle a few small stretches of 20% gradient. The other two ladies intended to head back. I opted for the 20% gradient. I had no idea what this meant. I don't think anyone really understands what 20% gradient truly means until they have faced it.

As we approached the first section, I looked up into a concrete wall staring me down. It looked very steep. I began to climb the stretch, and almost immediately I slowed significantly. The longer I kept grinding through the steep incline, the harder my heart began beating. I would have sworn that it was going to beat right through my chest. I felt dizzy. I panicked. Was I going to fall over?

Fortunately, I was able to regain my focus. Just breathe, I told myself, and so I did. I breathed, and I focused on the plateau ahead of me. I could do this. It took a lot of effort, but I did make it, all the while finding myself amazed at everything about my experience with a 20% gradient. All I can say is that anyone who has ever attempted this on a bike has a true appreciation for it. I soon joined the guys at the top of the climb, grinning from ear to ear, proud of my tiny accomplishment at making it up such a steep slope.

We finished off the ride, and in true Italian style found ourselves an outdoor patio where we could enjoy refreshing beverages and the warm sunshine. We chatted contentedly, and deepened the already strong bonds we had begun to forge with our new cycling friends.

A GAPING CLIFF

The first real test during our Italian cycling tour was the day of Monte Baldo. I approached this climb believing that it would be just another day, just another mountain. By this point we were completely comfortable with our new cycling buddies, and were really enjoying the experience of our first supported cycling tour. To have such support was a gift, really. James could take off a few of his hats, worry less about navigating and coaching, and focus more on his riding. We had the comfort of food, water, and encouragement just when we needed it most. Best of all, we had motivation to make it to the top where we would be congratulated by our fellow cyclists.

Things became interesting when we were already deep into the climb of Monte Baldo. I found myself on a long stretch where I could see the support vehicle and James waiting for me ahead. I felt slow and lethargic, and as I pedaled I pondered why this climbing felt so rough. Despite my difficulties, I kept grinding forward until I came to a halt beside James, who shared that he was finding this climb really tough. I agreed, and we both wondered why it was so hard. We debated the possibility that it might be the heat of the day, but it was undeniable that we both felt we were not performing up to par.

From our stopped position, we looked forward at the next stretch ahead of us. I took a gulp, and felt a bit of fear tingle through my veins when I saw that the mountain opened up to a gaping cliff. The view was spectacular, but the road that we were to cycle up was not. It was extremely narrow for the two way traffic that it was supposed to support. We would be cycling on the cliff side, of course, which made it even scarier thanks to the lack of any safety rail.

Perhaps the most terrifying part about this stretch of the climb was the steepness. To me, it looked like a wall. To fully validate my fear, there was a sign that indicated the next stretch was 19% gradient. I thought back to the small sections of 20% gradient that I had battled through a couple of days ago, and felt my heart begin to race as anxiety shot through me. In my mind's eye, I could picture myself unable to move my bike forward and falling over into oncoming traffic or plunging off the side of the mountain. My fear was so complete and intense that I actually contemplated getting into the support vehicle.

Fortunately, James put on his coaching hat once again and gave me a short pep talk to let me know that he believed I could do it. As we replenished ourselves at the sag wagon, the two lovely ladies supporting us provided some much-needed encouragement. They made it clear that they believed in me. I wasn't sure that I shared their belief, but I followed my husband's lead and got back on my bike anyways.

Off we went. I concentrated on talking myself through this, reminding myself over and over again that I could do it. We cycled towards the wall that seemed to face us down, and then started our ascent. As we began to climb, I thought back to the feeling of my heart wanting to escape from my chest on the 20% gradient two days ago and I reminded myself to breathe. I had no choice but to concentrate on the task at hand, to tell myself that I could battle through this, and to keep hyperfocusing on drawing in a breath, letting it out, and then repeating the cycle over and over again. I ground out every pedal stroke as I took the wall straight on.

I was partway through as I turned a bit of a bend. I dared to look to my right and caught a glimpse of the gaping nothingness below me. My stomach leaped to my throat, and I realized that this one little peek had been a huge mistake that I couldn't afford to repeat. I only looked straight ahead of me the rest of the way up. As I continued on and neared the top, it dawned on me that I had thrown everything into this ascent and that I wasn't going to stop until I made it through. I looked up to see that I was approaching the support team, and once I rejoined them and came to a halt I breathed a huge sigh of relief. Wow! That was *really* scary, but I had done it! I was excited. I was elated. I felt alive!

Monte Baldo was not an easy feat. It was my first long climb in the Italian Dolomites, and it was an incredibly difficult beast to tackle. When we had signed up for this cycling tour, I had had no idea what I was getting into. Each day was a new challenge, giving me the opportunity to surprise myself again and again with what I was capable of accomplishing.

That evening over another fantastic Italian meal, one of our fellow cyclists shared the data that he had collected during the ride that day. As he showed us how much 19% gradient we had cycled that day, it became clear to both me and James why the climbing had felt so difficult. While we were chatting, our fellow cyclist also shared his experience at the wall. He told us that he had contemplated getting into the support vehicle and taking the easy way up, but then he had thought to himself, "Julie is going to do this, so I guess I have to as well!" When he asked me if I had taken the wall head on or if I had resorted to a zigzag track, I was able to proudly reply that I had tackled it straight on. I had never felt more like a champion.

A RACE WITH THOUSANDS OF ITALIANS

I was unbelievably nervous. My stomach tingled and churned. I could feel beads of sweat on my face. I wasn't sure if I was going to wet my pants or vomit.

There I stood, deep in the middle of a sea of cyclists in the little town of Feltre. I was directly surrounded by several hundred women, all of them decked to the nines in fancy cycling gear and straddling flashy rides. To my right was the front platoon of several thousand men. Since the number of women taking part in the event was far fewer than the number of men, the women were placed up at the front alongside the fastest men, the ones who were competing for points and attempting to turn pro.

This was the first time in my life that I had ever participated in a real athletic event. I had never seen so many cyclists in person in the same place at the same time. There I was, just a girl in a matching blue cycling outfit, straddling my Trek 2000 and wondering what was going to happen when they said "go."

The next thing I knew, the magic word had been spoken and we started moving. I thought about the advice that had been given to me: Take your time, don't clip both feet in, and anticipate a lot of stop and go. I watched the cyclists around me like a hawk. I kept one foot out. I took my time.

I was extremely relieved when the pack started to pick up some speed and I was able to find my way over to the far right where I could cycle at my own pace on this long stretch of flat road surrounded by trees. I breathed in the fresh air and took in the beautiful Italian countryside. Thousands of extremely fit Italian men in tight clothing whizzed by me on custom-painted carbon. What a scene. Knowing this was going to be a long day, I paced myself and went out of my way to take it all in.

A couple of weeks ago, I had had very little knowledge of the Granfondo race. When I learned of it, I wasn't sure that I would participate since it was an optional part of our cycling tour. When the two other ladies in our cycling tour signed up without hesitation, however, I felt that I couldn't give up this opportunity to try something new even if I didn't have a full understanding of what I was agreeing to.

The idea of a big cycling event was foreign to me. Back home, this type of event was unheard of. Nestled here in the Italian mountains, though, it was common to shut down roads and towns to give thousands of cyclists the full run of the roadways for an entire day.

Not long into the ride, my bladder got the better of me. My nerves had churned up a bit of a dam in my system, but now that I was on my way things were moving again. I wasn't really sure what to do, so I kept cycling while looking around for any opportunity to relieve my situation. Soon we approached a town, which was totally shut down for this event except for the tables of food and water that the locals had set up. I stopped at one table and asked a woman for a "toilette." Fortunately, she was eager to help me out. I was so grateful.

As I was attempting to deal with my situation quickly so that I could get back on my bike, someone started banging at the door and yelling in another language, probably Italian. I could only respond in my simple English to ask him to hold on a moment. I think tone of voice is what communicates the most in these situations, but it was still funny to come out of the facilities and find myself face to face with a bewildered looking man in cycling gear. Laughing to myself, I made my way back to my bike and kept pushing on.

Soon after that, we began the first ascent. I had signed up for the "medio" course, which consisted of 116 km and three climbs. I knew from past experience that I could do two climbs, but I didn't know if I could handle a third. This race would be a personal challenge, which is why of course I had had to sign up for it.

On this cycling trip, I had come to understand that a climb in the Italian mountains would absolutely include some steep gradient. I had also learned that the afternoons were hot and humid. It was still early when we began our first ascent, so at this point the air was still cool and crisp and perfect for cycling. I looked up at the switchbacks winding their way up the mountain of lush green. It was perfect. I found a wonderful flow, and my physical and mental beings became one with my natural surroundings. I felt strong. I finished the first climb without a hitch.

We were now traversing a flatter area, and I knew that soon enough we would be on to our second ascent. One of the other ladies in our cycling tour had joined me by this point. Rather than stopping at the crowded fuel station to accept the refreshments being offered by volunteers, we decided to pull over onto a stretch of road and eat the bars that we had brought with us. We were about two hours into the ride, and I was so glad that I had taken the advice that had been given to me early that morning. At first, eating a plate of pasta at six in the morning had sounded absurd, but these guys obviously knew what they were doing. A heaping plate of simple pasta without any heavy sauce somehow miraculously fuels the system with the burst of easily accessible energy that the body needs to cycle up a mountain alongside thousands of Italians first thing in the morning. I now took the advice of another fellow cyclist on our tour, and ate a bar full of protein and carbs in preparation for the next ascent.

Off we went. It wasn't long before the second climb was upon us. I could tell right away that this one was going to be tougher than the first. There were steep sections, and the day was getting warmer. I still felt strong, though, and at that point I was in a flow that seemed unstoppable. I had learned enough by now to know that I had to keep my body fuelled, and that I had to pace myself. I made sure to do exactly that, but I also let myself push when I felt that I could.

By the end of the second climb I was feeling exhaustion creeping in, but I was mighty determined. I was able to fuel up with fresh oranges and cold water, and chat with the friendly volunteers at one of the fuel stations. I was very grateful to the local bar owners for their willingness to let me use their facilities so that I didn't have to deal with not-so-private bushes. Everyone was just so friendly and eager to help. It was amazing.

Despite the lovely hospitality that I was enjoying, not everything was perfect. The day was growing hotter by the minute. I was getting tired. There was still a third climb looming between me and the finish line. I had to start taking more frequent breaks.

All day long I had been playing hopscotch with two cyclists from Australia. They would take off on the descents, but I would often catch up to them on the stretches of climbing. As it became apparent that this last climb was going to be a true test of my limits, I happened upon those cyclists again. At this point, one of them commented that I was really tough. All I could say was, "that's what my husband keeps telling me." In retrospect, I guess that they were right.

By this point in the ride, continuing forward had become an example of mind over matter for many of the cyclists participating in the event. It was becoming common to see groups of cyclists who had packed it in for the day sitting on the side of the road. I am proud to say that I didn't contemplate that once on this ride. It got very hot, and some the sections of road were quite steep. I did have to stop at times, hang my head over my handlebars, and breathe. As I was taking one such break, one of the support vehicles pulled over to ask me if I was ok. I gave them a thumbs up and indicated that I was fine. I must have been more convincing than I felt, because they eventually continued on. I was still determined. I wanted so badly to finish this.

The last several kilometres were even steeper than the first two climbs, running right around a 20% gradient. By the time you reach such a steep gradient, your body is all in and you have to focus and convince your heart not to jump right out of your chest. Piece by piece, I dug away at this last section. I had come this far, and I was not going to give up. I wanted this so badly. I knew I could do it.

I put everything I had into moving forward and getting ever closer to the finish line. I cannot explain how excited I was when I rounded the final bend and saw that I was at the top of the climb. I had made it! My heart was so full of joy and my whole being was yelling out in celebration. This was definitely the hardest thing that I had ever done in my life up to this point. I was so completely satisfied that I can only describe what I felt as a perfect moment in time. From here, all I had to do was coast into the finish line.

I pumped my hand into the air triumphantly and then turned my focus to the descent. I was reaching speeds of 61 km/hr, which for me was a decent speed. I pushed and I pushed as my mental image of the finish line grew increasingly vivid. I was anticipating that home stretch so much that I was barely able to hold back my excitement and finish off the last bit of cycling. As I rounded that final turn, I saw before me a crowd of people on either side of the fence and a huge banner to indicate the finish line. People were applauding for me! I realize that they were probably there to see the fast guys that had finished hours earlier or perhaps people that they knew, but they were clapping as I came down that final stretch and in those moments I absorbed the emotion and the sense of victory. Best of all, there was James, running along with his jersey fully zipped open and flapping in the wind and his camera in hand. What an emotional high. What a moment to forever hold in my memory.

Across the finish line I went, and James guided me to the huge tent where they were serving refreshments. Another lady from our cycling tour spotted us and came over to join us as James found us a wonderfully shaded spot and then went to get us some food. To my amazement, he returned with a full and delicious pasta meal that was being prepared for all of the thousands of cyclists that had completed the event. My heart brimmed with appreciation to all of those people who had made this event possible, and to those who had encouraged me and given me advice along the way. I will never forget that day, and all of the details of my surroundings and how I felt at the various points along the journey.

Someone told me once that you won't remember what you were doing at work two years ago, but that you would always have vivid memories of certain moments in your life. They were right. To this day, in my mind's eye I can see the thousands of cyclists racing along a stretch of road lined with trees. I can feel the crispness of the air as I ascended the winding switchbacks surrounded by lush green on that first climb. I can feel the heat, the depletion, and the determination inside as I hung my head over my handlebars and realized that I *needed* to finish this course. I can see the people lining the cobblestone street towards the finish line and, of course, I see my husband running along the cobbles, jersey flapping open and camera in hand as he raced to get a picture of me crossing the finish line.

Start Point: Feltre 271 m

Climb 1: CastelloTesino: 600 m ascent

Climb 2: Le Ej: 14.49 km, 5.7% average gradient, 820 m ascent

*Climb 3: Passo Croce d'Aune 8.57 km, 7.8% average gradient,
605 m ascent*

SINKING INTO THE MOMENT

The day following our huge cycling extravaganza with thousands of cyclists, we relocated our base of operations to a tiny hotel nestled on top of a mountain. The only way to get to the paradise called Bolzano is to take a cable car up the side of a mountain. Once we checked into our cozy little room, we made our way to a patio and basked in the sunshine. I saw this lovely old, shaggy dog completely sprawled out on the deck taking in every bit of warmth that the glorious sun had to offer. One of the restaurant servers commented that he would not move, even if people tried to get around him. This dog was smart! He knew something about taking it all in.

It wasn't long before I found myself in our room looking out at the mountain panorama before me and down into the little town in the valley below. I felt like my whole being had taken an incredibly long deep breath, and then exhaled out every bit of anxiety, stress, and nervousness. I felt completely and utterly satisfied, both physically and mentally. In the last 24 hours I had experienced things that I had never even known existed. If you had told me even a few years back that I would someday cycle 116 km over three Italian mountains alongside thousands of cyclists, I would never have believed you. Now it just seemed like this was an integral part of my life and of who I was.

Allowing my fatigue to overtake me, I crawled into the snug bed. The puffy white cover engulfed me like I was being wrapped in a cloud. The sun streamed in through the open window, and covered me with warmth. I fell into one of the deepest sleeps I have ever had the luxury of experiencing.

That evening, my husband and I went down to the restaurant area prior to dinner time. We ran into Ed, one of our fellow cyclists on the tour, and invited him to enjoy a beer with us. He thought this was a lovely idea, and next thing we knew we were sitting, enjoying cold, delicious, frothy beers in tall glasses.

The dinner was nothing less than amazing. There was a fantastic resident chef who fed us pastas, rabbit, cheeses, and much more. The food itself was spectacular, and the company was equally wonderful. The experience of a large group dinner, of enjoying the food and wine and swapping stories of the adventures we had partaken in over the last week with our friends, is definitely a memory that I hold dear in my heart.

NERVES TURN TO CALM

Of all the rides that I did with the group, I think I was most nervous at the start of our Umbrail climb. After a drive that took up most of the morning, we finally stopped for lunch. Our guides indicated that we would have extra time today, which would allow us to disembark part way up a climb known as Umbrail and ride to the top. My stomach was uneasy from the driving, but since I knew that we had a climb ahead of us I forced myself to eat anyway. I felt better.

We had a little more driving to do before starting to ride, making our way up treacherous switchback after treacherous switchback. It was nauseating. At one point, we were delayed by construction. Cyclists and motorbikes were able to get through, but we had to wait. We sat there as we watched a car drive off of the tight little road into a deep dell to get around. We watched several cars and vans make the precarious trip around a tractor and a steam roller on the narrow mountainside road, and with each vehicle that passed my anxiety grew. Finally it was our turn. My teeth were clenched as the van maneuvered its way upwards. My stomach was queasy, and I had some serious jitters, but we made it past the construction without incident and continued on our way up the mountain.

I am not quite sure why I was so nervous. I don't know if it was because I hadn't been able to anticipate this climb in advance, or if it was because we had been driving for hours that morning and I found myself feeling a bit lethargic. It could have been from the teeth-clenching drive up the switchbacks and around the construction. It could have been some combination of all three of those factors, or something else entirely. Sometimes I simply get nervous.

Over the years I have tried to control my nerves with mixed success. I do think it is a good thing to keep your nerves in check, but I also think that sometimes a little nervousness is not necessarily a bad thing. Confronting your fears and pushing yourself out of the safe haven of your routine is good for you. Every time I have ventured out of my comfort zone over the years, I have been very glad that I did it. I always end up grateful that I took on a new challenge, and I usually learn something about myself. No matter how many years I continue to be a cyclist, I think that I will always find myself feeling nervous before certain rides. This might be a good sign that I am continuing to challenge myself. It might also be a good sign that no matter how much confidence I build, I can still be humbled.

Finally we pulled over on the side of the mountain and started preparing for the ride. My nervousness grew. In an attempt to calm myself down, I tried to find a somewhat private place on this very open area. It felt like we were literally in the middle of nowhere, but it was still difficult to be alone. Grassy spaces spattered in rocks were in every direction of the wide open space.

Soon enough, we were off. There we were once again, me and my little Trek 2000, attempting to summit a grand mountainside. Even though we were only doing a portion of the climb, Umbrail was challenging. Once I started cycling, though, I found my legs as I always do. The queasiness in my stomach began to subside, and my nerves began to calm. After only a couple of switchbacks, I was completely in the moment. This is one of the most amazing things about cycling. If you truly give in to it, your physical being starts to flow as one with your natural surroundings. Your mind calms and finds a restful place. All clutter vanishes. You find your entire being in the present.

I continued to climb up each switchback while taking in the beauty around me and sinking into the wonderful feeling of climbing up the mountainside. I could see the others ahead of me. We were a scattered string of cyclists, each conquering the mountain at our own pace.

Now that my nerves were calmed, I completely and utterly enjoyed this climb. Eventually, the others disappeared ahead of me, and it was just me on the mountainside. I wasn't sure how much further it was. I sank further in the tranquility of the moment. My breathing, my pedal strokes, and heart rate were flowing harmoniously with each other. It was wonderful. Just as I was wondering how far ahead the others were, I saw our cycling guide and one of the other cyclists poking their wheels around the corner. They had come to check on my status, and were surprised at how close I was. The three of us cycled side by side up the final few stretches. What a glorious feeling.

We took a moment to bask in the beauty of the summit and the feeling of having achieved this reward for our hard work climbing. There we were, on the top of a mountain, just over the border separating Switzerland and Italy. Once again I had climbed, and I had loved it. During this cycling tour, my limits had definitely been challenged.

Soon we began our descent down the other side. We were actually descending down part of Stelvio, which we would be taking on in its entirety the next day. We looked before us, and we saw a never-ending series of neatly stacked switchbacks. There were 48 of them, to be exact.

Down we went. The switchbacks are long and open. We were able to see quite far ahead of us, so the first part of the descent went smoothly until we approached what would turn out to be a series of intimidating, gaping tunnels. As I entered the first tunnel, the darkness began to engulf me, and I felt panic and fear creeping up on me. What if the drivers behind me couldn't see me? What if there was something in my path and I couldn't see it?

I slid my Rudy Project sunglasses down my face a little to expose my eyes to as much light as possible and found that the situation wasn't as bad as my initial panic had suggested. It wasn't completely black, so I could see well enough. It was unnerving, though. Being in a tunnel always, to this day, makes my adrenaline soar. Very motivated to get through the other side, I pedaled quickly. Soon I saw a burst of sunshine ahead and I could feel myself calming once again. We had to go through a series of these tunnels, and I didn't particularly enjoy any of them. I did, however, enjoy reaching the bottom of the mountain and seeing before me the absolutely spectacular town of Bormio. This would be our home for the next few days.

Bormio is quaint, quiet, and relaxed. Little houses and hotels are scattered across the grassy fields, a bubbling brook flows through the town and underneath little wooden bridges, the main street is lined with little shops and restaurants, and the main square is a wonderful place to sit on a sunny patio. The hotel that we were staying in was an old-fashioned building with small balconies and a lovely yard of green grass and colorful flowers. As we made our way into the lobby, my nose was filled with the scent of lavender, and my ears were treated to the soft, sonorous sounds of relaxing music. We were greeted by the sisters who run the hotel with their mother. The atmosphere was warm, inviting, and extremely relaxing.

We quickly settled in our cozy rooms, and ventured out onto our individual balconies where we enjoyed the view of the mountains surrounding us and the small houses scattered all around us. What a lovely place.

That afternoon I had one of the most amazing massages I have ever had in my life. After all of the riding and climbing I had been doing, my muscles were wound tight. I entered the massage room in the basement of our hotel, and was welcomed by the warm glow of candlelight, soft music, and my friendly masseuse: a diminutive Italian girl, soft spoken and friendly. She guided me into the massage room and gave me instructions in Italian paired with hand gestures. I understood well enough, and soon she went to work on my aching body.

Despite her slight physical appearance, my masseuse was strong. She worked my tight muscles, and even though she was pushing quite deep I could tell that she was holding back. I knew how tight I was, and I was a regular participant in sports therapy massage. I struggled to find the words to indicate to her that she could go deeper, but wasn't sure how to indicate to her that we had been cycling and I would be perfectly comfortable with her unleashing her full power. I am not sure what word eventually escaped my lips, but she understood. Soon, she was working so hard on me that I could hear her breath get heavy. I was engulfed in warmth, and every last ounce of tension was released from my body. I don't think I have ever been so relaxed in my life. Feeling like jello, I lethargically returned to our room.

That night we were introduced to the dinner routine in this wonderful hotel. The salad bar was magnificent. A long table of cheeses, breads, olive oils, fresh vegetables, varieties of beans, and other delectable foods was laid out before us. The dinners consisted of a choice of appetizer and a main course. The dishes were made locally by the in-house chef, and were prepared with fresh ingredients. Dessert was also a buffet of a multitude of items. Even I couldn't possibly try them all.

My aching body was rejuvenated. My hungry belly was satisfied. I was relaxed. I slept very well that night, nestled in the Italian mountains.

Umbrail: 13.2 km, 8.5% average gradient, 11% maximum gradient, 1126 m ascent

48 HAIRPIN TURNS

Famous for its appearances in the Giro d'Italia, Stelvio is a monster of a mountain consisting of 48 hairpin bends. The mountain's foot begins in the outskirts of the town of Bormio with a few switchbacks to quickly help the cyclist warm up. It then opens up to a few long and unforgiving stretches dotted with dark tunnels. If you make it this far, then you will see laid out before you a series of never-ending switchbacks snaking their way up the side of the mountain. The final stretch is hidden from view behind a corner, leaving you to wonder the whole time that you work your way up this beast what unseen challenges might await you before your victory at the top. When you finally make it around the corner, you find a few more solid switchbacks winding their way through snow-spattered grass and rocks. It is breathtaking. It is daunting.

Despite its intimidating appearance, this climb was a very peaceful one for me. Perhaps at this point I was starting to believe that I could simply get up, have breakfast, get on my bike, and climb up a mountain. Perhaps I was simply in awe of the sight of the switchbacks laid out before me. Whatever had caused it, I had found some sort of stillness.

On the morning of the climb, my little Trek 2000 and I warmed up with the group by riding through Bormio before making our way towards the base of Stelvio. It was a cooler day, I was surrounded by beauty, and I simply slipped into a wonderful flow. It was hard work, and the first few switchbacks were quite unforgiving. If the stroll through town hadn't warmed me up, the first part of the climb would have definitely done the trick.

The tour guide stuck with me up the initial part of the climb, so I had a companion all the way. Together we slipped into the pace that I set as I concentrated on finding a flow that would enable me to gracefully ascend this monster of a mountain. We stopped a couple of times for replenishment from the wonderful sag wagon that paced us on our way up, and each time we got going again we eased ourselves back into that nice flow.

Climbing Stelvio was gruelling work that tested my endurance and my strength. It seemed that the switchbacks would go on forever. Even with those challenges, I still feel a sense of peace as I think of the mountain. No matter how difficult the mountain seemed in a given moment, I simply believed that I was going to slowly work my way up, and I did. We bit off one switchback at a time, and then quickly moved on to dig into the next one. I had complete faith that eventually we would make it up the final switchback if I just kept moving.

As we made our way up our winding path, we were soon surrounded by snow and felt a chill in the air that nipped at us that made me glad for the cycling jacket I had brought with me. I was surprised by how quickly I encountered the final section and rounded the corner to see the hidden last bit of the mountain. I could see now that there were only a few switchbacks between me and my goal. I continued to climb. It is really funny how you can dig and dig and dig for hours to make your way up a mountain, and then all of a sudden the challenge is over when you reach the summit.

I remember one of our cycling companions, Ed, coming over to us as we arrived at the top. I'll never forget his comment to me: "Well done. I am proud of you." He later admitted that on the first day of riding he had wondered if I was aware of what I had gotten into, but that I had gone on to prove that first impression of me wrong.

At the summit, we found ourselves surrounded by shops, restaurants, and a buzz of activity. We had a delicious pasta lunch on a patio as we took in the breathtaking view. James and I did a little shopping and bought t-shirts and a special mug to commemorate the experience.

The descent was just as scary as it had been the day before. After all the hard work climbing up the mountain and the relaxation at the summit, it is very important to be very careful on such a descent. It is incorrect to assume that descending is easy and fun. On the contrary, descending is tough and can be quite dangerous. You have to fight your depleted state in order to put a lot of energy into staying focused and alert. It is always a relief to reach the safety of the bottom. In fact, I still feel more anxiety when I think about the descent than I do when I think about facing the climb.

Stelvio: 21.5 km, 7.1% average gradient, 1533 m ascent

GAVIA AND GELATO

On our last day of riding in the Italian Dolomites, the plan was for the whole group to take on Gavia. Once we reached the top, those who wanted more could go on to climb Mortirolo.

Over the last couple of weeks, we had already conquered Baldo, Umbrail, Stelvio, and completed the Granfondo event. I had experienced so many climbs, and I knew that nothing was going to stop me from getting to the top of Gavia. I felt almost unstoppable.

Looking back now, I don't exactly know how I made it. Gavia is long, steep, and rugged. It is nothing less than a brute! I remember climbing, and climbing, and climbing as the never-ending switchbacks kept on coming. I remember feeling exhausted and depleted.

Just as I was feeling like I wanted to quit, I spotted the sag wagon. Like angels, the beautiful support ladies were there with cold water, fresh fruit, and chocolate. Oh, that chocolate! It was just the burst of joy and energy that I needed to give my poor, depleted body some hope. Refreshed from my break, I valiantly mounted my bike and continued on with verve! My upbeat attitude lasted right up until the next switchback, when I once again had to face my fatigue. Given the number of mountains I had climbed so recently, I just couldn't believe how hard this was.

By this point I was becoming emotionally numb. I think it is a defense mechanism of the human body to disengage the mind from the physical being. In fact, James once told me that when the physical body feels pain or discomfort, it constantly sends signals to the brain. This goes on for a while until the mind realizes that the pain is not going to stop. At this point, it somewhat numbs itself from what is going on. It is a defense mechanism. In this case, the numbness was a welcome relief.

Becoming numb to the pain allowed me to freely take in everything around me, leaving me in awe. At one point, I looked around and realized how ridiculously high up I was. I mean, there were patches of snow around, and nothing but really rugged mountaintops covered in rocks in the distance. It was somewhat barren and spooky. I wondered to myself what I was doing up here. How had I gotten here? Why was I here? My legs just kept pedalling while my mind worked overtime. I knew I couldn't stop, that my precious numbness would be gone if I stopped and had to start again. I think that I started to believe that this final challenge was never going to end.

My mind continued to disengage from my physical being. My numbness grew more pronounced. I was moving forward in a sort of dreamland, looking hazily around me. I climbed higher and higher, and the gradients remained unforgiving. Apparently, the hardest gradients are during the last third of this climb. I thought I was starting to get close to the end, but in my fuzzy condition I could not be sure.

All of a sudden, my nose started to bleed. I pulled over, and I laughed. Blood was dripping, and I was laughing. I think I was a bit delirious. Somehow I managed to staunch the blood, and on I went. I reached the point where my dreamlike state seemed more real than the reality around me. Ahead of me, I could see James, coming towards me! There he was, in all his glory, cycling beside a beautiful lake and heading my way. He approached and told me that the end was just around the corner. I couldn't believe my ears!

Side by side, we approached the summit. Everyone was there. I sat down on a bench, felt the sunshine on my tired body, and in my numb state I pondered how I had made it up this crazy climb.

When it was time to decide whether or not to carry on, I decided that I was done for the day. In my numb and depleted state, I could not picture myself riding safely down this mountain. The thought of another climb was almost incomprehensible. The next climb was the very famous Mortirolo, a 13 km wall, but it was not in the cards for me today.

Rather than bike down the mountain, I chose the much safer route of laying in the back the support vehicle, taking in the steep switchbacks and the rugged beauty of the beast that I had conquered. Well, I didn't really feel like I had conquered it, but I had at least willed myself to the summit. Meanwhile, James and the other three guys left riding for the day screamed down the mountain and across the valley! Their energy was incredible.

The two support ladies and I made our way to the bottom, and found ourselves in a slumberous town where we would hang out to wait for the guys. There was a cute little street market in progress. In my cycling shoes, I perused up and down the tables and found myself a spectacular souvenir. To this day, I absolutely cherish the soft, black t-shirt crested with a sparkly red heart and the words "follettina girl". For ten euros, this was a prize. I wore it to dinner that night, and the girls running the hotel were very helpful in translating for us. It turns out that "follettina girl" means 'Elf Girl'. Since I am a measly four foot ten, this was just too much for my cycling friends. They burst out in laughter at how appropriate my shirt was. I hadn't even known it when I made the purchase.

Once we were finished with the market, the support ladies and I sat ourselves down outside a gelato shop and enjoyed the sunshine. I entered the gelato shop, and my eyes grew wide in astonishment at the variety laid out before me. I came back out with a bowl piled high with three delectable flavours and devoured my prize. I had definitely earned every bite! As the boys were off conquering Mortirolo, we sat and enjoyed the afternoon. I reflected on all that I had accomplished, and slipped into a relaxed, exhausted state.

Going home the next day was really hard to stomach after such an incredible trip. In order to make it back to work for the beginning of the week, we had to fly out before enjoying the last meal that the rest of our cycling companions would have together. From Bormio, we had a fairly long drive to get back to the first hotel we had stayed at, which was where our bike cases were stored. Once we arrived, we had to work hurriedly to pack up our bikes and ready ourselves for the flight. We didn't have a lot of time to say goodbye to our newfound friends. Everything just felt like it happened so fast. It was a whirlwind of activity, and next thing we knew we were giving quick hugs and saying short goodbyes.

That evening in our hotel with just the two of us, my heart felt sad. I think I left a piece of it back in Italy with our cycling friends. I just can't begin to explain the bond that forms when you cycle up the side of a mountain with others. There you are, performing physical feats you never thought possible. Your emotions are completely exposed, and you are quick to rely on and to support those around you. You open a secret door that only few know about, and you make your way to the other side. You experience something that the other people back home in your normal life just simply don't understand outside of a few special moments when you find a person who gets it and you end up engaged in an excited conversation that takes you back to the side of that mountain.

My heart was a little broken, but it gradually healed in time. Little did I know as we flew away the following day that Italy would eventually become a very significant part of my life.

Gavia: 25.6 km, 5.5% average gradient, 1404 m ascent

SWITZERLAND

'Never too bad, never too old, never too sick, to start from scratch once again.' – Contributed by Barbra Chakos

A YEAR OF BEING SICK

I was volunteering for a small and wonderful organization whose main source of fundraising is to sell beautifully crafted handmade jewellery, scarves, and other lovely items at the many fairs that take place around Calgary during the summer months. The proceeds of these sales go directly towards housing and education programs for the communities in Guatemala where the items on offer originate. The amazing woman who runs this small operation is extremely dedicated and hardworking, and it was my privilege to help her out by running some of her fundraising operations.

My duties consisted of setting up shop at each fair. On this particular day, I made it to the fair with table, tent, and loads of jewellery in tow. I was able to get everything set up, but once the day began and people started to mill past our table I realized right away that something was seriously wrong with me. I couldn't eat, and I was experiencing bouts of dizziness. I'm the kind of girl who likes to talk and eat, so when I can't do one or both of those things I know that there's a real problem.

As the day wore on I felt worse and worse, but I couldn't articulate exactly what the problem was. I am usually very in tune with myself and know exactly what is going on. This time I didn't, which was a frightening experience.

My discomfort must have been obvious, because another volunteer encouraged me to go home while she looked after the table. I took her up on her kind offer and went to have a rest. Later, I returned to help pack up the display. It was a very difficult day. I felt terrible about not helping more, and deeply concerned by this strange and elusive malady.

As the week progressed, my condition did not improve so I went to see my doctor. I had been going to the same doctor for a long time, so she knew a lot about me and my medical history. I am also, as I mentioned, very in tune with myself and very descriptive about it when required to be. In other words, the doctor had a lot of information to work with once I was done explaining my symptoms. We did a full physical and a slew of bloodwork, but all of the results came back negative.

I strongly believe that we must take our health and wellbeing into our own hands, and that we must be very proactive about it. In spite of this initial setback, I wasn't about to give up and accept what was happening as my new normal. When things did not improve, I continued to see my doctor and simultaneously obtained a number of other opinions. I put any reasonable course of action that I could think of into play.

The whole situation was very scary. The symptoms, including strange pains that left me bedridden and useless, would creep up out of nowhere and then simply disappear for a while as abruptly as they had started. The stress of my physical symptoms fed into my anxiety and fear over the mystery of what might be wrong.

Thankfully, my doctor was able to get me in to see a very good specialist in a very reasonable amount of time. The specialist was able to identify the problem before we even did any tests, and then of course carried out the tests to confirm his initial suspicions. He was very complimentary about how descriptive I was and the amount of information I was able to provide while relaying my symptoms, which further emphasizes the importance of being in touch with your body and of *not* being shy about speaking up when things are not right.

It turned out that I had picked up a parasite. I did a little research on the Internet, but I quickly abandoned it as I started to look at pictures of this thing and to read the details. My stomach churned and I started to feel twitchy and panicky. Taking a deep breath, I forced myself to focus on the positives: I had a diagnosis and a solution. This was one situation in which ignorance was bliss and it was absolutely fine to simply move forward without digging deeper.

One thing that I was surprised to learn was how common parasites like the one affecting me really are. People get them all the time without even travelling to distant places. They find their way into your body through fish, meat, and leafy produce, to name a few routes of entry. I had had no idea!

Unfortunately, the only way to get rid of the parasite was to take medication that would kill *all* of the bacteria in my body, including the good bacteria. I was going to get sicker before I got better, so I was going to have to take some time off of work. I had already stayed home sick quite a bit due to the spontaneous behaviour of my symptoms, and I will forever be grateful to my wonderful managers and colleagues who were extremely understanding during this time.

I took the medication, and the impact was even worse than I could have imagined it would be. I could barely eat or move for weeks. I watched a lot of movies. In my weakened state, it was really the only thing I could do to distract myself. Still, despite my fragility I knew that the medication was working. At the end of the whole ordeal, I was finally on the mend and gradually getting back to my normal self. Well, as normal as I would ever be.

It was such a relief to be starting to feel healthy again, and to know that nothing serious was wrong with me. I looked back to the days where I laid in bed, feeling terrible. Not knowing what was wrong had been really scary. My ordeal had only been a few months long, and had come with a resolution at the end. I honestly have no idea what it must feel like to face a serious ongoing health issue, and my heart goes out to anyone who has been in that position. I can only imagine that it must feel like all of your power and control over your being has been taken away. I will forever be grateful to my dear husband for his support during the several months that I was ill. He was so patient and kind, and he did exactly what I needed him to do to help me get back to my old self.

Once the parasitic invader had been vanquished, I started to take my life back. Falling in love with cycling and conquering other pursuits that had seemed so very far out of my reach had left me much more open to trying new things, but my sickness had left me unable to enjoy many of my passions, including cycling. During my time of enforced rest and reflection it had become very apparent to me that out of everything that I loved to do, cycling was at the very top of the list.

I absolutely longed to be back on my bike. I didn't even care if I had to cycle inside, I just wanted to feel that part of me again. I missed it so much. During my recovery I would sit in the bike room, just looking at my bike as I mentally urged my body to heal already. When I was finally able to start engaging in normal activity again, the first thing that I wanted to do was get back into cycling shape.

My immune system was still weak from my ordeal and needed time to rebuild the healthy bacteria that had been removed. I had to take it very easy and exercise a lot of patience to avoid overdoing it. This was one time when I absolutely had to find a way to hold back my fire because the results of pushing myself too hard too fast could result in a big setback.

The first time I got onto my bike, despite the fact that I was enclosed within four walls and going nowhere, I fell in love all over again. I knew that I had to ease back into my cycling routine, so I was careful about how many times a week I got on my bike. I balanced out my spinning sessions with healing activities such as yoga. I made sure to eat enough food, and to focus on very healthy meals cooked at home.

Despite my best efforts, it was difficult to hold back. I was so excited about the upcoming cycling trip that James was planning out. This time we would ride through Austria to Switzerland, and then spend some time exploring there. It sounded wonderful, and my entire being felt joy as James's plan slowly took shape. It took some serious effort to do my part in getting ready for our trip by focusing my energy into a slow, patient approach to recovery. Slow and patient simply was not my natural way of doing things!

When the weather started to warm, I ventured outside for my first outdoor ride of the season. It was just going to be a low key hour with a few small hills, but even that short excursion felt like heaven. I felt so free. The fresh air filled my soul and my Trek 2000 once again became an extension of my body. I had waited for what felt like forever to feel this again. I knew then that I could not live without my bike.

At the end of this battle against a parasitic intruder, I was left longing for my bike. I wanted, needed my strength and my fire back, and I yearned for a new chance to rebuild my health and take better care of myself.

BACK IN THE SADDLE AGAIN

I had just experienced one of the scariest times in my life. My body had been taken over by a parasitic intruder. Throughout my battle with the parasite, my symptoms would vanish into thin air in one moment only to resurge with ferociousness in the next. The situation had been unpredictable and quite out of my control. All I had been able to do was to undergo all of the tests that were sprung upon me, and then wait. Just wait.

I have always been a proactive person. I like to take control of a situation and to fix whatever needs fixing. In the case of my parasite, I was powerless to even identify the problem, let alone to fix it. That is why it was such a relief when I finally received an answer and a solution. By the time I was certain that I was finally on the mend, I was so extremely relieved. I will never be able to fully express how I felt. I had my life back.

There were two things that I absolutely longed for as I slowly recovered: to reconnect with my husband, and to ride my bike. Of all the things that I loved to do, it had never been more apparent to me that my biggest passion was my bike. On more than one occasion over my long months without cycling I had sat on the floor of the training room, staring longingly at my Trek 2000. All I wanted was to be on it, chasing James up a climb and feeling the wind on my face as I whipped down the other side. I wanted the fresh air to fill my lungs. I wanted to feel free. I wanted to feel alive.

All of that frustration and yearning was now behind me. We arrived in Munich, the perfect transit location, and then shifted our belongings around while we were still at the train station. We unpacked our bikes and refilled their cases with anything that we did not absolutely need for the next three weeks so that we could leave them at the train station to await our return. Our backpacks were loaded with only the essentials. It would just be us, our bikes, and one backpack each for three weeks.

Given our space and weight constraints, we had had to pack very carefully. Our trip would take us from Munich through Austria, and would end in St. Moritz, Switzerland. Whatever we carried with us would have to see us through the duration. Due to those restrictions, our cycling pants would double as our fancy dinner pants, and our fleece cycling jerseys would also be our fancy dinner sweaters. It might sound ridiculous, but we weren't going to be hitting any glitzy joints. Setting out with so few possessions to last me for such a long time was one of the most freeing experiences of my life.

Then we were off. We had five consecutive days of cycling ahead of us to get to St. Moritz. I was a bit nervous about how I would handle the upcoming trip, and I knew that I had to be very careful not to overdo it. After the roughest year of my life, it was important to hold back, find a comfortable pace, and save up my energy for necessary moments.

The route was picture perfect. We planned to stay in tiny Austrian towns along the way. Near the end of our first day of cycling as we headed towards the town of Kufstein, it started to rain. It wasn't too heavy, and we didn't have too far to go, so it didn't really bother me. I was completely unaware, however, of what happens when cobblestone gets wet. We were very close to Kufstein when we transitioned from the road to a stretch of cobbles. It turns out that wet cobblestone is very slippery, especially to slick road bike tires. I went down instantly.

Blood dripped from my elbow, and I looked around in shock. As I was composing myself, a man drove up and asked me if I was ok. He wasn't speaking English, but it was apparent that he was concerned. I pointed ahead and explained that my husband was nearby and that I would be fine. As I climbed back on my bike and started moving forward again, I saw James heading quickly back in my direction. He stopped to inspect my wound, but since the town was so close we agreed to simply pedal on.

We approached a hotel and I waited outside with the bikes while James inquired about a room. My elbow stung like crazy, and blood trickled down my arm. Soon enough we were settled into a cozy room and I was able to tend to my wound. I will admit, I felt a little badass for having my first real fall. This would be the first experience that would teach me that a little blood is not a big deal.

Kufstein is a beautiful, amazing place. That last little push with a bloody, stinging elbow had been completely worth it to reach this haven! We walked through the cobble streets of the little town, enjoyed a delightful meal, and completely immersed ourselves in our surroundings.

The next morning we woke up to a cloudy, wet day. The weather was less than ideal, but we had to keep moving if we were to make it to our dream destination of St. Moritz. We shouldered our backpacks, and off we went on our bikes.

The rain was relentless. Within a short time we were quite drenched. We simply carried on for a while until we reached the town of Rattenberg and decided to take a break. We traveled down a quaint cobblestone street, and found ourselves some warm apple strudel and cappuccinos to enjoy on a cozy patio. By the time we were finished the rain had let up some, and I took the opportunity to leverage the hand dryer in the restroom. We weren't completely dry, but we were no longer completely drenched either. Somewhere in between was not too bad.

Looking around, it was hard to not feel peaceful and enjoy the surroundings. We had known going into this that the path from Austria to St. Moritz would probably leave us facing the elements. We had anticipated some wet weather, but it was nice to be mostly dry again.

Our afternoon was spent cycling through a valley while enjoying the warmth of the sun that had finally graced us with its presence. We enjoyed the lovely pathways along the river as we made use of cycling infrastructure that was far more extensive than what we have back home. When we made it to the town that we had planned on staying in, we looked around and realized that it was a less than desirable place to stop. We could either accept it, or dig deep and carry on to the next town, which should be less than another half hour away. I was so hungry and tired by this point that thirty minutes seemed like an almost insurmountable obstacle, but as I looked around I could plainly see that the town we were in had nothing to offer. So, I dug deep and pushed on.

Once again, I was in a position where I had to separate my mind from my physical being. I had to look deep inside to find my inner strength, and to convince myself to focus and put forth an effort that seemed beyond natural. It is only at this point that the separation of the physical being from the mental being can begin so that I can reach a state where I can turn off the physical senses for a while and achieve my goals through sheer force of will.

Despite my aching, fatigued body, I put my head down and started to pedal. Soon enough I found a good heart rate and flow. I looked straight ahead and found a deep focus as I urged myself to just keep going and reminded myself again and again that I could do this.

It wasn't long before the beautiful town of Schwaz came into sight and I realized that my effort had paid off. This place was much more hospitable than the town we had originally planned to stay in. As we enjoyed a lovely meal and gradually relaxed, I realized that that last little push had been completely worth it!

LEARNING WHAT I AM

We had enjoyed four evenings thus far, each in a different lovely little Austrian town. My body had responded well to the first couple of days of riding. On the third day, I was struggling a bit, and my stomach wasn't feeling great. We found a lovely patio around lunchtime, and I made myself eat a reasonable meal despite my lack of appetite. We continued on for a little while after, and I focused on just getting through the day.

A little while later when we stopped in the town of Telfs, James indicated that we were making great progress and that we had a couple of options to choose from: we could either continue to where we had planned to be that night, or we could stay where we were for the night and take the afternoon off. Normally I would be fine with pushing on, but given the circumstances it seemed like the wisest choice would be to rest. We decided to stay. It was a great opportunity to enjoy the lovely town, and my body was very grateful for the break.

Perhaps in large part because we had taken it easy on our third day in response to my body's needs, the remainder of our trip went smoothly. Our fourth day of riding went off without a hitch, and we spent a wonderful evening in the fairytale town of Pfunds. As I had the previous three evenings in Austria, I felt like I was in a picture perfect postcard that had come alive.

Now, here I was on my fifth consecutive day of cycling. We had started in Munich, made our way through Austria, and our destination on this fifth and final day was supposed to be St. Moritz, Switzerland. Throughout our trip I had been patient with myself, and as a result I had done quite well over the last four days. I hadn't been able to train for real prior to landing in Munich, but I had been able to commit to a reasonable and regular workout routine that had me back in decent shape. I just needed to be careful to not overdo it as I didn't know how my body would react.

We had been cycling for several hours throughout the morning, and when lunchtime rolled around we found ourselves on a nice little patio enjoying our midday meal. There was another cyclist going in the same direction as us, and he had also stopped for some refuelling. We watched in amazement as this guy inhaled a huge plate piled high with food and gulped down a couple of very large beers. We were both wondering how well he would be able to bike afterwards as we knew there was climbing ahead of us.

We headed out, and soon we reached the expected climb. It wasn't a hot day, but it wasn't terribly cold either. It was kind of in between, a perfect temperature since climbing when the temperature is moderate is less taxing on the body. Less water is required, and the lack of heat prevents the body from becoming sluggish.

Up we went, climbing, climbing, climbing. After a while, I looked around. Here I was in the beautiful Swiss countryside, working my way towards our destination. I realized how quiet my mind was. It was not filled with worries and concerns, nor was I questioning my ability to complete this climb. I was simply moving onward and upward. This was the peaceful and profound moment when I realized that I *am* a cyclist and that I *do* climb mountains. I fully accepted my capabilities, and I simply trusted that I could take on what lay ahead of me.

At one point during the afternoon, I passed by the cyclist that we had seen gorging himself on the patio. There he was, walking beside his bike and pushing it along this long, steep road. I thought to myself that it was going to be very, very long day for this guy. I just couldn't imagine pushing a bike and walking all of this way. I hoped that his destination wasn't too far.

Time passed and I started to get hungry, but I had a feeling that James wasn't too far ahead of me so I held off on eating. Sure enough, I rounded a corner and there he was, sitting in a lovely little spot surrounded by colourful flowers on the side of the road. I joined him, and we sat there replenishing ourselves together and enjoying the moment.

Travelling through new places while surrounded by the beauty of nature, filling my lungs full of fresh air, and knowing that every bit of progress was completely dependent upon each pedal stroke provided the perfect conditions for me to completely rid my cluttered head of any thoughts of my usual life. It wasn't often that I found this kind of clarity, this kind of calm, this kind of peace. In my normal, everyday world, my schedule is full and all of my time is accounted for. There are time limits, there are deadlines, and there is always something that needs to get done. I am usually immersed in a long to-do list.

The to-do list honestly ruled my life. While I was ill, that list was set aside for a while as I was simply unable to do any of the tasks I wished to accomplish. When I started feeling better I was able to maintain a better balance between my passions and my to-do list for a while, but I soon found myself once again completely overtaken by a very hectic work life. At the time, it had seemed like the right thing to do.

Sitting on the roadside surrounded by flowers in the middle of a climb in the Swiss mountains, the only things that made sense in that moment were a clear mind, a strong connection with my surroundings, and my inner peace. It was easy to see from this unique physical and mental place that no matter how important that next work task may seem, it pales in comparison to finding time for the things that matter. Whether your passion is your children, your life partner, your sense of self, your creativity, your health, or something else entirely, it is vital to set aside time to pursue it. It's funny that all I needed to do to achieve that moment of clarity was to take a couple of weeks away from my usual life to immerse myself in European mountains.

Soon enough it was time to carry on, so we did. I continued to enjoy my beautiful surroundings and the feelings of strength and calm that overtook me. It was bliss while it lasted. Of course, a cycling trip just isn't complete without a little adventure.

A Cloud Bed, Chocolate, and Sparkly Wine

I pulled up beside James and we came to a stop while we waited behind a line of cars for our turn to proceed. He looked at me and declared that we had done it! We only had about twenty minutes more of cycling and we would arrive in St. Moritz, our resting point for the next week. I was ecstatic! I had worried for so long about how I would do and if I would make it here after my battle with the parasitic invader that it seemed almost unreal that we had reached our destination.

Soon we were off again, and before long it started to rain. No problem, I thought. We have been wet on this trip before, and we were fine. This time, however, both the rain and the surrounding air were cold. Very cold. We were quickly getting drenched, and the crisp air was nipping at our fingers and toes. It happened so fast. I was getting wetter and wetter, and colder and colder. Almost before I knew it, I was losing feeling in my toes. This frightened me so badly that I pulled up beside James and exclaimed in a panicked voice that I was so cold that I didn't know what to do! Of course, the only choices available to us were to sit there and continue to get wet, or to continue on as we got wet. On we went.

As we approached St. Moritz, we came to a climb. Of course, there seems to *always* be yet another climb in our adventures. When I saw this climb approaching, at first all I could think was how tired I was. Once we started ascending, however, I realized the benefit of pushing myself harder: I could feel my toes tingling. A warm, fuzzy feeling surged through my extremities. The work that I was doing in ascending this hill was generating heat, and that heat was warming my frozen toes. As quickly as it had come, the cold that had shot painfully through my fingers and toes was gone. Now I found myself in a very familiar place. I needed to find a pace, focus, and work towards making it up this climb.

We finally made it to the top and found ourselves in St. Moritz. I was so relieved, so excited. As we rode around looking for a place to stay, these feelings of triumph were short-lived. Little did we know that there were two sides to this town: the fancy side and the quaint side. In our ignorance, we had started searching for accommodation on the fancy side. As I waited outside in the rain with the bikes, James went into several hotels, and each time re-emerged expressionless. My heart sank a little deeper each time. All I wanted was to be inside and out of the rain. Once we had stopped cycling, the cold had shot through me again. I was so chilled that my teeth had started chattering, and my arms were making involuntary twitches. I honestly hadn't known that teeth could actually chatter on their own.

We eventually made our way to the other side of the town. James has a keen sense of direction and some sort of inner intuition about finding things, which has given him the honor of being my horseshoe on our traveling adventures. Once again, his luck served us well. We found the quainter part of town and James disappeared inside the sweetest little hotel. In he went. I was feeling rather desperate by this point. I looked up at the sky, and in my exasperation I begged the clouds for James to bring back good news. When he came out and told me we had a room, I almost didn't believe him. In my hazy state, I thought I was in some sort of dream. I followed him with my bike down into an underground garage. Soon we were making our way into the hotel, up the elevator, and into our little room.

I went into immediate action. I rid myself of my soggy cycling attire and embraced the steamy, hot relief of the shower. I had no intention of coming out anytime soon. The warmth of the soothing water on my skin helped my body to wake from its cold stupor. My toes began to regain feeling and the chattering of my pearly whites finally halted. The desperation and panic began to leave my inner being, and a sense of peace filled me. I began to feel calm and complete again.

As I basked in the luxury of the hot, steamy hideaway, a sense of accomplishment and happiness filled me. I had made it. We had made it together. I still had it in me. I was, and always would be, a real cyclist.

Finally satisfied, I left the warmth of the shower, and found a warmth of a different kind. Donning my warm fleece, I nestled myself into what I can only describe as a cloud bed. Two, small individual beds had been pushed together to look like one. Each had its own white, poufy comforter. I crawled in, and engulfed myself in this soft cocoon. I lay there in complete bliss, warm and fuzzy inside.

To my delight, while I was warming up James had gone back out into the cold, wet world and had found me a Toblerone bar and a bottle of sparkling fruit wine. As I lay there in my cloud bed, eating every last morsel of that sweet, chocolatey nougat and sipping sweet bubbles, James slipped into his own dream world next to me. This was a moment that I would never in a million years forget.

CELEBRATION AND YODELING

We spent almost a full week in the Swiss town of St. Moritz. Nestled in the valley and surrounded by mountains, I felt like I was living in a postcard picture. We had the perfect little room for which James had negotiated a good deal as our home base.

We had an absolute blast exploring this wonderful town. We completely submerged ourselves in the local cuisine. Donning our fancy pants and sweaters (which may have looked like warm cycling pants and fleece jerseys to the untrained eye), we enjoyed many cozy dinners including perfectly wood fired thin crust pizzas and rich cheese fondues. Just like the bakery, produce, and meat sections in our grocery stores back home, I discovered that the local grocery stores had an entire section dedicated to chocolate! This simply amazed and delighted me. After dinner, we would often stroll through the peaceful town and find a place for a digestif, or try our luck at the local casino.

As the week went on, we observed that there were many tables and tents being set up all over town. We also took note of the growing number of people arriving at our hotel dressed in traditional yodeler attire and toting alpine horns. By the end of the week, yodelers were literally streaming into St. Moritz in large groups. With so many people coming into town, it was a good thing that we had our hotel room booked right up till the end of the weekend! We still had no idea what exactly was going on, but our curiosity was piqued.

Most of our time in St. Moritz was spent strolling around the lovely town and taking it all in. Surrounded by mountains, it was impossible for James to sit still. He had quite an adventure of his own when he took off on his bike one day and ended up conquering three peaks.

I was able to join him on one occasion, where we found ourselves making our way up Bernina pass. It was a very peaceful climb for me. I was so much at peace with myself and my surroundings. I felt so grateful that I had been able to cycle through the spectacular countryside all the way from Munich to St. Moritz, and that I now found myself working my way up yet another one of earth's wonders.

My ascent up Bernina pass was the perfect experience. I found a flow, and sank into my surroundings. When I passed by a fellow female cyclist, it felt so good to know that I was still strong and able to indulge my competitive side. When I neared the top, I passed a young male cyclist training with his team. He was pulled over to the side in tears. My own memories of moments of complete defeat flooded my mind. Not today, I thought. Not today.

During our Italian cycling tour about a year ago I had learned about a wall of a mountain called Mortirolo, the very last mountain that the guys had gone on to tackle after we finished our climb of Gavia that morning. At the time, it had definitely been the right decision for me not to join them. I will never forget, however, the look on James's face that day as he and the other guys sped across the valley towards Mortirolo. Neither will I ever forget the look of defeat as he rejoined me later that day where I sat enjoying the sunshine and a mountain of gelato. Raw emotion had taken over his entire demeanor, and trickled its way out of his sad eyes and down his salty, hot face. Mortirolo was the biggest beast that he had ever taken on at this point, and that day the beast had won.

Honestly, I believe with all of my heart that the two weeks of serious climbing, the climb up Gavia that morning, and the unreasonable speed at which they had screamed across the valley had all taken their toll. Top this off with some scorching Italian afternoon heat and humidity, and my dear James had fallen victim to an uncontrollable heart rate at key moments when tackling the wall that stared him down. I hadn't known any of this at the time. I only knew then that James, my warrior who has never shied away from a challenge, was shattered. My heart had dropped. To this day I get tears in my eyes when I think of that look on his face.

It is amazing how opportunities present themselves at just the right moments. Being in St. Moritz, we were only about 80 km from Bormio, an Italian town close to Mortirolo. It turned out that a good friend of James's had signed up for the same Italian tour with the same company that we had used the previous year. It also turned out that they would be in Bormio to tackle Mortirolo during the time that we would be in St. Moritz. They had eagerly invited James to join them for some riding, so he had arranged to ride from St. Moritz to Bormio on Thursday, stay overnight with them, and then make his second attempt at Mortirolo on the Friday. This time, they would be starting their day early before the real heat settled in and the first agenda item would be Mortirolo.

Off he went on his little adventure. I can't even begin to imagine what must have been going through his mind. How would this second attempt turn out? If he was afraid, as usual he did not show it. The weather wasn't very good, and as I stood in the doorway of the visitor center in the heart of St. Moritz watching the pouring rain turn to hail, I wondered where James was on his journey and I hoped that he wasn't too wet or cold. I never had a doubt that he would be ok.

I learned later that he rode for a while, took a train for a while, and then rode some more. Of course, he found himself right in the middle of the rain and hail. He did make it to Bormio safely, though, and enjoyed a lovely evening with the tour group. It was really odd talking to him on the phone that night. I was tucked into my cloud bed in our cozy room, watching Hollywood movies, eating chocolate, and drinking sparkly wine. I found it hilarious to hear the actors and actresses I knew so well talk to me in strange foreign voices. James sounded so far away, and even though it hadn't even been 24 hours, it felt like we had been apart for a very long time. I couldn't wait for him to get back the next day. I told him I loved him, and wished him good luck on his feat the following morning.

The next day, I lazily arose from my sleep and strolled through town. I carefully selected a variety of delectable items from various little shops to create the perfect picnic lunch. My excitement at seeing James again was mounting, and I just couldn't wait to hear all about the climb up Mortirolo. I eventually made my way back to our room and waited there anxiously. The afternoon wore on, and with each passing minute I longed even more for James to appear through the door.

Then he was finally there, wearing an expression that was quite different from the one he had worn when he approached me at the gelato shop a year ago. He definitely looked hot, tired, salty, and finished, but he also looked happy, triumphant, and satisfied. He described to me how difficult the climb was, how he had been forced to stand on his pedals, and how there had been moments when he had wondered if he would make it. He told me how challenging it had been to control his heart rate, and the feeling of his heart pounding hard as though it was trying to escape from his chest. He told me that the climb up Mortirolo had been the most uncomfortable thing he had ever done, but that he was glad he had done it and he would never do it again. He showed me the picture of him and his bike in front of the Mortirolo sign at the top. What a day of triumph!

That night, it finally became apparent what all of the tents and tables set up around town were for. We found ourselves in the middle of an International Yodeler Festival. The yodelers had streamed into town all week from all over the world. As we strolled through town that evening, we heard the most beautiful sounds as groups of yodelers would spontaneously break out into song. We walked by table after table of delicious food, and our nostrils were delighted by the juicy smells.

Over the course of the weekend, we experienced all kinds of amazing sights. We watched a guy carve an alpine horn out of wood from scratch. We found ourselves inside a tent, sitting on a picnic bench, drinking beer, and chatting excitedly with the mounds of people around us. We occasionally found someone who spoke English, but it is truly amazing how much you can communicate without understanding each other's words. Everyone was in celebration mode, and so, with hundreds of our new friends, we joined them as we celebrated James's victory in reaching the summit of Mortirolo.

Bernina Pass: 20.4 km, 7% maximum gradient, 600 m ascent

COLD, WET, AND SLIPPERY - FURKA PASS

Ever since my first encounter with Furka Pass, it has loomed in my mind as a great beast that completely exposes and humbles the cyclist. For years I wondered if I had an exaggerated image of this monster of a mountain in my head, but when we returned there some time later I only found validation that it truly was everything I had painted it to be in my mind.

After our wonderful stay in St. Moritz with thousands of yodelers, we made our way to the itsy bitsy town of Andermatt which is nestled between multiple mountain passes. The next morning we found ourselves back on our bikes, making the short trek from Andermatt to the base of Furka Pass. Looking up at the first part of the climb, I saw a series of switchbacks carving their way through the beautiful countryside. It didn't seem like it would be all that bad. The switchbacks were actually really pretty. We got started on our climb, and soon I found that magical flow and become one with nature. It was hard, but it was peaceful.

Soon after finishing off the switchbacks, we paused and found ourselves staring up at a much different scene. A long, daunting stretch of road perched precariously on the side of a cliff, staring me down and looking me right in the eyes. I felt the first flutter of nerves, but I also knew that if this trip had taught me anything it was that I am a girl who ties her pigtails, and then gets on her bike and climbs up mountains. We got moving again.

Furka Pass was hard, very hard. This stretch of road felt like it went on forever. You could see a building at the top, but it seemed so very far away. It was almost like in those kids movies where the evil guy lives up in the castle way, way up in the sky. Everything at the top of this beast looked very, very far away. I kept myself going one pedal stroke at a time, and on and on and on we went.

Reaching the top felt like the ultimate victory. Of course we felt ecstatic. We sat down in the formerly-distant restaurant that now looked life-sized and had some lunch. Before we knew it, it was absolutely pouring. Sheets of water pelted their way onto the pavement.

We waited for a while, but the rain showed no signs of slowing down, let alone stopping. My uneasiness grew the longer we waited, and soon became full-out panic. Was it my fate to slip off the side of a slick cliff on my bicycle? The images of falling to my death were growing in my head. In my mind's eye, I could see myself sliding to my doom.

It was clear that the rain was not going to subside anytime soon, and we simply could not stay on the top of this beast all night. We had no choice but to mount our bikes. I was extremely nervous and scared. James told me to relax, to take it very easy, and to stay behind him. He assured me it would be alright. My stomach was in knots, but I followed his advice.

Furka Pass: 41.2 km, maximum gradient 17%, 956 m ascent

I started moving slowly and controlled my speed very carefully. This was not going to be a fast descent. As we crept down the long, daunting stretch of road, I tried not to look to my right at the nightmare-inducing gaping cliff of doom. I tried not to think about sliding off the edge into nothingness. I focused on the road in front of me, worked to keep my speed in check, and stuck with my partner. Since we only had summer riding gloves on at the time, my hands were absolutely frozen from the cold, pelting rain, and my knuckles screamed in pain from the constant pulling on the brakes. It was crazy. To this day, it was one of the scariest descents I have ever experienced.

Finally we made it to the bottom of the stretch of road on the side of the cliff. We were back at the set of switchbacks carved into the beautiful countryside. I am sure I have never been happier to see a set of switchbacks in my life. We still had to be careful, but, there was no longer a gaping cliff to my right.

We carefully wound our way down to the base of the mountain. The whole time I wanted nothing more than to stop and give my aching hands a good shaking to relieve the pain and the pervasive chill. When we finally reached the valley floor, my whole body started to relax as I gradually let go of my nerves and fear. We made the easy jaunt back to town and cautiously navigated the slippery cobblestone streets.

I will never forget Furka Pass, for it made me face my fears straight on.

Mele Kalikimaka is the Thing to Say

'There are thousands to tell you it cannot be done,
There are thousands to prophesy failure;
There are thousands to point out to you, one by one,
The dangers that wait to assail you.
But just buckle in with a bit of a grin,
Just take of your coat and go to it;
Just start to sing as you tackle the thing,
That "cannot be done," and you'll do it.'

- Edgar A. Guest - Contributed by Kate Morse

While I was recovering from my parasitic invader, James and I took a vacation to Maui. Of course we had a wonderful time. After driving along the winding coastal curves of the Road to Hana and traversing the beautiful switchbacks to the summit of Haleakala, however, we both longed to enjoy these roads by bike. Thus, when an opportunity presented itself to return to the beautiful Hawaiian island for a wedding, we jumped at it. We planned the trip so that the first four days of our time in Maui would be completely dedicated to cycling.

My previous cycling season had been a very cautious return to aggressive physical activity after being bedridden for the better part of a year, and had culminated in our trip to Switzerland. When we returned home, the ice and snow of another Canadian winter had forced me into the offseason. Still riding the high of my success on that trip, I found myself extremely motivated to improve my fitness during the winter months and thus I committed myself to a fairly hardcore training season.

I dug up the amazing nutritional spreadsheet that James the Excel Wizard had built, dusted it off, and spent long hours updating the food database and tracking everything that went into my body. After being so sick and observing in great detail the way that my body reacted to different foods, I was determined to treat it with the utmost respect. I planned out both spinning and weight training workouts and slotted them carefully into week-long segments to ensure the proper balance between core, strength, and cardio training. I essentially became my own nutritionist and physical trainer, and it was a lot of work. After being physically out of commission for so long without knowing when I would be able to ride my bike again, my desperation to get back to cycling had now transformed into motivation.

Since I was working full time, my meals and snacks for the next day needed to be planned out and packed the night before. Between all of the food and gym gear that I schlepped to work every day, I often felt like I was packing up to leave for a week! Snacks and lunches were eaten at very regular times throughout the day to keep my body fuelled. Lunch times became weight training sessions in the on-site gym. After work, I would gun it home, have a snack to refuel, and then hop onto my bike in the training room. When my workout was finished, I would proceed to make dinner and pack up everything again for the next day. By the time I reached my nightly quiet time stretch session followed by a luxurious soak in a hot bubble bath, I was always completely depleted.

Between a full time professional career, and what had effectively become a second full time job planning out and preparing for homemade healthy meals and workouts, I was constantly spent. At times it was difficult to slot in other important things like time with family and friends, cleaning the house, and hanging out with my husband. I am sure that there were points when other people did not fully understand how torn I was between my commitment to training and my desire to see them.

I knew that if I could get in the right quantity and quality of sessions each week, then when I arrived in Maui the results would speak for themselves. Our four days of cycling would be capped off by an ascent up all 3055 metres (10,023 feet) of the famous volcano Haleakala. I was extremely determined to show up fully for this ride.

My inability to ride my bike while I was sick had made me want to do nothing else but ride my bike. My passion had been magnified. All winter I dreamt of riding along coastal roads, and of making it to the top of the volcano. I am not sure that I recognized myself anymore. What had happened to that frightened girl who didn't think that she had any athletic ability or sense of adventure?

THE ROAD TO HANA TAKE II

Our first ride in Maui was along the winding coastal road of Hana. We had driven this entire road during our first visit to Maui years before, and while we hadn't really enjoyed the actual driving we had loved the beautiful stops along the way. This time, we would be tackling the road's incredible curves on high-end Lite Speed bikes.

It had been many years since the last time I had rented a bike, and I was unsure about riding a bike that wasn't my own. As soon as we started the ride, however, all of my trepidation vanished. This bike was light as a feather and handled unbelievably well!

The rental bike worked out so well that the seedling of a thought was planted in my mind. I wondered if I was ready for a new bike. Although I could never see a day that I would completely part from my Trek 2000, I began to think that I might welcome a carbon fibre beauty into my life. These thoughts became reality the following Christmas, when James presented me with a brand new Trek Madone 4.5 women's edition. Shiny silver and baby blue, this girly yet tough stead would help me graduate onto tougher rides.

We whipped along the coastal road, zooming up, down, and around tight curves. We often moved faster than the traffic due to the close confines of the curves and the narrowness of the road. The entire time I felt like I was flying through the air. My dedication to my training regimen had paid off. I chased James as he ascended up a hill or disappeared around a tight corner. No matter how fast he moved, I would simply turn up the gas and soon have him in my sights again. I felt light, I felt fast, I felt free. This was the ultimate playtime. It just couldn't get any better!

We stopped for a rest in a tiny coastal town about halfway to Hana. Dramatic white waves crashed against steep, rocky cliffs. We were on the very edge of coast. It was breathtaking! It was as if we had opened a secret door into an unknown land. As we sat in the warm sun and listened to the soothing waves, the energy of the ride soon turned to a relaxed calm. Our resting place felt like a hidden treasure of existence where the earth turns to sea and everything moves at its own pace. The crazy Monday to Friday churn and dash to get everything done didn't exist here. This was a rare opportunity for me to connect with my inner being, and to completely be in the moment.

After purchasing some some delicious banana bread that was still warm from the oven from a little street vendor, we enjoyed our snack and were ready to roll. The ride back was just as invigorating as the ride out. Once again we flew on our Lite Speeds, up and down, and around and around. The thrill and excitement mixed with the fresh air of the ocean was invigorating. I had never felt more alive. The entire time I didn't hesitate, I didn't question. I just completely trusted my ability to ride hard to the end.

TWO STINKY CYCLISTS AND A BEACHSIDE PARADISE

The next day, to my delight I was raring to go again. We did a slightly more relaxed ride that day, part of which covered about a third of the famous volcano Haleakala that would be our goal in two more days.

We were cycling in a small group consisting of my husband, myself, our tour guide Ralph, and his friend, Frank. The ride was fantastic with a fair amount of climbing on the way out. My legs were tired from the day before, but I felt steady and remained motivated. I simply kept on pedaling through the soreness.

We were rewarded for our hard work at the turnaround point as we pulled up to a lovely little coffee shop known as Grandma's House. I enjoyed a chai tea and more banana bread. I had worked so hard for so many months to get here, and I definitely wasn't going to hold back on indulging in the occasional treat.

Our return journey was mostly downhill and quite relaxed. As we began the drive back towards the hotel, James mentioned that he would like to stop at Mama's Fish House, a restaurant he had read about. It was located right on the coast close to the bike shop where we began and ended our rides. We arrived still in our bike gear, hot, sweaty, and less than fresh, but our understanding was that the fish house would be similar to the informal patios that we were in the habit of stopping at after a ride for a couple of fresh fish tacos. We couldn't have been more wrong.

As we pulled up to this famous fish house, we were greeted with a valet parking attendant. He cheerfully whisked away the keys as we looked around, stunned by our upscale surroundings. We looked at each other, decided to shrug it off, and headed down towards the beach.

Mama's Fish House, to this day, is one of the most magnificent hidden gems that I have ever experienced. Located right on its own little stretch of beach, facing the ocean, it is much more than a house. Both the beautiful outdoor patio and indoor sections feature spectacular ocean views. Every bit of the culinary experience is out of this world.

We did feel a little uncomfortable having shown up in gross, wet, smelly bike gear. However, as my husband quickly pointed out, we were already there, and the outdoor seating would give us a great option to avoid offending other diners with our smell. So, as I had been repeatedly learning to do since I first starting cycling, I let it go. I sat down, ordered an Island Girl martini, and relaxed. As I sipped the vanilla and coconut flavours and appreciated the fresh island flowers, all thoughts were banished from my mind and I completely sunk into the moment.

Once again, cycling had opened up a new world for me. After the physical exertion and experience of connecting fully with my natural surroundings, all tension and anxiety that may have existed within me was nowhere to be found. All that remained was calm, peace, and a complete connection to the present moment.

CLIFFS AND FRESH BANANA BREAD

The hilly, winding curves of the road to Hana are smooth, which makes them an absolute joy for the cyclist. On the more westward side of island, the hills are steep, the curves are dramatic, and the roads are rough and much less travelled. These were the roads that we tackled on our third day of cycling.

For this ride, we were once again accompanied by the happy, energetic Frank and his cycling buddy, Ralph. It was just the four of us. Off we went, embarking on another adventure. This may have been one of the most exciting rides I had done at this point in my life. We climbed, we descended, and then almost immediately began climbing again. The road wove up and down, up and down. The turns were tight, and as my Lite Speed easily handled around each curve I wondered how a vehicle would possibly be able to make such a maneuver. To my left were ragged, rocky walls, and to my right steep, jagged cliffs plunged into the ocean. There wasn't much room for error. One truly had to have a sense of adventure for this ride, and I was definitely feeling it! We had a ball maneuvering our bikes through this beautiful scene, looking out over the white foam of waves crashing into the cliffs below.

Our turnaround point was a tiny booth dangling on the side of a cliff where fresh, warm banana bread could be purchased. Of course we each gobbled down a piece of the warm, delicious delight before taking off again.

Getting moving after our break proved to be a little challenging. We had stopped right at the very bottom of a steep ascent. The only way to get going was to start pedaling with one foot clipped in, and then very quickly get the other foot clipped in to continue through the rest of the circle. This was going to be tricky indeed.

I did feel a moment of panic as I started pedaling and hoped that my other foot would make it and that I wouldn't find myself in a clumsy mess in the road. I heard the click, and felt the pressure of my foot contacting the pedal, then pulling up backwards. Relief flooded through me as I realized that I was in! I stood up on the pedals and pushed through the steepness in front of me.

Soon we were all safely past that ascent and back to what we loved best: climbing, descending, and turning back through the sharp curves that had brought us to the banana bread booth on the cliff. Exhilaration surged through my veins. I couldn't believe I was in such a beautiful place and riding on such an adventurous route. I was elated, and knew in that moment that this was my reward for all of the hard work that I had put forth during those long winter months.

As I made my way through the winding turns, I approached one of many summits in this roller coaster of a ride. Off the side the road was a sight unlike any I had ever seen. A small car was parked on the side of the road, its windows fully clouded up. The car door opened, and an old Hawaiian man stumbled out and clumsily made his way to his feet. A cloud of dense, sweet smelling smoke followed him. He caught sight of me and cheered me on as his dog lazily followed him out of the cloud. Hilarious!

As I descended down the final and most significant climb of the day, I felt free, like I was flying. I descended the switchbacks far faster than the traffic behind me. I didn't hesitate. I didn't break a sweat. Who was I? Who was this girl flying down a series of switchbacks on a race bike? Where had the frightened, unathletic Julie gone?

I was once so scared of everything. I was once so uncomfortable with my physical being. I was once the last person on earth who would ever believe that I could be an athlete. The warm sun on my skin and the warm wind with its salty tang of the sea were my new reality, and in that moment I could barely comprehend how foreign the person I had been in the past seemed. I had emerged from my chrysalis to become someone completely new.

JULIE VS THE VOLCANO

When we awoke on our fourth and final day of riding, James looked over at me and said, "You are going to make me climb this thing, aren't you?"

I had spent months preparing for and thinking about this day. We were to climb from 0 to 3055 metres (10,023 feet) up to the peak of Haleakala. In my mind, it was me versus a volcano. I prepared a lovely breakfast of Hawaiian-style omelettes and rich Kona coffee. Soon enough we were dressed and fuelled, and it was almost time to depart. I looked out from our hotel balcony and took in the wonderful ocean view one last time. I was ready.

The last time we visited Maui we observed first-hand that Haleakala is a dangerous mountain. At the time, we had observed tour companies that herded tourists onto buses early in the morning to enjoy the sunrise from the top of the volcano. After that scenic adventure, those companies would kit the tourists out with inadequate bicycles and have them ride down the side of the volcano. This might sound like fun, but the reality is that the side of Haleakala is a series of steep roads and sharp switchbacks with no guard rails. It very much reminded me and James of a climb in the European mountains, so we were not surprised to learn that those companies had been responsible for serious injuries and even a few deaths. It would be very easy to get going too fast and lose control on a switchback.

Due to the carelessness of those tourist scams, all tour companies, including the reputable ones, had been banned from the national park. Therefore, the tour company that we had signed on with would be supporting a group of cyclists up to 1981 metres (6,500 feet), which was where the national park officially began. We met up with the group, and after a round of introductions we began our trek up the volcanic beast. It was hot near the bottom, and even the first stretches of incline felt steep. I knew right away that this was going to be a long, hard day, but after all of the preparation there was no turning back.

James and I had a bit of a rough start as he had a flat early into the ride, followed by another one soon after. We were separated from the pack as a result, but we remained intent on enjoying the day and refused to let our bad luck hold us back. Soon we found a flow and moved past the troubled start. We stopped for a break when we caught up to the support vehicle, refuelling our bodies with protein bars and bananas, and topping up our water bottles. Then we were off again.

The road soon transitioned into switchbacks as we begun the real meat of the climb, allowing me to put all of my new knowledge to the test. I found a nice flow and set myself on a pace that I was certain would take me all the way to the top. I refused to let my confidence falter or to question my ability to make it. After the brutes that we had taken on in the past, I had learned that the question I should ask wasn't, "Will I make it?" but rather, "When will I make it?"

Our tour company had a number of guides to help ensure that everyone riding had support along the way. The tour company was absolutely outstanding, and I would highly recommend it to anyone wanting to ride on the Hawaiian islands. It was simply a small misfortune that James and I were paired up with a guide who had a totally different way of thinking than we did. To this day, I still vividly remember my frustration with her. She asked each of us multiple times if we would be disappointed if we did not make it. She actually talked to us as if we wouldn't. I could hardly believe my ears!

Fortunately, this woman's negativity did not cause either of us to falter or ruin our experience in any way. It was me versus the volcano, and I was determined to win. All I wanted was to keep cycling until I reached the top. In fact, looking back, it was a real eye-opening experience. I will never forget her words, and as a result I will never question another person's ability to accomplish something that they have set their mind to. Questioning the abilities of ourselves and others is really a psychological game where nobody ever wins.

As we approached the 1981 metre (6,500 feet) mark, we saw the support van ahead. We pulled over, refuelled again, and were loaded up with arm warmers, leg warmers, and jackets. Our final ascent would be cold and windy, as would the first portion of our descent.

Fully outfitted for the remainder of our trip, we pushed on. I was getting tired and my legs were feeling the accumulation of several days of cycling the hilly routes of this island paradise. I was struggling, but I stuck to my guns and found my flow once more. I willed myself to keep going, and allowed the separation of mental and physical beings to begin.

Looking ahead, I saw James literally vanish into white cloud. Soon I was engulfed in white, fluffy mist. It was spooky. As I emerged on the other side of the wall of mist and continued to climb, I soon realized that I was looking down at the cloud line. Looking ahead, I once again located James. I was so tired, but I carried on. I didn't even contemplate stopping as I had finally learned that such thoughts would always bring me to the conclusion that stopping simply wasn't an option. On we went.

It felt like forever, but we finally reached the main visitor center. Despite this small victory, our journey wasn't over yet. We were at 3048 metres (10,000 feet). Ahead of us was a final, excruciating 7 metres (23 feet) up a short, steep path to the observatory. I had not come this far to stop now. I dug deep and found my power.

As I passed by the sign that indicated the summit, I was filled with relief and excitement. We sat up at the observatory level and looked down into the Mars-like red swirls of the inside of the volcano surrounded by the thin white strings of cloud. After taking it all in for a few minutes and having our photo taken together to solidify our accomplishment, we knew that it was time to be on our way. It had been a long day and we still had a very long descent ahead of us.

We bundled up with all of the warm clothing that had been stuffed into the back pockets of our cycling jerseys and then got back on our bikes. It was cold and windy, the road was steep, and the turns were sharp. I was tired and depleted, so I took my time and carefully descended section by section. Back into the spooky white haze we went, and then out the other side. Soon the cold air turned warm and we felt the heat of the sun beating down on us. We gradually discarded pieces of clothing again as we made our way down the 3055 metres (10,023 feet) that we had climbed.

When we finally made it back to our starting point at the bike shop, I was consumed with fatigue, relief, and an overwhelming sense of accomplishment. We had completed about 20 hours of cycling and almost 7000 metres (20,000 feet) of climbing over four days. I had prepared for and thought about this trip for so long, and it was hard to believe that it was now over. It felt pretty incredible.

We were reunited with the tour guides with whom we had rode and befriended over the past four days. Such a short time can feel like much longer when you are completely submerged into an experience and exposed to pure nature and such wonderful, friendly people. After chattering excitedly about this last adventure, we said our final goodbyes and we were on our way.

We realized then that we were absolutely starving. We found a place to stop and gobbled down fresh fish tacos like animals that hadn't eaten for days. The delicious food replenished my body, but once that need had been met exhaustion began to take over. We ate and ran, knowing that we still had to drive to another part of the island, our luggage in tow, and settle into a new place that we would call home for the remainder of our trip.

When we showed up at the condo that we would be sharing with James' old high school buddies, we were sweaty, stinky, sunburnt, and gross. After refreshing ourselves and resting up a bit, I felt a little more human again. We ventured out for the evening to find some dinner and ended up at one of our favourite joints, Fred's Mexican cantina. The fish tacos from earlier had vanished into my system as if they were a small tidbit of a snack. I was famished and ready to eat.

I have always been a good eater, and cycling up mountains had only encouraged my fiery appetite. There were times when James was astonished at what I packed away, and this was definitely one of them. After months of strict eating and four days of aggressive cycling, I was ready to take on something big. I ordered a margarita as big as a fish bowl and a massive burrito oozing with fresh fish and melted cheese. I don't think that James' buddies anticipated me eating the entire thing, but that burrito didn't stand a chance. I packed away bite after bite of cheese-covered fish and tortilla. I cleaned up that plate until there wasn't a morsel left. Then I looked one of James' friends in the eye and inquired whether or not he would be eating dessert. I had met this particular guy a long time ago when I first started dating James, and he had always been able to out-eat anybody. I simply assumed that he wasn't done yet. That night, however, I actually had to twist his arm to order dessert. I dug into that fancy dessert glass filled with ice cream, chocolate sauce and whipped cream like I hadn't eaten all day. Like the burrito, that sweet treat wasn't long for this world.

As we left the restaurant, I felt like I was going to explode. Oh, but it was so good! I finally felt full and satisfied. As I waddled along behind the group, we walked around the town in the beautiful night air. When I finally fell into bed, I was out for the count practically before my head hit the pillow.

The next morning, I was so excited. We were now moving into the second part of this trip, which meant that we would have several days to relax and enjoy the sunshine. Today was a beach day. Of course, with all of the training I had done, I was actually

145

excited about that. I had finally bought a bikini and I was ready to wear it!

When I was all changed, I looked into the mirror and gasped in horror. Eight hours in the hot Hawaiian sun on the side of a volcano had left me looking like Neapolitan ice cream with bright red legs and arms that turned sharply to white at the lines where my cycling jersey and shorts began. My lips had been seriously sunburned and were swollen to several times their natural size leaving me looking like a cartoon caricature. Oh, my.

After staring at myself for a few moments, I decided that I hadn't worked this hard *not* to wear my new bikini. Once I was lying on the sandy beach, listening to the ocean waves and letting my accomplishments sink in, I didn't care what color I was.

Haleakala: 56.9 km (starting from Paia), 5% average gradient, 12% maximum gradient, 3055 m ascent (10, 023 ft).

TAKING IT TOO FAR

Only through experience can the soul be strengthened, ambition inspired, and success achieved.' – Helen Keller

When I took my very first cycling trip, I was thrust into action without even a basic understanding of critical concepts such as training and eating to fuel the body. That first trip was one time in my life when my stubbornness and persistence paid off as mind over matter got me to the peaks of several mountains in the French Alps. It was also an experience in unpreparedness that I didn't care to repeat.

Taking into account my lessons from that first trip, I completely threw myself into a training and nutritional regimen prior to my second cycling trip. While cycling to the top of some of the brutes of the French Pyrenees, I was definitely aware of the benefits of the regimen that I had followed. On that trip I also found myself up against some unexpected challenges and had some eye-opening experiences that would never have occurred in the training room back home. This was the trip where I learned to pace myself, to harness my fire, and to unleash it slowly on the switchbacks of a French mountain. I also learned to celebrate each accomplishment along the way, and to allow myself to become fully immersed in the cultural surroundings I discovered as part of my travels.

Prior to my third cycling trip, I was more laid back about my eating and fitness regimens and instead chose to focus on finding balance in my routine. As I cycled up some of the most ferocious beasts of the Italian Dolomites, I trusted myself to make it even if it wasn't graceful. My only goal was to simply reach the top. By the time that trip wound down, I had sunk so deeply into my surroundings that it was very difficult to pull myself out and get back into my regular life.

Between my third and fourth cycling trips, my body was invaded by a parasitic intruder. I used that opportunity to learn patience, and to prioritize the important things in my life as I gradually returned to good health. I longed for my bike as my body healed. Our next bike trip was always on my mind. When I finally made it to the quaint towns of Austria and climbed up and over the mountains that would lead me into Switzerland, I completely accepted the fact that I am a cyclist and that I live for the climb. I finally fully admitted that this is simply what I do.

With a fully healed body and a renewed passion for cycling, I once again thrust myself into a training schedule in preparation for my fifth cycling trip. I was completely committed, and was nothing less than amazed by the results once I had a chance to put my training into action. I took on a Hawaiian volcano and walked away triumphant. The level of success that I experienced in Hawaii encouraged me to take on my next training season with a high level of aggression. Looking back, I think that perhaps I still had a lot to learn.

For our next cycling trip we were planning to return to Italy, one of our favourite places. This time we would be visiting Lake Como and Tuscany. After my successful training season the year before, I was very eager for a repeat performance. Our upcoming trip to Italy was the perfect goal to set my sights on to keep my motivation high.

I embarked upon a similar routine as I had the year before with regular trips to the gym. My workouts encompassed both intense cardio and weight training. As the cycling season drew closer, I spent an increasing amount of time in the training room at home spinning on my bike.

Saturdays were a prime opportunity to spend at least half of my day executing a perfect training session. Both the composition and timing of my breakfast were planned out carefully to ensure that my body had just the right type and amount of fuel for the physical exertion. I also allocated time post-training to allow for proper re-hydration, stretching, and physical recovery. I was totally committed. I was all in. As I saw the results of my efforts, I continued to push harder and harder. I had learned many things so far on this journey, but two concepts that remained foreign to me were those of rest and balance. These were simply not part of my nature.

About a month before we were to leave for Italy, I completely crashed physically and mentally. My body was so exhausted that I could barely even complete a simple workout. I was starving all of the time, but it seemed no matter what I ate I just wasn't satisfied. I was mentally exhausted as well, and had lost the motivation to continue to push myself.

I took another look at my nutritional spreadsheet and revamped it according to my current calorie intake and exertion. When I had first started the training season I had had a bit of winter weight to lose, and so the numbers had added up. As the training season had gone on, however, I had leaned up, gained muscle, and increased my metabolism. The numbers no longer added up. I had reached a point where my goal should not have been to lose weight but to maintain my current weight, and to fuel my strong body for the powerful workouts I was executing.

I was burning more calories on a daily basis than I was consuming, but I was at a point in my training where I no longer needed a caloric deficit. In fact, this deficit was hindering my performance. I should have been fuelling my body, but instead, I was starving it! To top this off, my continuously increasing motivation had prevented the thought of a rest day from even entering my head. As a result of my pushing myself so hard without proper fuel or rest, both my physical and mental selves went on strike. I crashed. I had no choice but to take a step back from the hardcore training and to increase my food intake. My body went into full recovery mode. My overly enthusiastic approach had resulted in my overdoing it.

By the time we left for our trip to Italy, I had recovered to a more stable place. I was able to work out more aggressively, and though I was trying to stick to eating healthy, I had taken a step back with regards to how strict I was being. My body was simply craving something more substantial than I had been providing it.

As part of my process when I reconsidered my nutritional spreadsheet, I did some research with regards to nutrition and sports. It turned out that the low fat and low calorie framework I had used to lose weight with a moderate amount of activity was completely wrong for training for an intense sport. It seemed that perhaps I wasn't taking in enough fat. The super lean eating approach was not working for me. This was a problem I had never dreamed of encountering.

It turned out that there was a lot of evidence to support the idea that female athletes require a certain amount of healthy fat. I had not been getting even close to what was being recommended in terms of daily fat intake for the types of activities that I had been doing. In trying to be healthy, I had taken a wrong turn and had done some damage to my body. As we prepared for our trip to Italy, I was ready to ride, but I was also full of trepidation. Unfortunately, my naïve and inexperienced approach to fitness had left me with a lack of confidence regarding my upcoming adventures with my bike.

THE LONGEST DAY EVER

I stared at the soft foam bobbing on top of the rich espresso that was creamy with milk. I wasn't quite sure if I was awake, or if I was still deep within a dream. After a long flight to Amsterdam during which I had not been able to find any sleep, I felt extremely foggy. The coffee was a welcome treat which at least jolted me enough into reality to function through the next leg of our journey, a short flight to Milan. Thankfully we were able to nap on that flight and by the time we were at the car rental counter we were feeling somewhat human again.

Bike cases in tow, we made our way to the car lot. We stopped at the spot to which we had been directed, and stared with surprise at the small sedan that awaited us. We were expecting a decent-sized hatchback that would accommodate our bikes. The cases weren't heavy, but they were bulky in such a way that we weren't sure they would fit into this car.

Always the problem solver, my husband went to work on this expert-level game of Tetris. As it became apparent that this was one game he wouldn't win, he left me with the bikes and went back to the rental counter. I stood there beside the little four-door until the light rain began to crescendo and hard pellets nipped at my face. Luckily there was a canopy close by. I dragged each bike case underneath, then found shelter myself.

Luckily the rain and hail were letting up by the time James returned. He didn't have good news, though. Apparently the little car was the only available means of transportation for us. Despite the specific reservation of a larger vehicle with a hatch, the woman at the counter had declared that it was this or nothing. Well, I couldn't see us walking our bike cases from the airport to Lake Como, so James went back to work trying to make them fit. I will never understand how he got those bike cases into the back seat of that car, but he managed somehow.

We were finally on our way, or so we thought. I hopped into the driver's seat while James slipped into the passenger side and pulled out a map. When I looked to the right, however, my heart sank. The vehicle was a standard and I only knew how to drive an automatic. The plan had been for James to navigate and for me to drive. This was generally the most effective setup for us, but now it looked like we would have to adjust. We had no choice but to switch spots.

Next thing you knew, I was staring at the most confusing and cluttered map I had ever seen in my life, and my normally calm husband had transformed into a crazy Italian driver. Off we sped. I had no idea where we even were on the map to begin with, which made conveying anything of use to my driver nearly impossible. My panic rose as we wove through roundabout after roundabout, and my confusion increased as I stared at the clutter of information in front me. Finally, we pulled over and regrouped.

In addition to our unexpected swap between driving and navigating, other matters were conspiring to make an uncomfortable situation even more challenging. James was really not feeling well, and neither of us had gotten much sleep up to this point in our journey so we were both exhausted. Usually I was the one tearing straight into things with complete irrational emotion and without applying any forethought or logic. Today, that person was James. Where was my rational husband, and who was this nutty driver who had replaced him? Usually logic was his guide, but at this moment it seemed that logic could not reach him. I tried to take a couple of deep breaths and calm myself down.

I'm not sure exactly when the turning point was, but somehow we managed to find a means of communication that was at least reasonably effective. We finally found our way onto the main highway and started heading towards our destination town. Now that we were truly on our way, a sense of relief filled the little four door.

A period of calm followed as we drove, and as the sun began its descent we pulled into Lake Como. We were able to find the rental office and get the key and directions to the villa that we would be staying in. We had no idea at that point that our adventure was only beginning.

I flipped through the pages and pages of directions, trying to decipher little tidbits such as, "turn left at the white house with the hen." My sense of ease was quickly vanishing. We kept on going as I attempted to translate the many pages of information into usable directions. It soon became apparent that we needed to head up. As the little four-door slowly zigzagged its way up the side of the mountain overlooking Lake Como, we did our best to puzzle through each piece of the direction manuscript.

It was getting darker, and we were both getting quite anxious to reach our final destination. The road itself was making me nervous, too. When I looked to my right and saw a brick wall inches from the window, and then to my left only to find a gaping cliff, I could only hope that a car wouldn't come down towards us on this road that was barely wide enough for one. Up and up we went, winding and weaving up the side of a cliff. We finally rolled past the villa that we were looking for, whereupon James realized that the paved parking spot was literally at a 90 degree angle to the tiny road that we were on. It was impossible to make it into the spot, so he kept driving on. My hope for easily finding a turn around point vanished instantly as the little car soon found itself mired in deep, thick mud.

I kept silent and wrestled with my feelings of panic internally. James was somehow able to kick up the gas a notch and bull his way through the black, sticky mess. Next came a move that to this day I am unsure how he pulled off. He whipped the four door up a steeply inclined driveway, then starting backing up. I had a vision of us plummeting off the cliff behind. I took a deep breath and waited. When the car came to a halt, then gained forward momentum once again, I exhaled a sigh of relief. We plowed back through the mud with more luck than I thought we had left. Finally, James pulled off one last amazing manoeuvre to get us into the ridiculous parking space. I don't know how, but we had made it.

Wearily, we made our way into the villa. I felt a little stunned by the day's events, and was quite surprised to actually be at our final destination. Of course there wasn't any food in the villa, and going back into town was not even a consideration. I suggested that we bring in one bike case, retrieve a couple of protein bars, and then call it a night. The best thing we could do at this point was to get some rest and reconsider our situation in the morning. It was hard not to think about the ridiculous drive up the side of this mountain, and how we would do this every day for the week. Somehow I got my mind to quiet down, and my exhaustion finally took over.

THE CALM AFTER THE STORM

I was alone in the bed down in the basement of the villa when I awoke the next morning. I realized that I had slept alone. What I didn't know was that James had been up all night stressing about what to do. He had put so much work into planning this trip, and finding ourselves perched on the side of mountain with a ridiculously dangerous drive between us and any sort of food, bike ride, or sign of civilization was a huge disappointment to him. Of all the pictures and information that had been provided about the villa, the drive had never been mentioned.

Doing our best to put our concerns aside for the time being, we drove down to the town and had a glorious day. We took a ferry ride to one of the other towns along the lake. We relaxed and enjoyed the sunshine and beautiful scenery. In the backs of our minds, however, was the drive that we had ahead of us to get back to our destination for the evening. We were hesitant to stay out too late since the last thing we wanted was to make the journey in the dark again. The stress loomed in the background of our otherwise wonderful day. As afternoon turned into evening, we picked up some food to cook, and then headed back up the mountain.

This time, we were making the drive in daylight and we knew what to expect. As we once again wove our way up the side of the mountain feeling like we were barely clinging to the road, we confirmed that this drive really was as scary as we remembered it being the night before. Not too much later, I attempted to cook dinner but could not get the stove to work. My trepidation about how this week was going to work out continued to grow. I eventually did get the stove fired up so that we were able to have more than just power bars for dinner, but that small victory did little to sooth my growing uneasiness.

As I waited for the water to boil for the pasta we had purchased, I flipped through a guest book that had been set in the dining area by one of the windows. I came across an entry written by a man who had brought his entire family to stay here. He had commented that they had a nice time, however, that that drive up the steep road was less than pleasant in his Volkswagon van! He had expressed his concern over the lack of information that had been provided regarding the driving conditions up to the villa.

We had a pleasant dinner, but that did little to improve my mental state. We had worked so hard all year to enjoy a short two-week vacation, and yet here we were, confined by our situation and worrying about how to make it work instead of relaxing and enjoying ourselves. It seemed absolutely ridiculous to be constantly stressed about getting down and back up this mountainside every time we ventured away from the villa.

The next morning when I couldn't get the stove to turn on so that I could make coffee, I finally admitted to James that I wasn't sure if this was going to work. He must have felt the same way, because practically the next thing I knew the car was packed, the mountain was descended, and we were checked into a hotel in the town overlooking the lake. Again, the problem solver in James had already found a solution.

As we enjoyed delectable wood fired pizzas on a patio overlooking the lake, we reflected on the last couple of days and laughed about everything from the inhospitable villa to the insane little car to the crazy Italian driver that James had become when he slid behind the wheel. Sometimes a situation can simply be reworked a little. Other times, when no amount of reworking is making a bad situation better, it is best to take another direction. Despite the roller coaster of stress and emotions, my bike had brought me to this wonderful place and now that we were settled the journey was just beginning.

POURING RAIN, SUNSHINE, AND A HAZY RIDE HOME

Now that we had settled into the lovely hotel overlooking Lake Como, we were able to prepare for our first ride. As we were getting our bikes ready, I looked up in the sky and expressed some concern about the lingering dark clouds. James gave very little response. Not much slowed him or his zest for adventure down. Despite my misgivings, we were soon off. Our plan was to cycle around and over to the other side of Lake Como. Our destination would be the town of Bellagio, almost directly across from our home base of Menaggio.

Not long after we had started riding, the rain began. As the drizzle quickly turned into a downpour, we found a little spot under an arch in the rocky cliff on the side of the road to shelter ourselves. We huddled in tightly and looked out at the pouring rain. I was so glad to be sheltered from the buckets of water pouring down in front of us. The rain just kept going on and on with no sign of letting up. It went on too long for James, who was eager to get riding. Without warning, he declared that we should continue. I was game, so we took off cycling through the pouring rain.

It actually wasn't that bad. The rain wasn't all that cold, so while I wasn't exactly warm I can't say that I was freezing either. I focused on the road ahead of me and cautiously pedaled through the water surrounding me.

We approached a tunnel and my nerves fired up a little. There is something special about cycling through a tunnel. It is scary, exciting, and exhilarating all at once. Every time I enter a tunnel on my bike, I feel my adrenaline spike. I guess it is a kind of high for me. I am frightened and I want it to end, but at the same time the thrill of having to fully concentrate on such a scary task feeds my sense of adventure. This tunnel was dark, but not completely black. My cycling sunglasses were covered in beads of water, and it became very difficult to see ahead of me. I slid them down my nose a bit and was relieved to be able to see well enough again.

As I pulled back out into the daylight, my adrenaline eased up and the tingling sensation charging through me disappeared. There is such a sense of relief followed by calm and relaxation that comes after the adrenaline vanishes. I soon caught up to James, who was waiting for me. We were both drenched but we didn't let that slow us down.

As we neared the end of the lake where we would be turning to come down the other side, the rain let up and the sun started to peek through the clouds. I was quite chilly by then, and was very hopeful that the sun would fully emerge and dry me off. We had to wind our way carefully through some heavy traffic in the town of Como at this point, so I soon forgot all about being cold. When we neared the edge of the busy city, we found ourselves back along a quieter lake side road. What a relief.

The sun now started to show its full strength, and I could feel the warmth all over my body. I wanted to be warm to the core, and so I willed the sun to continue to shine. The touch of the warm rays on my face and the view of the lake beside me left me peaceful and full of enjoyment. This was a nice part of the ride.

All along the lake we rode until eventually we reached Bellagio, a beautiful little town with cobble streets and patios dotting the main square. We found ourselves a seat on one of those patios and ordered some wine. Looking out over the lake, we chatted and relaxed. Despite the rainy start, it had been a wonderful day. I was so glad that James had gotten us out riding. If it had been up to me, I may have cowered from the rain to avoid getting wet and cold. At this moment, it seemed so silly to be worried about such things. If we had not ventured out we would have missed a lovely ride, some warm sunshine, and wine on a patio.

We were both getting hungry, so we decided that we would finish off the wine and take the ferry back over to the other side of the lake to find a nice little place for dinner in Menaggio. Following through with our plan, we polished off our wine and caught a ride on a ferry heading across the lake. We enjoyed the view and the anticipation of a nice meal as our hunger grew.

The ferry stopped a little ways from our destination town, so we waited as the passengers around us departed. Even after the ferry emptied out we continued to wait until one of the crew members approached and indicated that we should get off, too. James tried to explain that we were going on to Menaggio. The crew member shook his head and indicated that no, we were not going there. It looked like we would be cycling the rest of the way back.

We wheeled our bikes off of the ferry. I was quite fuzzy from the wine, and made sure that James knew that I would need to take it slow. No problem. It was only a couple of kilometres. We pedalled slowly towards the town in our hazy, giggly state.

Later that evening, we found ourselves sitting at a little table on a cobbled street surrounded by the warm chatter of our fellow diners. We looked up at the stars, sipped at another round of delicious wine, and enjoyed a lovely meal. We had a celebratory glass of limoncello, and completely sank into the moment.

JUST GO UP

We were completely settled into Menaggio and our lovely hotel overlooking Lake Como. We had done a nice ride with a touch of adventure the previous day. After pushing myself past the point of crashing during my winter training, it felt really good to be back into a cycling flow. I had no idea at this point that I had merely sampled a taste of the craziness to come on this trip.

The ride from the day before had simply whetted James's appetite. After all of our cycling trips together I was starting to realize that his big sense of adventure was more than enough to make up for my complete lack of one. His curiosity and driven attitude constantly took us to new places and unexpected challenges. My understanding of this piece of my husband's psyche deepened on our second ride of the trip.

We rolled out and made our way along the beautiful Lake Como once again. Before long, we started climbing. James' interest in climbing is just as big as his sense of adventure. It seems that almost every time we embark on a new journey, there is at least one climb involved. So, up we went. We climbed for a while, and found ourselves near a quaint town overlooking Lake Lugano. We took a break and soaked up the beauty of our surroundings. What a lovely day it was, and what an enjoyable ride we were having. Soon, break time was over, and we pushed on.

Next thing I knew, we were climbing again. We were really climbing this time. When I inquired about our route, James simply indicated that we were going "up there" as he pointed to a peak in the distance.

It turned out that we were climbing Monte di Tremezzo. At the time, all I knew was that I had a vague goal and that I really had my work cut out for me. I was game for this, so we climbed.

Despite the physically and mentally depleted place that I had found myself in not so long ago, it was now clear to me that I still had the ability to tap into the power of my own determination. I had thankfully allowed my body enough recovery time from the overly zealous training that I had committed myself to, and had not lost all of my strength or sacrificed the endurance that I had worked to build up over the years.

I found a flow that would get me to my destination in a reasonable time without prematurely depleting myself. I let go of all worry. I focused. I didn't think about how long it would take or how much further we had to go. At points along the way I couldn't see the top at all, so I was able to simply focus on the current piece of the whole. This had become my strategy for so many of the cycling related challenges that I had taken on: Breaking each overwhelming challenge down into small, accessible pieces. I took on each stretch one at a time, and some of them were definitely steep. I pedalled my wheels over gravel, around tight corners, and up walls. One bit at a time, I just kept chipping away at my ultimate goal.

As we approached the peak that James had pointed to hours before, I looked around. The view was outstanding. Way up here looking down at the lake and all of the surrounding towns it was just me, James, a few cows, and a donkey. It was serene and peaceful. What surrounded us was a reward that could only be earned with hours of gruelling grinding, one pedal stroke at a time. We were at peace with the earth, each other, and ourselves. My inner cyclist was finally free once again!

The descent was rather adventurous. In attempting to find the most direct route to the bottom, we wove our way down extremely steep and winding streets that took us through tiny towns nestled into the side of the mountain. We carefully navigated down each stretch, straining our arms as we wrenched on our brakes. The day was getting long, and I was getting extremely hungry and a little fuzzy. We just kept on crawling down the mountainside.

As we neared the bottom, my body began to relax. We had climbed for hours. We had experienced one of the highest points in the area, and had seen a view that most of the others around us were missing out on. We had cautiously woven our way down the mountainside. Now, with no food left and very little water, we had to make our way back along the lake to a place where we could replenish ourselves.

It is funny how the end of the ride, when the body and mind are depleted and all you want is a cold drink and some real food, can feel more challenging than the steepest parts of the ascent. This is the part of ride when I feel completely finished, but somehow I find a way to really dig deep. It always amazes me to realize that my limits are mostly psychological. After putting my mind to it and finding more energy where I thought there was none, we pedalled on towards town.

The warmth of a hot shower, the softness of my comfy clothes, the numbing effect of a glass of wine, and the satisfaction of delicious, warm food filling my hungry belly are all rewards of such hard physical and mental work. It is the biggest feeling of accomplishment that I have ever enjoyed in my life to reach a summit up in the sky, knowing that I made it there one pedal stroke at a time. It is such a feeling of reward to enjoy an amazing meal in beautiful surroundings while reminiscing about the ride of the day with my cycling partner.

The next day as we sat on the rooftop of our hotel enjoying a lovely picnic and each other's company, not an ounce of tension remained in my being. All of the excitement in finding this place and all of the hard work we had done to ride our bikes up the side of the mountain had left me at peace. We allowed ourselves to sink into one of the most important elements of hard exercise: the rest day, where you allow your body and spirit time to recover. Besides, when you discover such a lovely little spot as Menaggio you need to breathe it in. You just never know when or if you will be back. Don't let it pass you by.

Monte di Tremezzo: 1500 metres of ascent from Menaggio

THE CHURCH OF THE CYCLIST

Before departing from Menaggio, we had one more very special cycling quest to conquer. The day after our rest day, we prepared to take that quest head on.

Bikes in tow, we took a ferry across the lake back to Bellagio. We wove our way through the little town to the base of Monte San Primo, where I looked up at a series of switchbacks. This would not be the longest climb that I would ever accomplish, but I knew that it would be a tough and hot one.

Once again, our hard work in ascending that climb was rewarded. At the top of Monte San Primo lies the Church of the Cyclist, a very special little church with an indescribable collection of cycling memorabilia. The best way for the true cyclist to experience this is to cycle up the series of lovely switchbacks, dismount at the top, take a picture of the amazing view, and then embark on a journey within the little church. Putting in the hard work to make it to a summit and then getting a glimpse into the lives of those whose abilities are beyond my comprehension was an inspiring and emotional experience.

The riding that we had done over the past few days made me feel like I still had it in me. My passion for cycling was still strong, and my ability to succeed hadn't been entirely destroyed by my overly aggressive approach to training.

I enjoyed a sense of true serenity for the rest of the day. It was simply impossible not to take it all in as I descended the switchbacks, looking ahead at the lake laid out before me. When we finally rolled to a stop in the lovely square, we enjoyed a delectable lunch with a fantastic view. It was the perfect end to this small adventure.

Monte San Primo: 13.4 km, 6.9% average gradient, 923 m ascent

THE TUSCAN HILLS

After Lake Como, we moved on to Tuscany, a place that left me with oddly mixed feelings. My memories of that time are mostly of my fear of pushing myself and rides that didn't particularly stand out as important. Thanks to the fear that my overzealous approach to training had instilled in me, I hesitated to venture too far from our villa since returning after a long ride would involve several steep ascents. I worried about how far we would go, how long we would be gone, and how I would fare during the ride. I felt that I had partially regressed back to the scared little girl that still lurked deep inside of me after all this time.

Digging back into my travel journals to review the trip, however, I was quickly lost in a beautiful journey full of nature, culture, food, people, and cycling adventures. Yes, I experienced some trepidation in Tuscany, but I felt it while embarking on an adventure of hard work and cycling outings in a place of constant, steep climbs! As I digested each little journey that I had carefully documented in my journal, I was taken away into memories of magical moments. It seems that perhaps this part of my cycling journey was not the failure that I had filed it away as in my memory.

Looking back, I can see that I absolutely did experience some fear, some worry, and that I had lost a bit of feist in my riding. On the other hand, I also did three and four hour-long rides in the hot Tuscan sun. I faced the steep hills of the Tuscan countryside, and never once considered stopping or getting off of my bike. At the end of each ride, I took on a six km steep climb just to get back to the villa where we were staying.

Was I as fast as I normally was while I was in Tuscany? I don't know. Does it matter? I doubt it. Was my riding a failure? Hardly, or at least, not by the definition of failure that had become such a part of the way that James and I lived our lives. He had taught me that it was more of a failure to not even try than it was to not finish something the way that you had planned it.

I discovered a lot more in Tuscany than I had actually anticipated. We spent our days riding our bikes through the beautiful Tuscan countryside. We rode alongside vast fields with rows upon rows of luscious grapes. We rode past beautifully manicured olive groves and picturesque pastures dotted with quaint little homes. We sweated and grinded up the never-ending sequence of steep hills. At this point in my cycling journey, I didn't necessarily feel that I had it in me, but I dug it out and persevered each time.

When we arrived in Tuscany and were navigating for the first time towards the villa that we would be staying in, I couldn't help but think how romantic it was that we would be in the heart of the hamlet of Torsoli. I had never been to a hamlet before, let alone stayed in one. As we pulled up to our destination, I don't think I could completely believe what my eyes were telling me. Before us was an absolutely lovely, quaint villa surrounded by vineyards and olive trees. The perfectly-manicured grounds housed a fragrant, luscious looking rosebush, and a cherry tree in full blossom with an abundance of bright red sweet fruit. Each morning, birds would sing and roosters would crow. The magnificence of this place simply cannot be fully captured through words.

Unlike our experience in Lake Como, this home away from home was exactly the way it had been advertised when James had spent hours and hours researching for a spot for us to immerse ourselves in this lovely countryside. Many mornings were spent reading by the pool while sunning my belly. Years later I would look back on this and smile as I realized that "sunning my belly," or warming my whole being from the outside in, had become a symbolic staple of my life to represent times when I was able to rejuvenate myself. Adventurous days on my bike or exploring the abundance of Tuscan culture left us hot and tired, but those days also made the cool, refreshing relief of a dip in the pool even more amazing. I spent most of my evenings outside watching the sunset and sipping wine. During one such lovely evening as we watched the warm red and yellow glow, our ears were soothed by the sounds of a Zeppelin ballad emerging from a nearby town.

Over the course of the week, we immersed ourselves in the wealth of culture surrounding us. We simply had something that we usually didn't: time. We had time to explore a place that was entirely different than what we were accustomed to. We didn't have any schedule to stick to or limits to our time.

We visited the extremely old, untouched town of Sienna to see a place created with only quality and perfection in mind. Experiencing such a treasure truly gave a different perspective to someone who grew up in a society built on quick solutions and a focus on quantity over quality. The architectural magnificence was nothing like I had ever seen in my life.

We plunged ourselves into the artistic, poetic romanticism of the famous Florence. Wandering through a canopy of architectural remains from ages past into the magnificent square bordered by café patios and awe-inspiring sculptures left me feeling like I had walked through a tiny door into a make-believe land. After becoming accustomed to the steep inclines of the Tuscan hills on my bike, climbing the 414 steps by foot to the top of the belltower left me feeling exhilarated but not exhausted, and ready to indulge in the Italian fare perfuming the air.

We indulged in both villa-style home cooking over an open fire in the fresh air, and the lovely dining in a few of the many ristorantes that seemed to be everywhere. On our last evening in this magical world, we drove around to satisfy our craving for a little more exploration before heading back to our scheduled lives. We didn't have a specific destination in mind; we just let the evening unfold as it would. As if by magic, we found ourselves walking into the most lovely restaurant I have ever been in. We were a bit early for dinner by local standards, but they were happy to have us.

We were welcomed with a glass of wine and four kinds of homemade bread, and then seated on an outdoor patio decorated in blue scarves and tiny lights that tinted the roof blue as the sun slipped away. Paper butterflies danced over our heads in the slight breeze. Acoustic guitar serenaded our ears and our souls. The entire kitchen was open for all to see. Thus, we experienced art at its finest as the two culinary wonders behind the counter wove the simplest, freshest ingredients into creative masterpieces. The conclusion to this gastronomic symphony was a chocolate soufflé made from scratch. It was an evening of quality, creativity and the breath of life.

My bike has taught me a lot about myself. It has facilitated achievements that I never thought were possible for me, has taken me to many places, and has opened up new worlds in my life. My bike is many things to me, and in more ways than one it has changed my life for the better.

LEARNING SOME BALANCE

It had become clear to me that I was holding myself back from reaching my full potential as a cyclist. When I took things too far, over trained and under ate, I ended up crashing and burning. For a good month I was unable to complete even moderate workouts, and my calorie-deprived body craved mounds of food.

Even after recovering and completing some reasonably difficult rides, there was a part of my psyche that was afraid of pushing too far. I was terrified of crashing and burning again. As a result, I always held something back when going out for rides. I wasn't afraid to push hard in the gym because the gym is a safe place where you can always stop if get tired or push too hard. If your blood sugar gets low, you can always go and grab a snack. If you get dehydrated, you can simply walk over to the water fountain.

Riding outdoors, however, is another story. This is especially true when doing a longer ride or riding an unfamiliar route. You just can't be completely certain of how long it will take, of whether you will run out of food or water, or if anything unexpected will go wrong. I was afraid to push too hard on longer rides as I didn't want to find myself too depleted to continue. This was a far different state of mind than I had ever experienced in my riding days up to this point, and it simply wasn't working for me. My approach to training wasn't working, either. I had repeatedly thrown myself into months of hard training and strict eating. My physical ability would increase, and my body would become lean and toned. My insides would feel extremely clean from all of the dietary restrictions that I would place on myself. I would feel spectacular, but only for a while.

As long as this type of regiment was timed perfectly with a cycling trip, I would peak just as I needed to climb up the European mountains. If the regimen resulted in a peak in fitness at the wrong time, though, I would find myself struggling up a mountain or crashing before our cycling trip ever started. Even if I was lucky enough to peak at the right time, the regimen that I was following was so unsustainable that after our annual cycling event I would get lazy with my fitness routine and find myself eating too much of the things that hindered my performance. I figured that there just had to be some sort of balance, but I didn't know how to find it. I think I found it much easier to fully commit to an extreme program for several months at a time than to be dedicated longer term. I had no problem at all achieving a goal that was only a few months away, but when it came to the bigger picture and the years of cycling ahead of me I was at a bit of a loss for the best way to proceed.

As the next training season began, I was far from where I wanted to be. My dedication to a regular fitness routine had wavered. I had indulged in a few too many evenings of decadent food and drinks. I had put on some weight, and I definitely wasn't feeling very good about myself. I was so disappointed in how far I had regressed after many seasons of dedication to both my fitness and nutritional regiment. I had seen such amazing results in myself, and had completely surprised myself with what I had achieved on my bike. All of the hard work, all of those results, all of the accomplishments, just seemed to vanish into thin air. I didn't feel good about any of it.

I started by recommitting to a regular gym routine and eating a more balanced diet. I went back to what I knew, but I was careful to be less extreme about it. I didn't cut out anything that I really wanted, but I balanced out how often I indulged. I focused on how I felt, and thought about getting to where I wanted to be. Sliding back into some good habits was doable for the short term, but I still didn't know how I was going to tackle the long term.

I was going to the gym at my workplace during the lunch hour to do weight training, spinning on my bike at home, and getting back to the basics with my meals, but I knew that I needed something more to help myself out. I needed some sort of punch to add something interesting to my routine. A boot camp class that was being offered at the gym at work caught my eye, so I joined. It turned out to be the missing piece of the puzzle for me.

The class was absolutely fantastic. The instructor, Gillian, had a wonderful, positive energy that infused the studio and all of the participants. She had designed fantastic moves that were energizing and that challenged the entire body. The classes were really hard, and they were a lot fun! I felt like I was really starting to push myself again and feeling much more optimistic about my progress.

It turned out that Gillian was also a personal trainer and a nutritional consultant. Up to this point, I had designed all of my training workouts and meals on my own. I had learned a lot and

I was doing some things right, but I had so much more to learn. Despite my best efforts, I knew there were some key things that I was obviously doing wrong. I wanted so badly to learn how to find balance the right way so that I could maintain it for the long term, and Gillian became the person I could turn to for help in that quest.

I ended up working with Gillian for most of the training season that year. Her approach was perfect for me. She didn't just show up and bark orders at me. She taught me what to do on my own. She showed me different moves every time we met, and made sure that I understood how to do them correctly. She examined pages of printouts of my nutritional spreadsheets and offered very helpful insight about what I was eating. I was afraid to push myself physically and nutritionally. I wanted to find a more constructive approach that would give my body what it needed, enabling it to perform the way I wanted it to. Gillian kept it simple. She would teach me just enough each time we met to keep me interested and focused, and she would make very few key observations about my nutritional breakdowns.

With a few small adjustments, I was quickly on my way. I feel like Gillian helped me to really learn the value of balance. She guided me through cycles of training with proper rest breaks to allow the body to repair itself. She also taught me how to really look at food as a fuel for the body and not as an enemy to struggle with. When I asked her to, she also taught me how to visualize properly. It was a very constructive training season for me, and I could feel myself getting stronger.

The most important part about the whole training season was that I completely committed myself to patience. I knew that a slower, more balanced approach would not get me the quick, aggressive results that I was used to, but I also knew that those results were not sustainable. I completely believed in this new approach and trusted that it would work in both the short and the long term.

Just as I had hoped, my patience paid off. Years later I would realize that the fundamental lessons of patience and balance that I had learned from this training season would never leave me. Rest days would become a regular part of my life, and my desire to be in tune with how my body felt would override the short term cravings for greasy or fatty foods around me. I am not saying that I never enjoyed a delectable meal, but what I am saying is that my motivation to be balanced now stemmed from a deep desire within to take care of my body and to make my body feel good.

The slower, more balanced approach did bring slower results. I didn't see the pounds vanish as quickly as I had in the past. I did, however, start to feel really good. As our next cycling trip approached, I knew that this time I wasn't going to crash and burn just before we boarded our flight. I knew that this time I would ride my bike triumphantly up any climb that we decided to take on.

PRIORITIES CHANGE

'If you wake up two days in a row unhappy, change something.' – Contributed by Melissa Anne Paauwe

BIKE PATH OR RACE TRACK?

After a long haul of several years working in an intensely stressful environment, I finally made a switch. I just absolutely knew that it was time for me to break free into another place for a while. The position that I left was difficult, trying, even ridiculous at times, but it was also challenging and it led me to grow in many ways and to meet many amazing people. I committed to taking on a new, far less challenging position in an environment that was a cakewalk compared to any other that I had ever known as a professional.

Both the location of this new position and the time of year that I made this switch allowed me to ride my bike to work daily for several months after starting. I had never been able to do this before, and it turned out to be absolutely fantastic! Most of the riding that I had done to this point had been on the highways on the outskirts of Calgary and through the European mountains. This was something different altogether.

Prior to this, there had been absolutely no reason for me to use the bike paths in my hometown. Often crowded by rollerbladers, skateboarders, and all types of pedestrians including children and dogs, these paths just aren't for serious cyclists. On the bike paths, the situation is completely unpredictable, without any real rules that are actually followed. There isn't any penalty for forgetting to shoulder check before changing lanes, for travelling in the wrong lane, or for coming to a sudden halt. It was simply safer for us to cycle on the roads where there existed a set of rules that were followed the majority of the time. On the smaller highways, we were treated to long, open roads where we could see very far ahead, and where we could watch the light traffic like hawks in anticipation of any deviance to the road rules.

Commuting to work on my bike was like being exposed to an entirely new world. The first part of my route was on quieter residential roads. I would get out of bed at an unreasonably early hour, attempt to eat a banana in my sleepy haze, deck myself out in my cycling gear, and grab my backpack. Mounted on my little Trek 2000, I would bike down our street, and take a left at the end. Immediately after that turn I battled with a climb. It was always tough to start climbing first thing in the morning, but every day I would reach the top and feel exhilarated from the exertion and fresh, crisp air. Once at the summit, I would cycle on a path along a ridge. I could see everything from up there: the mountains in the distance, my neighbourhood below, and all of downtown sprawled out before me.

Next up was another section of residential roads. This part was a lot of fun. These roads weren't that busy, and there were only a few stop lights. There was one longer, flatter section where I could really gain some speed as long as I was lucky enough to hit green lights. Here, my more aggressive, competitive side would occasionally show up. It is quite amusing how human beings are naturally competitive. I have seen it in others during many bike rides, and I see it come out in myself whenever I spot another cyclist ahead. If I find myself gaining on another cyclist, I can feel my adrenaline soar and my heart race. Having never been even slightly athletic before I discovered cycling, it is just so exciting for me to actually beat someone at a physical activity. If only that silly gym teacher could see me now!

After this stretch of racing, I would turn off towards the bike path. A steep descent and a sharp turn later, I would find myself immersed in a world of cycling that I had never imagined existed. The first time I used the main bike path during commuting times, I felt like a deer in headlights. I was bewildered, intimidated, and quite frankly scared for my life!

During commuting hours, the bike path isn't a bike path at all; it's a race track! You would see every sort of cyclist on this path. There were road cyclists wearing lycra, which is what I was accustomed to. There were riders on heavier mountain bikes, and riders who clearly cycled year-round through the snow, ice, and rain. There were riders with an elastic band tied around their dress pants who only rode a bike to and from work. There were also many people who were somewhere in between who defied categorization. The point is that all of these riders now found themselves scrambled together in a citywide race to get to the downtown core.

My first ride to work was a slow one, but I learned quickly and I soon found myself deeply embedded in this strange racing culture. It became a game for me, and I often found excuses to compete with other cyclists even if I was the only one who knew that we were racing. If I saw any sign of a reason that I should be faster, this became motivation for me to step it up. If the bike was heavier, if the rider was out of shape, if they were carrying a heavy pack, or if they simply didn't look like a road cyclist, then I should be able to win this race.

This part of my commute might sound dangerous, but honestly, it was not. The only people who were on this path during this time were commuters. Almost every one of them was on a bike. Those who were walking were doing so far to the right. The safest thing to do was to follow the pace being set and to be very decisive and clear about my actions. So I did, and I definitely enjoyed it! By the time I reached the downtown area, I only had a few blocks of road to travel, and the traffic was still light at this time of day.

I mentioned that I was riding my Trek 2000 during my commutes. I had decided to give my Madone some time off. The summer of commuting back and forth to work gave me several months to fully renew my relationship with my old friend, my first real bike. My 2000 had gotten me through my first bike rides and training seasons. My commuting time resulted in a whole new appreciation for how powerful this little bike really was. It would rest all day safely locked in a bike cage in the underground parkade in the building where I worked. When I was ready to go home in the evening, I would once again gear up in my cycling clothes, pack up my backpack, and head down to the bike cage. It was so wonderful to end the work day out in the fresh air, enjoying the sunshine and letting go of any work-related thoughts from the day.

James had mapped out some great routes for the trip home to lengthen the ride and to insert some additional climbing. I would take the same race track bike path all along the river each day. Then I would take whichever turnoff corresponded with the route I wanted to ride that day.

My favourite turnoff was right near a park, and would route me directly to a good climb that was regularly traversed by many cyclists, some of whom were commuting home and others who were doing hill repeats. After this good climb, I would cross over into the nice, quiet residential area near my home. The rest of the ride was mostly climbing. The first ascent right after crossing the busy main street was a short but very steep stretch. Many a time I would find myself digging deep to try and catch up to any cyclists in front of me. I wasn't always successful. When I was, it was exhilarating. When I wasn't, I would try as hard as I could and then admit that the cyclist in front of me deserved the win.

Win or lose, after that climb I would be rewarded with some flatter road through the quiet neighbourhoods where the scents of other people's barbeques would float into my nose and arouse my hunger. I had one more climb to face before coasting home.

A bit longer than the previous climb but still reasonably steep, this ascent was the perfect way to build some strength and willpower as I battled fatigue and hunger. As I found whatever smoothness I could in my final ascent of the day, all my thoughts would be on the wonderful sunshine and fresh air, and the delicious dinner I would soon be eating. This was the perfect way to end a day of being cooped up in an office. It was so much better than being stuck behind a steering wheel in bumper to bumper traffic. Near the top of this final stretch of steepness, my body always relaxed. It was all coasting from here, and I would often find myself whipping triumphantly down the last few hills towards the home stretch.

When I was tired, I would cruise down the final block and take in the scenery. When I still had some punch left, I would enter an imaginary sprint to the finish of a pro race. Every time, I would be so happy so see the little balcony outside of our house beckoning me home and inviting me to enjoy the evening ahead.

The Perfect Trainer

The warm summer turned to fall, and the mornings started getting darker and crisper. I knew that my days of commuting to work by bike were coming to an end, and that soon I would have to turn to indoor training once again. In anticipation of this is, and also to provide a place for me to transform myself from cyclist to professional every morning, I had joined a gym right across from my workplace. For several months, I had only used the change room and shower facilities as it had seemed absurd to me to use a cardio machine when I could simply get on a bike and ride. Now that the weather had turned, and it was no longer safe for me ride outside, I began to explore all that the facility had to offer.

It turned out to be a fantastic setup. Every lunch hour, I headed over for my hour of cardio or weight training. I dug out old workouts from the past and tried to simulate climbing up mountains on an elliptical trainer or a treadmill. It all went well enough for a while, but eventually my workouts started feeling tedious, like they weren't enough for all my punch.

Right around this time, my husband found himself released from his professional situation. This was a long-anticipated occurrence that provided an opportunity to change directions. Talk of finally doing a big adventure began to surface around our household. Deep down I knew that something was going to happen, but I had no idea exactly what. I did, however, know that I had to be ready for whatever was coming. I needed to step up my training because whatever we were going to do, I knew it would be true James-style. People who have never experienced a true James-style adventure can't possibly comprehend what this means, but the long and short of it is that these types of adventures require a lot of physical and mental toughness since they are demanding and have surprises around every corner.

When I purchased my gym membership, I also purchased a training package in response to a gut feeling that I would eventually need and really benefit from it. Knowing that there was something big coming my way, I knew that it was time to cash in on these sessions. I went into my gym and inquired about who I would be placed with. They soon presented me with this very young guy. My gosh, I thought, what can this kid possibly do for me? We were introduced, and I asked him if he had some time at the moment to chat about what I was looking for. He did, so we sat down and I proceeded to run through with him what my goals were, and exactly what I expected out of training sessions. To my surprise, and delight, this "kid" looked me right in the eye, took notes, and asked questions. I began to have some hope that this might work out. We booked our first session.

You have to understand that over the summer I had been a free bird, cycling to and from work every day while trying to take down other cyclists along the way. Now I was caged behind a desk all day long with no fresh air, no hills to climb, and no one to compete against. I have always been a bit fierce, but now my energy was pent up during those long hours behind the computer. Plus, I had a fitness goal to work towards, and when I have a goal I become seriously motivated. My gym sessions were only an hour long, which was just not enough compared to some of the incredibly long days I had experienced on a bike.

For my first session with the trainer, I arrived in the gym filled with punch and ready to rock. My new trainer, Mikey V., had me warm up on the treadmill, and then we were off. Circuit-style combinations of lunges, squats, push ups, weight training, and core moves were interlaced with periods of serious cardio that had me buzzing. This "kid" had me seriously working hard. It was so much fun and so motivating to have specific exercises to focus on and work through.

The further we got into the workout, the harder I tried. Just to finish off each set successfully was a rush. I had worked harder in an hour than I could make myself work alone in the gym, and the moves were so effective that I could practically feel myself toning up and getting stronger. That first session left me craving more.

I only met with Mikey V. once a week for most of our time spent training together. It wasn't until closer to the approach of the crazy unknown adventure that I started meeting him multiple times per week. I learned so much from the moves that he came up with and strategically grouped together that I had lots to work on by myself during the week. To top it all off, he always seemed to find me and make sure that I was working hard enough when I visited the gym on my own.

As time went on, Mikey V. always had something new for me to challenge my body and continuously upped the intensity, sometimes even running me through multiple workouts in one session. This kid actually had the ability to shut me up. Yes, this fierce little fireball that always had something to say was left absolutely unable to speak at the end of a session with Mikey V. I will never forget the first time this happened. I actually thought he was trying to kill me during the workout, but struggled through nonetheless. Not only did he know how to push me beyond my limits, but also he knew how to deal with my attitude. He just didn't back down. He wouldn't have any of it. I felt so put in my place, and it rocked! It was so impressive that he took my fitness goals so seriously.

Just when I thought I couldn't really go any harder, I managed to do just that. I showed up for my session as usual. We warmed up, and then we headed to the back weight training area. Mikey V. shows me that has set up a *real* weight training set, the full bar with the huge weights on each end. This kind of weight training set brings to mind those guys in the little one-piece leotard type suits with big arm muscles lifting these bars over their heads.

Mikey V. started by showing me the Clean portion of the Clean and Jerk. The Clean portion of the move consists of a low squat and a harnessing of power in the legs to launch the bar up to shoulder height. I squatted down and attempted to do as he instructed, but the bar didn't really move. I looked at Mikey V. and said, "Are you serious?" He looked me right in the eye and replied, "Yes, now do it."

I really tried, and as I did I was overcome by a very familiar feeling. I was facing something dead on that I didn't believe that I could do. How many times was I going to be here? And what valid reason did I have not to try my hardest?

I listened carefully to Mikey V.'s guidance and concentrated on my form and on harnessing all of my energy to getting this bar to shoulder height safely. It took a few tries, but I did it once, and then again. I was completely pumped up! I was so excited. I had just been introduced to something that never in a million years would I have thought of even trying, something so out my realm of what I thought I could do that to have succeeded was almost unbelievable. Best of all, this was something that required an all in attitude and focus, a perfect addition to my training!

We did more of these sessions, and I continued to work on my Clean. Eventually I mastered that move enough that it was time for the Jerk. This is portion of the move where you move the bar from shoulder height to above your head. I had the utmost trust in Mikey V. to guide me through this.

The first time I tried the Jerk part of the move, I couldn't believe how difficult it was. I couldn't get the bar high enough over my head. I wanted to complete the move so badly, but it just wasn't happening. I got it almost right once during the session, but I knew I had a lot to work on in terms of posture. I was pretty sore the next day and felt a bit like a beat up old woman. but my hunger to get this move right was strong.

There is absolutely no feeling in the world like trying something that you can't completely comprehend in your mind. Failure doesn't matter. Failure is how we learn and grow, and embracing it can open up new worlds. We kept on going with these sessions, and even slotted in serious weight training sessions every so often to mix things up as I worked towards my goal of completing this move.

We both knew when it was the right day to go all in and attempt the full Clean and Jerk. Slowly and surely, my form improved and I would feel the results in the right places. The first time I really got it was incredible. It went something like this: Squat low, focus on proper placement of hands, make sure the power is coming from the thrust of your hips and that nothing else around you is distracting, focus deeply within, breathe in, commit, and pull. That got you up to shoulder height. Next, relax, refocus, breathe and commit your entire being to the rest of the move. Use your power and your thrust, and visualize that bar moving over your head as you execute.

Completing the Clean and Jerk was an incredible feeling of power, focus, and achievement. Like I said, this move is an all-in activity. It won't work if you aren't completely committed both physically and mentally. What a confidence builder it turned out to be for me. I wish that everyone could try this. All those hours on the cardio machine with no time spent working on your physical and mental strength will not get you as far as you can go.

To top all this off, I was ultra-impressed when I saw the photos of some of my most successful Clean and Jerks. Mikey V. had taken some shots and provided an in-depth analysis of my posture so that I could continue to improve. I couldn't believe how strong I looked. I thought back to those days in elementary school when gym class struck fear within me. I thought back to my university days when I felt like a blowfish and was so uncomfortable with my physical being. It was just so empowering to accomplish such moves. I wish that all women could feel this way. I truly believe that there is something out there for everyone, something out of their realm of comprehension, that can open up new worlds for them. I wish that every person could find their inner athlete. At this point, all of my worries about pushing too hard were gone.

My bike changed my life. If I had not learned to ride that little Trek 2000, I never would have cycled up Alpe d'Huez. I never would have climbed mountain after mountain after mountain. I never would have embarked on my extreme nutritional ventures. I never would have purposely signed up with a trainer, and I never would have attempted the Clean and Jerk. I never would have found out that I really was an athlete in my own way. I never would have realized that my understanding of the word failure was entirely wrong.

I now identify *failure* as not attempting something because you are too afraid. Failure does not refer to the times when you do not finish something or when you do not finish as quickly as you wanted to. Failure actually refers to those times when you didn't even try.

A ROCK GOD RISING FROM THE WATER

I had finally found it, the activity that perfectly channeled my aggression, attitude, and the fire that burned daily in my belly. Cycling was an activity that *required* me to be all in, and that rewarded me equally for the amount of effort that I put in. I'm pretty sure there is a side of me that is a little crazy, a side of me that has a switch turned to overload. This side of me just longs for something out there, something wild, something unimaginable. It turned out that cycling up European mountains was exactly the something that I was looking for. Ever since my first ascent up Alp d'Huez, my passion for cycling has only grown. I had developed a deep love for my bike, and day after day, stuck behind a desk, I longed for the freedom to climb mountains.

Having committed myself fully to a year of consistent training and knowing that some wild adventure was lurking just around the corner, I had become very passionate about putting every bit of myself into my workouts. From my perspective, there were absolutely no excuses to hold back during that one little hour in the gym. After the long rides that I had survived and all of the unknowns involved in cycling in the heart of nature, one hour in a gym was simple. There was always water. There was always food. If you had to, you could stop any time. There was no such thing as having to make it to the destination regardless of how depleted you were. This was an opportunity to dig as deep as possible in a very safe environment. There were absolutely no excuses.

Day after day, I showed up and tried to push myself as hard as I could. I was so grateful to have my trainer there for my last session of each week to absolutely push me beyond my limits. After a session with him, I would feel like I had been beaten up in a really good way. Knowing that I had gone as far as I could, and then a little further, left me truly believing that I was on the right path. I didn't know what lay ahead of me, but I knew that I had better be ready. This time when I could take all my sass, all my punch, all my fire, and harness it into pushing my physical and mental limits, became the most exciting hour of my day.

All of the gym time was fantastic, but I knew I needed to add on a cycling component. Time on my bike would let me get all of my body parts accustomed once again to spending long hours in certain positions. I knew it was vital to get comfortable with a nice pedal stroke once again and to hone my mental ability to sit on my bike for a long time.

I will admit, I wanted to feel that rush of pushing my heart rate into a high zone. I wanted to feel the high of being able to complete a target number of intervals, of being able to spin my legs continuously for a full hour or for the full length of a movie. Despite a long work day, and having already spent an hour in the gym, I craved the time when I could go home and get on that bike. I now understood and shared in the drive that had kept James going during those early sessions when I had struggled so badly.

It may come as a surprise, but one of my favourite movies of all time is *The Fast and the Furious*. It is nothing but fast cars, hot girls, loud music, action, and very bad acting. There is just something about it that I find fantastic. It could be that the first time I saw it I was with James and we attended the opening night expecting nothing. We loved it. Afterwards, cars peeled out of the parking lot and we were reminded of our younger years when my husband used to drive a cool little red Honda Civic all pimped out with a tonne of audio gear.

It turns out that *The Fast and the Furious* is the perfect training movie. If you can make it in the endurance heart rate zone throughout the entire running time of 1 hour, 42 minutes, and 28 seconds, then you have accomplished a fantastic base training session. The loud soundtrack, fast cars, and action provide some excitement and motivation, and since the acting is so poor the story line doesn't require much attention. This worked well for longer spinning sessions on a Saturday morning.

For weeknight spin sessions, one hour on my bike was plenty. These were the harder sessions. I had already been at work all day and had likely already spent an hour in the gym. I would come home, eat my snack, and get my riding clothes on right away. Putting the session off was dangerous since my motivation could slip away quickly. Some days were easier than others. On particularly hard days when I was tired or longed to simply sit down and cozy up on the couch, I needed something special to motivate me.

Finally I found something to help encourage myself. I really am a classic rock chick at heart. I will never let that go. Thus, one of my favourite training videos is *Welcome to the Videos*. This is a collection of the top videos of Guns 'n Roses. There is just something so raw and real about this perfectly matched and explosive combination of the band members, the timing, and the circumstances that will never be recreated. *Welcome to the Jungle* was on top of the charts when I was in grade eight. My parents never understood why a quiet, shy, studious schoolgirl wanted more than anything for Christmas a poster of Axl Rose decked out in leather and chains, long red hair wildly flaring. The rawness, the realness, was just what resonated with my inner being.

Now here I was twenty years later, and the voice of Axl Rose was still exactly what I needed. Decked out in my Lucky Charms training jersey, I would climb onto my Trek 2000, now mounted to a trainer, and let that raw, emotional voice take me to higher heart rates. No matter how bad a day had been or how tired I was, every time I saw Axl stepping off of that bus, with his red hair wild and his tight leather pants, and heard that deep, dark, introductory riff of *Welcome to the Jungle*, my legs would just start spinning and my heart would just start pounding. By the time I made it to the video of *Estranged*, it would be exactly what I needed to push me over the edge. I mean, really, when you see Slash decked out in leather and literally rising out of the ocean, face hidden behind dark curly locks that are tamed by his signature black top hat, perched on top of the waves and ripping away an out of this world riff, how can you *not* pedal harder? I may not have actually been moving, but in my heart, I knew that I was going somewhere.

EAT LIKE A MAN

I was finally learning to put all of the pieces into practice. I was pushing hard. I was focused. I was taking rest days. I was completely in control of my nutrition. Despite the rigor that went into each weekly schedule of workouts and the meal planning for every breakfast, lunch, pre- and post-workout snacks, and evening replenishment, the most important ingredient was my ability to listen.

I was listening, listening, listening to my body in a way that I never had before. When it started telling me that it was starving, I responded. I hadn't eaten any red meat, pork, or even chicken for some time. I had still been eating fish and some dairy, but had been especially avoiding heavy red meat. That had been cut out of my diet long ago when I wasn't very active and when I found meatless dishes easier to digest. Now, as I executed an aggressive training schedule, it seemed that no matter what volume of food I consumed I simply could not get full.

I had learned from my previous crash and burn that this was likely an indication that I was missing something in my diet. I did some analysis and consulted with a few knowledgeable people. The same verdict consistently came back: I needed some meat. It had been so long since I had eaten any, so I started with something lean by picking up some bison on the way home and cooking up a lovely dinner. The minute I smelled the meat cooking, my entire being responded. It smelled so good that I imagined I could already feel it fuelling me up.

It wasn't long before meat was once again a regular part of my life. I will always have those days when I simply want fish, fruit, or dark leafy greens, but I will also always have those days when I have been doing back-to-back rides all week and all I want is a nice juicy burger.

Years later, on the last evening of a several-week stint in Switzerland, I found myself devouring a burger and polishing off a pitcher of beer with James. I sat there for a moment, contemplating the vigor with which I was demolishing off this large plate of food and impressive pint. Gone were the days of ladylike, low fat eating. Don't get me wrong, there would always be a place in my life for green smoothies and granola bowls, but now there was also a new space for climbing mountains, devouring burgers and drinking beer.

Getting Serious – The European Cycling Adventure

'Lord what fools these mortals be.' – Shakespeare - Contributed by Paul Moore

Each year since I started on my journey to become a cyclist, my husband and I would spend our short two or three weeks of vacation time pedalling through some of the most famous cycling routes in the world. I would throw myself completely into months of training just so that I could make it to the peaks of mountainous beasts commonly summated by the Tour de France and Giro d'Italia greats. I would plan out each week so that I could fit in enough sessions in the gym and spinning in our training room at home to be at the top of my game. I would spend hours shopping for ingredients and preparing snacks and meals that met my nutritional requirements. Day after day I would spend every extra moment I had pushing my physical limits and evaluating everything that entered my body.

Throughout these weeks and months of preparation, I would be thinking about that short timespan during which I would have to complete as many of the challenging rides as possible in our geographical location of choice. Every trip we took, the time absolutely whizzed by. It just never felt like enough. James and I both craved more time in the world's greatest places to take part in our greatest passion. Our hearts longed for it.

For years we talked about our dream of cycling through all of the most famous areas, and of taking our time to do all of the climbs in each area. Our vision was to take on some of the most challenging routes, and then to witness the pros in action. We just wanted time, time to fully sink into our passion for cycling and to live our dreams.

Eventually, an opportunity came along to do just that. Some things in our lives had changed, and that allowed everything to simply shift into place. We had worked so hard for so long, committing most of our time to professional careers and putting our dreams in a safe little place in our hearts to wait for the right moment. When the moment finally came and we realized that it was time to dust those dreams off and give them life, it didn't feel real at all. I mean, I knew it was happening, but until we were actually on the airplane it felt like I was dreaming.

We had stayed focused and worked hard for so long. We had both gone to school for what felt like forever, and then immediately transferred into professional careers to which we dedicated large amounts of our time for many years. Finally, we found ourselves with this opportunity to take a break from our regular lives and invest some time doing something entirely different. We were free. We had a clean slate, and we could write whatever agenda we wanted on it.

We talked about many different options. There were just so many possibilities. Then, we went to see a documentary on the professional cycling team HTC. Mark Cavendish, my favourite rider of all time, rode for HTC at the time the documentary was filmed following the team's pro riders during the Tour de France. We watched in amazement as hundreds of cyclists battled through stage after stage, climbing the toughest mountains in the world. We recognized many of places in the film, and our own memories of some of the summits washed over us.

We watched in awe as various riders took on some brutal challenges. The one that sticks vividly in my mind is George Hincapie as he suffered through a broken collarbone, but finished the last few stages of the race in spite of it. Watching him talk as he was interviewed prior to one such stage, I was in absolute awe of the mental and physical toughness that he

189

displayed, and at how calmly he behaved the whole time. We left the theatre completely inspired, and it was settled right then and there that our gift of time would be used to do our own cycling and to catch some of the pro races.

For the next few weeks, I was caught up in a whirlwind of activity. We weren't sure how long we would be gone, or exactly where we would end up going. We had a rough plan, a rough timeline, and lots of preparation to do. Before I knew it, we were celebrating the eve of our departure with our wonderful friends. I was always very grateful to everyone who showed up to wish us well, and to spend some quality time with us before we left. Next thing I knew, I was on a plane heading to Spain.

GETTING SERIOUS – SPAIN

'The impediment to action advances action. What stands in the way becomes the way.' - Marcus Aurelius – Contributed by Darren LaRose

FIVE DAYS IN BARCELONA

At first I missed the soft-boiled eggs and rye toast that constituted my normal routine, but I soon became accustomed to a perfectly combined morning injection of sugar and caffeine. It could have been that delectable little blueberry cake disguising itself as a muffin topped with frosting, or perhaps it was that gooey apple strudel, but somewhere along the way I abandoned the thought of eggs and welcomed the morning sugar rush.

The best part of the morning routine was the cappuccino. I couldn't get enough of such good coffee topped with a beautifully whipped froth of cream and dusted with sugar and cinnamon. The atmosphere in the cafes that serve up these treats was also of the utmost importance. One in particular stood out for me. It felt like we were in the middle of nowhere on this particular street, but there was a constant stream of customers and a background chatter of friends greeting each other warmly. This cafe was obviously a neighborhood hangout. The little old lady running the place shuffled her feet along the floor in pace with the size of the line, speeding up and slowing down as the volume of customers demanded. I even witnessed the exchanging of a loaf of bread as it failed the poke test of freshness performed by both the customer and the little old lady.

At least our sugar-caffeine highs were balanced out by ample protein thanks to our love of the fresh-grilled seafood that is a staple of the popular tapas-style dining in Barcelona. Our first experience of this was on our first evening in Barcelona at a lovely little restaurant. The squid was marinated and grilled to perfection. As we sipped local red wine, we started to sink into the experience of being in this amazing place. I think we both took a deep breath and let everything go. Here we were, at the very start of our adventure. There was so much to see, so much to do. There was so much life to live!

Over the next five days we digested mounds of art, architecture, scenery, culture, frothy lattes, sweet pastries, and a lot more tapas. Everywhere we walked in Barcelona we were completely surrounded by absolutely amazing architecture. I could go on and on. My first exposure to the Rambla left me in awe as we walked street after street lined with intricate brick buildings filled with restaurants, bars, shops, and apartments. The complexity and detail of the entire place were overwhelming and whisked me into a totally different world from the cookie cutter streets back home.

The streets of Barcelona were filled with the works of various artists, most notably Gaudi. We visited the famous Sagradia Familia, an amazing cathedral that we had visited once before about seven and a half years earlier on our honeymoon. As we entered, I was overwhelmed by the progress that had been made in creating this masterpiece. The complexity and detail had lead me to believe that it would take forever to make any visible progress when we initially visited, but over the past seven years Gaudi's vision had been significantly more realized. Looking up in awe, I found myself staring at a giant forest. The columns blossomed into a blanket of leaves, literally forming a cement forest as they reached towards the sky.

We were disappointed that they had stopped allowing people to walk up the spiral stairs, but we were able to go into a basement section that we had not yet seen to view a quiet prayer area where they hold mass. The room glowed with candles surrounding a statue of Jesus. After taking in the warmth of this place, I found myself overwhelmed with emotion. It was the kind of setting that closes out the whole world and everything that is very important to you immediately becomes apparent. It was quite an experience.

In addition to the amazing architecture everywhere, we continuously stumbled across outdoor markets and displays of local art in squares filled with Spanish guitar music. We were able to check out a very large outdoor market filled with people moving in every direction and incredible displays of food everywhere our eyes landed. We wandered through rows and rows of large, luscious produce, immense steaks of red tuna, whole squids, fresh shellfish that you could take home or have cooked for you to eat right there, dried fruits of every sort, and a plethora of candies. It was wild, and I just wanted to buy it all!

Of course, a trip with James would not be complete without an outdoor adventure. After having our fill of the main attractions, we started our last day with a walk to the outdoor Gaudi park. It was a lot of fun climbing Gaudi's signature spirals as we passed by quirky buildings to reach a great view at the top.

Thinking that lunch and a siesta were in order, I followed James in search of a place to eat. For a couple of days, he had been eyeing a church on the top of a rather large hill. We began walking and soon realized that a series of switchbacks that wound through a town would apparently take us up to this church. We started climbing.

After walking for a while and seeing no sign of anywhere to eat, we gratefully snacked on the oranges and water that we had bought at a store before we began our ascent. Eventually it became clear that this so-called hill should be under consideration to be categorized as a mountain. We climbed and climbed, enjoying the seclusion of our surroundings but wondering how anyone lived up here with nothing around. We found our answer when we reached a bustling area of restaurants, trains, and buses.

We continued on. Soon the road narrowed so that it was barely wide enough for two-way traffic. Despite this narrow passage, cars were parked all along the side so that there was just enough room for a single vehicle to pass through on this two-way road. Needless to say, it was a complete jam with traffic in both directions at a standstill!

Eventually we came to a crossroads and chose the route that we believed would take us to the top and thus the church. I don't know how long we walked before arriving at our destination, but it felt like forever. The last section of our climb was steep, and we were starving and exhausted. After a subpar lunch in the one restaurant that was operating at the top of the mountain, we were ready to explore the church and enjoy the fruits of our labor.

We climbed the stairs in spite of the pain that shot through us with every step, and we took in everything about that church. The building was amazing and beautiful, and the view was equally so. Satisfied, we started down the mountain.

We didn't get very far before we discovered a multilevel amusement park built into the side of the mountain just below the church. It was so bizarre. We thought there might be a gondola to take us back to the bottom, but it turned out we were wrong. We kept walking.

On our way down we found a series of shortcuts that were obviously less-travelled than the main road but that combined to shave a lot of time off of our trip. You have to understand that James's style of shortcuts are sometimes very fruitful, sometimes not, but are always adventurous. One such shortcut had us scaling down a steep dirt path. As we approached a turning point, several mountain bikers whizzed by at top speed. Another shortcut was definitely designed for me as James ducked his way through a blanket of low hanging brush.

Thanks to those shortcuts, we found ourselves back at the busy hub we had passed by on our way up just as a trolley was leaving. We sat down just in time. The rickety old trolley car crawled down the hill at a snail's pace. We could have walked faster. We traveled only a very short distance before we reached the end of the track! We had no choice but to get off the trolley.

Now we were far enough down that it made sense to us to keep walking. We ended up wandering in search of some dinner, a goal that took an incredibly long time with every step bringing a fresh wave of pain courtesy of our sore feet. I remember mentioning this to James and him replying that he couldn't even feel his feet and that he was sure they had fallen off a while ago and he was walking on nubs. I was past the point of feeling hungry well before we found a place to eat. All I could think about was how badly I wanted to stop walking.

We actually ended up passing by the chocolate museum that at one point we had thought we might get to. We took a quick peek inside, but we were too tired to do the tour so we continued on in search of food. We ended up back at a strip of restaurants along the water not far from our hotel. We were given a slick sales pitch by every host as we made our way down that strip, and we finally settled in the one that offered us a free glass of champagne and what they claimed to be the best service.

Finally off our aching feet, we had some delicious mussels and seafood paella under a tent decorated with little white lights on the pier. That glass of champagne went right to my head in my weary and depleted state. After dinner, we made our way back to the hotel where I enjoyed a nice stretch and a hot bath. Soon after that, we were both sound asleep after a long day of travel to the top of a random mountain to explore a random church.

TRAINS, PLANES, AND TROLLEYS…AND A CRAZY RIDE

We had spent five days in Barcelona taking in all of its beauty, but now it was time to move on to the first bit of cycling in our European adventure. We knew we had a crazy day ahead of us as we made our way to the island of Mallorca, a real cycling hub where many of the pros were known to spend time training. We took a metro, a bus, an airplane, another bus, an old train, and, finally, a trolley to reach our destination.

The old train was definitely the most concerning as I looked around at the rickety car and wondered when it had last been inspected. It did its job, though, weaving its way right through the heart of the island of Mallorca where we found ourselves surrounded by beautiful mountains. From there, we finally reached our destination town of Port de Soller which is situated right on the edge of the island. What an adventure it had been just in getting here. Little did I realize that the adventure was only beginning.

We found a bare little room with two twin beds, a couple of pieces of furniture, and a little balcony with a view of the water. Nothing else! Our next step was to find ourselves a couple of bikes to rent, and to plan out a route for the next day. We walked to the only bike shop in this tiny little place where, to my astonishment, there was a women's Trek in my size waiting just for me! James found himself a decent ride as well.

As James worked out the details with the guy in the bike shop, I browsed around. I overheard them talking about routes for the next day, and I heard James indicate that he wanted a long, hard ride. I knew well enough by now that rides with James could be rather adventurous, and I wondered what was in store for me. I had definitely gotten myself into good shape with my gym routine, but the challenges of an outdoor ride in the European mountains far outmatched those I faced in the gym, especially when they involved cycling a route that was designed by my riding partner.

With our bikes acquired, we were soon on our way. The next agenda item of the day was to grab a couple of beers and enjoy them while taking in the view from our little balcony. I just couldn't believe the sight before me. In this tiny port town on the edge of the water it felt like we were at the end of the earth. As I gazed out onto the ocean, I was very aware of how far away from home I was. It was so serene and peaceful. No television. No radio. All we had was a beautiful view from a little balcony, and each other.

The next morning we arose, put on our cycling attire, and went down to the hotel breakfast room. At first we only found yogurt, fruit, and cereal. I was a bit concerned about being properly fuelled for the long day ahead if we dined only on those light breakfast items. Then, right on cue, one of the waiters brought out a big tray of hard boiled eggs. I was so excited. I knew my body, and I knew that it needed some oomph in a breakfast before a long ride.

A typical person might ease into riding in the Spanish mountains. James, however, is not the typical person. As I had suspected in the bike shop the previous afternoon, we would be tackling a rather hefty ride that consisted of 100 km of riding and 2100 m of climbing over four summits: Coll de Soller, which was 7.4 km in length with an average gradient of 5.7% and a height of 497 m; Coll d'Honor, which was 5.4 km in length with an average gradient of 5.9% and a height of 550 m; Coll de sa Batalla, which was 7.9 km in length with an average gradient of 5% and a height of 576 m; and finally Tunnel a Monnabe, which was 5.0 km in length with an average gradient of 5.3% and a height of 880 m. Phew! I had a long day ahead of me for my first outdoor ride of the season!

The first climb felt great. I was really able to tap into the power I had gained from training. Everything I had learned over the years fell into place. My mental state was positive and encouraging, my physical being felt strong, and I was confident as I gracefully made my way up to the first summit.

The next climb felt pretty good too. I appreciated the beauty of each switchback. The strong flow I had found on the first climb continued, and practically before I knew it I was at the top of the second summit. We stopped for a quick lunch on a patio, and as soon as we finished eating we were off once again. All in all, the morning went pretty smoothly. I wasn't feeling at the peak of my cycling game, but I was feeling like I had tapped into a nice flow given that I was once again getting accustomed to riding outdoors.

There are many things to think about during a long ride. When doing a ride in a foreign place that you don't know well, the list of things to think about grows. How long will this take? How hard will the terrain and the elements be to handle? Did I eat enough before we started? Will I have enough food to get through the day? Will there be any places along the way to replenish? Will I stay hydrated enough to prevent leg cramps, but not so hydrated that I have bladder pressure at the wrong time?

If one can truly get in tune with their own system, then for the most part their body will tell them what to do and when. It isn't always simple, though. During the third climb, the mental aspect came into play for me. I was getting tired. My mind was telling me to stop. The little rented Trek wasn't set up quite right, so parts of me were hurting and I couldn't go too low in the gears as the chain kept falling off. Did I mention how tired I was?

Despite my fatigue, I kept pushing on. What else was I to do? Curl into a ball on the side of the road? Once you commit to a ride like this, just you and your cycling partner versus a series of

European mountains, you really don't have any choice other than to finish it. There isn't a support van around the corner waiting to rescue you when you discover that you have overestimated your abilities. All you have is your own two legs to get you to the finish line.

I thought about all of the climbs I had done that had been harder than this. I thought about how I had recently learned to conquer weight training moves that I had once thought were way out of my league without fear. I thought about all the times that I had found myself on the side of a mountain, depleted and trying to find a way to go on. Using those thoughts, I tapped into my power source and willed myself into a flow. One pedal stroke at a time, I continued to make my way up, up, up, until I finally reached the top of the third summit. I was so happy to see the end of this climb. I didn't realize yet how much climbing I still had left!

At the top of the third summit, James gave me an update. I was so tired, and I had really started to feel it on that last climb. I knew I had to go on, but I was a bit nervous about how much climbing we still had ahead of us. On top of that, the afternoon was beginning to fade so we would have to step it up a notch or risk cycling in the dark.

I had no choice. I needed to continue to tap into that internal power source that had gotten me this far. I was grateful for the burst of energy I found after gobbling down some chocolate. It was just what I needed to perk myself up and get back into my flow to make it to the top of the final peak of the day. I silently celebrated the end of the climbing, but in the back of my mind I couldn't escape the fact that there was still some work to do to get to the finish. The 15 kilometre descent was hard on the arms as I worked to keep my balance. I couldn't feel all of my toes, either, due to the cold wind. It took some grit on my part to get there, but soon enough we were at the bottom with only a couple of kilometres to go. When we finally rolled into the bike shop we realized that we were just in time as the sun was starting to get dangerously low in the sky.

Just like that, the day's adventure was over. We returned the bikes, and walked slowly through Port de Soller. I felt a little dazed and rather surprised at how much I had done that day. It was strange to think that we had only just set the stage for the riding portion of this crazy adventure we were on!

Our next task of the evening was to embark on a serious trip to the gelato shop near the hotel. As we sat on a bench, basking in waning sunlight and eating our prize, we talked about the day. I had known from the beginning that we were getting into a rather adventurous ride for our first ride of the season. I had to admit that in spite of my fatigue and how long it had been since I had done a real outdoor ride, I liked the adventure.

There really isn't anything like putting yourself outside of your comfort zone. There really isn't anything like accomplishing something that you aren't sure you can do. Cycling a good distance with a hefty amount of climbing isn't a trivial feat. It is just what I needed to put myself completely in the present moment.

During that type of ride, all of my focus is on the current pedal stroke and my physical and mental flow. Knowing the day is going to be long, and the climbing is going to go on for a while, the mind begins to focus on the small things. Each individual climb, each single switchback, and even each individual pedal stroke becomes everything as your perceptions narrow down to the next thing that needs to be done. The world is resized by the mind, and your immediate surroundings are magnified until nothing exists beyond them.

Coll de Soller: 7.4 km, 5.7% average gradient, 497 m ascent

Coll d'Honor: 5.4 km, 5.9% average gradient, 550 m ascent

Coll de sa Batalla: 7.9 km, 5% average gradient, 576 m ascent

Tunnel a Monnabe: 5.0 km, 5.3% average gradient, 880 m ascent

THE OUTDOOR TRAINING PLAN: PORT ALCUDIA

After setting the stage for our training time in Mallorca, we moved from Port de Soller to the other side of the island. We hadn't quite worked out how we were getting across the island, so after breakfast and checkout from our tiny room we mounted our packs onto our backs and began to walk. We initially perched ourselves at a bus stop just outside town, but it soon became apparent that the stop we were at may no longer be in use. Off we trekked.

It had become my custom to focus on trying to keep up to James as he charged ahead. That was the case that day as he found another bus stop for us to wait at. Luckily this stop was still in business and we soon found ourselves and our packs crammed into a very full bus. We were moving slowly, but we were on our way to the other side.

When we disembarked in Port Alcudia, our next order of business was to find our hotel. As we left the busy part of the town, we found ourselves walking along one of the most beautiful stretches of beach that I have ever seen in my life. The sand was a perfect soft texture and uniformly tan. The water rippled with the most incredible hues of green and blue. The sun shone down, baking us in our jeans and sweaters. We walked for a long time up the coast, following the green ripples. It was hot, we were hungry and tired, but the view was breathtaking and that helped to spur us on. Eventually we arrived at a strip of hotels. This was when the blue dot failed us.

The blue dot was exactly that. We had been using an application on James's cell phone to guide us. We plugged in our destination, and a little blue dot guided us from where we were. We followed the blue dot, but to our dismay it did not take us to our hotel. We knew that we were in the right area, but our exact destination was nowhere in sight.

By this time I was about to burst, so I wandered into a hotel lobby and found some facilities. Hunger was making me fuzzy, so I dug into my backpack and retrieved peanut M&Ms, the only snack I could find. It wasn't perfect, but it helped enough that we were able to continue searching for our hotel. When we did finally find it, we were nothing less than amazed by how wonderful it was.

This town was a major hub for cyclists of all abilities, amateur and professional, to spend the late winter and early spring months executing outdoor training plans. The hotel we had chosen was completely oriented around cyclists. There was bike storage and mechanical facilities across the street, and the breakfast and dinner buffets boasted an abundance of healthy options to provide more than adequate fuel. Our little suite was lovely, and was equipped with a small kitchen and fridge that were perfect for preparing our post-ride lunches. The cherry on top was a small balcony with an amazing view of the coast.

James, the ever-amazing trip planner, had once again found the perfect setup for us to keep the momentum going after our initial training ride up the four peaks. We were able to fuel up on hearty breakfasts and then walk across the street to retrieve our bikes and embark on each day's training ride. We could replenish ourselves with healthy options from the grocery store post-ride, then rest in the room or walk around the town. Sometimes we would treat ourselves with a thin crust pizza and beer on a patio if it was a sunny afternoon. It was idyllic.

The weather wasn't always good, but for the most part it was ok. There were some windy, wet days which limited our riding. All in all, though, we were able to execute some really decent training rides. Sometimes we simply braved the chilly air, and other days we were rewarded with some warm sunshine. My most favourite ride was a trek out to a lighthouse via a series of switchbacks. A coastal background as we made our way up those switchbacks provided a rather dramatic backdrop for the lonely cyclist slowly conquering each piece of the climb.

This portion of our cycling adventure was quite straightforward. Every day we got up, had our breakfast, and got on our bikes. One day at a time, we got reacquainted with pedaling out a route. Every day our bodies became more accustomed to the elements, the climbs, and distances.

Eat. Bike. Recover. Repeat. Don't forget to enjoy the amazing view and lovely surroundings. I knew I needed to execute this pattern each day, trying to keep up with James as best I could. I didn't fully realize how important these training days would be as preparation for the challenges ahead.

GETTING SERIOUS – IRELAND

'The greater part of our misery or unhappiness is determined not by our circumstance but by our disposition.' – Martha Washington – Contributed by Tracy Mehr-Muska

ST. PADDY'S DAY IN DUBLIN

After focusing on executing daily training rides in Spain, we decided to take a little detour that would let us relax a bit before embarking on the next cycling segment of our trip. As a result, we found ourselves on a plane heading to Dublin on the craziest day of the Irish year. We weren't there for long, but during this side-adventure I felt like I was whisked away in a furious hurricane, had my ass whipped, and was left exhausted on the side of the ditch.

James and I, two gentle Canadians, arrived in Dublin on March 17, also known as St. Patrick's Day. In order to get there we dragged ourselves out of bed at four in the morning and then took a bus, a plane, another plane, and another bus. Between our early start and the fact that we had just spent a week biking in the Spanish mountains, we were already pretty depleted. That didn't matter, though; we were here for an adventure and that meant we were up for anything. How fortunate that we had gone diving into this trip with that up-for-anything attitude, because in retrospect it is difficult to even describe the whirlwind!

We checked into our hotel then raced to grab the bus to get into the heart of Dublin. We had just missed the parade, but that was okay because the festivities were now in full swing and we were able to join right in. Our first order of business was to grab a pint. Here in the centre of the true celebration of St Patrick's day, they do not dye their beer green. Instead, their brew of choice is true, smooth pints of Guinness. They start drinking around midday and keep going until well into the following day.

Every pub that we stepped into was so crowded that we could barely move, but somehow we would still manage to find a spot in each one to enjoy the local band strumming and fiddling away on the stage. One of the most fantastic musical displays I have ever seen occurred as we watched a fiddler take it away on a very long solo while his band mate kept encouraging him to continue in accordance with the crowd's reaction. They kept urging him on with hoots and hollers, and so he kept going!

It was such a shock and a relief to finally NOT be the loudest one in the room. The Irish are not shy. They are blunt. They are also extremely courteous. A total stranger crawled across the floor in a crowded pub to retrieve a pair of shiny spring loaded shamrocks that had been knocked off my head in the commotion. The passion and fire all around me were spectacular.

At some point after a couple of bar hops and several pints of Guinness, James looked at me and said, "It's only 20 after six!" Before he told me what time it was, I would have sworn it was around midnight. If this was how crazy things were at such an early point in the evening, then I wondered how wild it was going to get! It was even more amazing to realize that St Patrick's day is a multi-day festival in Dublin, and that this was the pace that everyone would keep up the entire time.

Eventually, we needed a break and some food to help soak up the Guinness. We walked into a Thai restaurant with a tranquil environment that was literally like stepping into another world. We had to take a few deep breaths to come down from the whirlwind we had just escaped from and were still watching from inside this bubble we now found ourselves sheltered within. We enjoyed a spectacular meal. Realizing how exhausted we were as we finished up, we made our way back to our hotel and to bed. What a ride! I had totally fallen in love with this place and we had just arrived. I definitely had the celebration component of a successful training routine down pat.

We spent a few days in Dublin enjoying the architecture and culture in yet another new-to-us world. During this time, I made a grueling and rather unsuccessful attempt to plan out an itinerary to explore the rest of Ireland. Each coastal area was accessible by bus from the main hub of Dublin, but none of them were connected to one another. Driving didn't seem to be a reasonable option. Since it was ingrained in us to drive on the right side of the road, we weren't even comfortable crossing the street. We had to make do with public transportation options.

I felt like the reason that I had wanted to come here at all had been a purely emotional one so that I could explore where my family roots had come from. To accomplish that goal, I wanted to visit many of those coastal areas. I really worried that I had brought us over to a place that was just too difficult for us to explore, and that our situation had no answer.

Then, seemingly out of thin air over coffee, James produced a 10-day itinerary for a bus tour along the entire coast that covered everything I wanted and more. By the end of our coffee, it was booked. He had once again found a spectacular solution to a problem that had left me spinning my wheels, and had committed to something that I really wanted to do without a second thought. I felt like a weight was lifted as all of the internal strain I had been experiencing began to dissolve. I found that I also had a new and enhanced appreciation for how much effort it took for James to plan all of our adventures.

The rest of our day was wonderful. We walked along the water in downtown Dublin, making a couple of stops in memory of the potato famine. The Jeanie Johnston Tall Ship is a replica of the original ship on which Irish emigrants travelled in their attempt to escape death by starvation. It seemed too small to carry hundreds of people in such a state of despair. The Famine sculpture by Rowan Gillespie depicts life-sized sculptures of people walking along towards the ships during the famine. The sculptures are incredible in their detail showing painfully thin, weakened people who had lost all hope. They are so lifelike that I could almost feel their suffering. With the information from these memorial sites, and with James filling in the gaps, my family history pieced itself together. Many of the descendants of the potato famine sufferers migrated to Canada for the opportunity to become land owners.

We walked for a while, and then ended up at the oldest pub in Dublin for a pint. What a great little place. I sat perched on a small stool on an outdoor brick patio across from James as we continued to chat about the past and the present. The evening faded, and our tour bus awaited us the next morning.

FIERCE, DRAMATIC, PASSIONATE, AND RUGGED: NORTHERN IRELAND

During the first portion of our tour, I found myself hurled into a world of politics and violence that was completely unfamiliar to me. Growing up in peaceful, passive Canada, I had not fully realized how much of a bubble I had been living in. Seeing conflict in other countries when it's on TV is not the same as being in a place that is living it.

We spent an evening in Derry, a place that has suffered a long history of conflict between Irish Catholics and British Protestants. It was shocking to me that there are still 300 British Protestants living within walls to separate them from the Irish Catholics. These walls do not actually prevent physical contact with the Irish Catholics, but are more symbolic of the separation between the Protestants and the Catholics. The atmosphere of the entire town was very dramatic and the walls of the buildings were covered with large, daunting murals depicting the politics and conflict.

The IRA (Irish Republic Army) were still active. Their last bombing had been only four months prior, and had occurred at the end of the street near the hostel in which some of the people on the tour were staying. We walked by the site of the bombing every time we headed from our bed and breakfast to the restaurants and pubs, and passed it again every time we headed back. I found the atmosphere in general to be quite uncomfortable and a bit scary. We were provided with an in depth walking tour that left me feeling heavy with sadness and overwhelmed that these people lived in such a conflicted place. Despite the circumstances of their lives, the people of Derry were friendly and welcoming and we spent the evening in a small pub listening to live music and of course enjoying a pint of Guinness.

Belfast was in an even worse state than Derry. We took the Black Taxi tour, allowing us to see the areas that have seen the most drama and violence. The tour and the story of the city were very dramatic, serious and full of conflict. Dark, dramatic murals covered the building walls in several areas, again using images to tell the story of the politics and bloodshed that had occurred throughout the years.

The trauma had not yet ended. Our driver told us a story of being taken out by the IRA and waking up in the hospital where he discovered that he needed to learn to walk again. Here, too, the ongoing disputes had a strong underlying theme of Protestant versus Catholic. We saw gates that were closed and locked every night and weekend. At the beginning of the tour, we passed by a hotel that was apparently the only place that the foreign press were able to set up. It had been bombed 52 times.

As we listened to the wealth of information provided by our driver and saw for ourselves the dramatic atmosphere, I was overwhelmed. I felt sad and my heart felt heavy. This was really the first time that I had ever felt that I was actually physically in a place where violence has had a long history and is still not over. I actually could have been born here or within close proximity of this place if my great grandparents had not migrated to Canada. I felt overcome by a deep appreciation for the life that I had been given.

Later, upon reflection, I came to wish that I had been smart enough, aware enough, and mature enough to learn from my grandma what my great grandparents' lives had been like growing up in this place. I was very relieved to walk in the sunshine in the botanical gardens after feeling all of the darkness around me.

The landscape in Northern Ireland seemed to mimic the contentious atmosphere with its rugged and dramatic features whose beauty astounded me. We saw the remains of the Dunluce Castle whose entire sea-facing kitchen had been taken out by a storm. We walked the Giant's Causeway, which was formed by multiple layers of hot lava. The Northern coast was a series of dramatic cliffs plummeting into the sea below. We had the wonderful experience of watching a sunset from the top of old fort remains.

After a second night in Derry, James and I both felt a sense of relief to be leaving the North. It turns out that we skirted a bit of danger by leaving when we did. Later in the tour we heard that a car bomb had been found in Derry near the courthouse and safely defused several days after we had left.

ROLLING HILLS, SHEEP AND FAIRIES: MOVING SOUTH

As we moved towards the west coast of Ireland and then headed south, the atmosphere of the towns grew lighter and the soft rolling hills became soothing. The beauty of the large open spaces and spectacular coastlines and the friendliness of the people welcomed us. We had a fantastic tour guide who managed to take us to all of the famous spots as well as leading us to some additional little gems off the beaten path. Our group was great, too. We quickly made friends with the various Australians and the lone American travelling with us.

Ireland is rich in history, religion, and politics. We saw a wealth of monastery ruins, abbeys, Celtic crosses, cathedrals, and castles. We absorbed an equal wealth of historical accounts relating to the towns we passed through and the sites we saw.

Ireland has a magical side to it with all the talk of leprechauns and fairies and its many tales of folklore. This magical side is not to be taken lightly. In one small town we had the opportunity to throw a stone into the wishing well of a leprechaun house. As we drove by a fairy tree in another little village, we heard a story of multiple contractors who had refused to remove the tree as they did not want to upset the fairies. We saw Druid stone circles and pagan burial mounds. We both walked backwards down wishing steps with our eyes closed. It was all very mysterious and interesting. James even succumbed a little bit to whimsy when he kissed the famous Blarney stone at the Blarney Castle.

One of my favorite days of the tour was when James, myself, and another fellow climbed Croagh Patrick, the holy pilgrimage mountain. It took us an hour and five minutes of grueling climbing along steep slopes of loose shale. Of course, as usual I found myself trying to keep up with James as he charged ahead. What was absolutely amazing to me was that Chris, the guy who had joined us, kept up with James even though he had one arm in a sling. The loose shale demanded core strength, and often a hand or two to avoid slipping.

The pilgrims used to climb Croagh Patrick with bare feet to hear St. Patrick speak in the little church at the top. They would stop along the way to honor the stations of the cross. Some pilgrims to that church still do it. We saw one man beginning his trek with bare feet. I couldn't imagine confronting the loose shale with nothing to protect my feet. It was slippery and treacherous. I often had to use my hands to stabilize myself as the rocks slid beneath my shoes.

It took some serious focus and hard work to get to the top, but the sweat and effort were completely worth it. The view was incredible, and the little church where the pilgrims had come still stood strong. As advised by our tour guide, we chose a rock from the summit to bring back with us. Later in the tour, we placed these rocks at a memorial along Connemarra for the victims of the potato famine. The site was located on a stretch where these poor starving souls had walked. I was really thankful that I had the opportunity to contribute my own rock, which I had obtained at the cost of a small amount of my own suffering.

The smaller towns that we passed through were quaint and charming, and the rolling hills between those towns were filled with little farms and sheep. Parts of the landscape reminded us of farm areas back home in the rural parts of Alberta. We saw many little lambs running around, living proof that spring was definitely in the air. Again, the coastline was beautiful, and we even walked barefoot in some very soft sand and dangled our feet in the very cold water. The famous cliffs of Moher were definitely a highlight as we enjoyed the spectacular view while walking along them!

The pub is definitely the center of Irish culture. The pubs are full every night of the week. Within those walls, you'll find that the Guinness is flowing and the live music is a go. I can't think of anywhere else in the world that playing a flute at a live gig would be considered a cool pastime for a guy!

The plan for our European adventure was centered around cycling. Spending time on my bike had already taught me so much, including the importance of taking moments to celebrate the small victories in life. Training day after day was not something I had grown up doing. Now it had become something that I simply did to push myself towards achieving the big goals of climbing mountains that danced in my head. Allowing myself times of rest and looking back to take note of my accomplishments is a critical part of being able to move onto the next step, the next goal, the next mountain.

Plummeting into one of the craziest celebrations that we will ever experience truly allowed me to recharge, and will forever be an unforgettable experience. Exploring most of Ireland, seeing a part of the world that is so very different from my own sheltered home, and being immersed into an entirely different culture could only result in reflection and self growth. Without these side adventures, would I even know why I was climbing up the next mountain?

Taking the time to really learn and reflect is fundamental to my path. I am not sure that I would have ever experienced the places that I have been if I had never starting pedaling, one stroke at a time, up a foreign mountain. For me, my bike really did open up new worlds to experience and explore.

GETTING SERIOUS – BELGIUM

'If it doesn't challenge you, it doesn't change you.' – Fred DeVito

CHOCOLATE, BEER AND BICYCLES

Well rested from our training break, we moved on from Ireland. The next leg of our trip had not yet been planned out, so when James heard about a cycling tour in Belgium it seemed like destiny for us to sign up. The tour was to take place right at the time of Spring Classics, some of the hardest one-day races in the world. Luckily there was still room for us to join.

Belgium was an experience to say the least. My husband summed it up perfectly by describing our trip as a fine balance between chocolate, beer, and cycling.

Chocolate...

My experience with Belgium chocolate was a fine one indeed. While in Bruges, we chose which of the many chocolate shops we wanted to visit based on the recommendation of our tour guide, Holly. Immediately upon walking in, I found myself surrounded by a plethora of choices. It was overwhelming.

James, being the good husband that he is, knew exactly what I really wanted and encouraged me to order a variety of delicious creations. I asked the girl behind the counter if she could recommend an assortment, and she quickly went to work filling a bag. Each individual chocolate was a beautiful and unique creation, from lime-filled dark, to orange-topped milk, to strawberry and champagne cream. Back at the house we were staying in, we shared this wonderful treat with the others and took the time to delight in the magical flavours.

Beer...

Belgians are extremely passionate and serious about their beer. Their beers are local, preservative free, and served in a branded glass at the optimal temperature . The waiter will even ensure that the glass is turned in such a way that you can see the logo and name of what you are drinking.

We took a tour of a brewery in Bruges, where we were both educated and entertained. Andrew, our tour guide, was extremely proud of and very passionate about Belgian beer. As his hands waved about wildly and his voice took on a variety of dramatic tones, we listened in anticipation and hung on to his every word. We learned of the light, the medium, the dark, and the golden tornado that is created upon pouring. We walked up the many levels and saw a real working brewery where a lot of the brewing process was still done manually. The tour ended with a sampling of beers. Of course, every day in Belgium included some sampling, yet we only managed to scratch the surface.

Cycling...

Belgians are very passionate about cycling. Everyone in Belgium rides a bike, yet cycling is different there than anything I have ever done. There are challenges that you must be alert for everywhere, including cobbles, rough cycling paths, and backroads.

The famous Paris Roubaix professional cycling race includes one the roughest treks in the world, known as the Hell of the North. Even though the race is in France, it is close to Belgium and is usually won by Belgian cyclists due to their familiarity with cobbles. We had the opportunity to ride the last 85 km of the Paris Roubaix starting at the Arenberg forest and ending at the Roubaix velodrome. The route included 15 sections of cobblestone covering a total of 27 km.

As we started out on the Arenberg, I looked down at the widespread cobbles gaping up at me like alligator teeth ready to swallow me up. My nerves were almost instantly frazzled. I gingerly made my way to the end of the Arenberg at a ridiculously slow pace, but I remained unsure of my ability to finish the whole ride. On the other hand, I wasn't ready to give up. On we went.

We kept a good pace between the cobbled parts of our ride, and I did my best to complete each cobbled section without disaster. Riding a cobbled section is a psychological game, really. You have to convince yourself to pick up a reasonable speed and to loosen your grip on the handlebars, allowing your arms to relax as much as possible despite the constant fear of a wheel getting stuck in a gap and sending you flying through the air. If you hang on too tight, your hands will be ripped to shreds.

There were sections where I was really starting to feel like I was getting it, and others not so much. I just took each stretch one at a time. When we reached the 23 km mark with only a few cobbles left, I finally believed what my husband had been telling me all day: I could do this. Those laps at the Velodrome felt pretty good! My body was exhausted from the tremendous amount of vibration it had endured, but that was a small price to pay for the sense of accomplishment that suffused me.

A couple of days later we found ourselves back at the Arenberg, this time with a picnic of wine, cheese, and bread as we waited for the pros to come through. I stood and watched in awe as the first few came whizzing through at an unthinkable speed on such a treacherous stretch. In a closely packed peloton, these riders did not have the luxury of choice in placement on the cobbled terrain that varies widely as random gaps have burst open over time. We watched team support cars loaded with beautiful bikes bouncing by, and the main pack of riders clumped together and riding viciously towards us with no hesitation. What a crazy sport. I love it.

ADVENTURE WITH THE FOX AND THE SPARROW

On our first night in Belgium we met the Flanders Fox. A Scottish lad and a friend of the couple running the cycling tour that we had joined, he would be staying for the week and helping out with the Tour of Flanders. It may be his slyness that earned him his nickname, but I am not quite sure.

We met the Sparrow the next day. A fellow Scottish friend of the Fox, he came over to see Belgium and do some riding. He says that it is his tiny legs that got him his name, and of that I am quite sure! The two of them would often disappear for lengths of time, leaving us wondering about their whereabouts and about what adventure they may have gotten into. They were two of the most genuine and friendliest lads you have ever met.

One afternoon, the Fox and the Sparrow offered to take James and I to a bike shop that we were interested in. Of course we agreed! Our first stop was at a favorite bakery where we loaded up on delicious fresh sandwiches. Then, we headed to the bike shop where we spent a good amount of time.

When we were asked if we had to be anywhere, James casually put up his hands and said that we have no schedule. Our new friends took that opportunity to whisk us off to "The Palace," a cafe on a hill where we enjoyed a beer in the sunshine. We received an incredibly warm welcome because of course the Fox knows the people that run the place, and had even brought over some Scottish beer for them. I was entertained thoroughly by the Fox's story of the Koppenberg Cross, which began with bratwurst, cakes, and loads of heavy Belgium beer, and ended with an unwelcome explosion!

When we were finished at The Palace, we were off to another friend's house. When we arrived, the Fox engaged in a lovely discussion with the neighbor across the road. The house we entered was beautiful with a spectacular view of the countryside, a huge back yard, and some chickens. We toured the yard and relaxed into this wonderful Belgian moment. The friend, Haute, offered us some of his private stash of Trappiste beer. Dark and rich, it was a delightful and amazing treat! To this day, I have not tasted a beer with such complexity, flavor, and completeness.

From there we all headed off to dinner. We found ourselves in a lovely little wonderful restaurant. Haute, our new friend, really wanted to have the mixed grill of seafood, but it required two people. Of course I shared it with him! It was a platter big enough for four. I am quite sure that Haute could have stayed late into the night as he gulped down his heavy Belgian brew, but alas, we had to get back as we had the "Hell of the North" to bike tomorrow!

140 KM OF PAIN

Of all the riding I have done, I have never before encountered anything like Belgian-style cycling. Rough bike paths and old farming roads made of cobblestone comprise a good portion of the common cycling routes. Cobblestones separate over time as part of normal wear and tear, and each side of the road begins to slant downwards. This leaves the cyclist with the option of cycling precariously on the apex, or on one of the sides. Both situations present their own risks, especially when surrounded by other cyclists.

James convinced me to embark on a 140 km amateur version of the famous Tour of Flanders. This amateur course was composed of 15 climbs, some of which were cobblestone roads. The climbs ranged from 360 to 2200 m, and from four to 22 percent gradient. There were also some sections of flat cobblestone, a few sections of downward cobblestone, and many sections of rough bike path that we all had to pile on since the roads were not closed and the rules about using the bike paths are strict. To top this off, there were over 33,000 cyclists in the event.

Give me a long climb of switchbacks and tough gradients, and I know how to deal with it. This, on the other hand, was an entirely different world. The accumulation of so many short climbs really adds up, especially when those climbs are paired with the flat cobblestone that made your entire body shake to the point that you just want it to stop. The sheer volume of riders participating in this event resulted in severe congestion on the extremely steep and narrow cobblestone climbs, resulting in ferocious battles to make it to the top. All of that, combined with the multitude of cyclists that you had to constantly watch around you, added up to a very long day. It was definitely one of the most challenging rides I have ever done.

I was able to complete most of the climbs. The cobblestone climbs were very tough as it was a fine balance between avoiding gaps, maintaining grip between your wheels and the stones, and riding as fast as you could despite the steepness. I accomplished the ones that were not too congested. The severely steep ones, however, belonged to crazy madmen. These steeper climbs were clogged with cyclists due to those that had fallen or who had had to stop. A few crazies were fighting their way through the crowd, yelling at the others to get out of their way. When I encountered such messes I chose to step out of the way. We were at the beginning of our adventure, and I did not intend to become injured by some silly situation that was completely avoidable.

I also had to be constantly vigilant of those around due to the sheer volume of participants. Unfortunately, despite my caution a French guy attempted to pass me without regard for an oncoming car, and then chose to push right into me in order to avoid the vehicle. Our wheels touched. As I was flying through the air, I thought to myself, "Wow... This is going to be a bad landing." I really thought that was it for me. Luckily, I landed primarily on my well-padded ass, and secondly on my hand and knee which left me to suffer only cuts and bruises.

As blood oozed from my fingers and people helped me off the road, I was in a bit of shock. Fortunately, however, nothing major was wrong with me or the bike. After a strange discussion with the Frenchman in which he simply indicated that he had had to push into me due to the car, the people around made sure I was ok. I was, so back into the saddle and the race I went. It was only blood. I still had climbing to do and some of the longest sections of flat cobbles!

After eight hours, about six of which were spent in the saddle, I finally made it to the finish line. I meekly made my way to the beer tent to join the others in our group. I'm not sure a beer had ever tasted that good. Later, as I sat on the bed feeling like I couldn't move, I couldn't help but think that I had never felt more beat up. It took me a good solid five or ten minutes to get my pants on to go out for dinner, but all the soreness was worth it to say that I had completed the amateur Tour of Flanders.

The next day, we watched the pros do the real version. Our tour guides provided us access to the VIP breakfast where I definitely got my fill of pastries! After this, we were able to get into the area where all the team buses were parked and from which the riders were departing for the race! When I arrived, my husband was already in there somewhere. I was pretty sure he was stalking his favourite rider, Thomas Voeckler, so I decided to leave him to it. Upon the advice from our tour guide to try and see my favourites before the riders were all gone, I made my way over to the HTC bus.

There weren't too many people there as the biggest bustle was around the Quick Step bus where Tom Boonen, the Belgium champion, was. I was able to lounge around until it became apparent that the riders were coming out of the bus one at a time to make their departure. I noticed someone getting autographs. I had a pen in the backpack that I was carrying and a cycling newspaper, so I was prepared to get some signatures of my own. As I watched the bus door in anticipation, I wondered if I really would get to see Mark Cavendish. Next thing you know, he was poking his head out of the bus door. As he came through the gate on his bike in all his glory, I took my opportunity and handed him my pen and paper. I was in too much awe to really even say a word! Yes, me, the girl who always has something to say, could not find words. I will always regret not at least getting out something like, "Good luck on the race today." As I walked away with my signed paper, though, I had no regrets. I was elated.

The rest of the day was a mad rush to get everyone into the vehicles and off to the next point to watch the race come through. Our tour guide's knowledge of the back roads and fearless rally-style driving got us to both the Koppenberg and the Muur in plenty of time.

As we whipped at ridiculous speeds around tight, winding passageways, James and I were squeezed into the front seat holding up a TV so that everyone could continue to watch the race between stops. When we arrived at one of the steepest cobblestone climbs, the Koppenberg, it was still early in the race. Perched about 2/3 of the way up and watching them come up this treacherous climb at a smooth pace was incredible. The

Muur, otherwise known as "The Wall," was the last major push in the race, and thus a very key point.

We were a good portion of the way up this 475 m stretch that ranged from 9.3 to 19.8% gradient. We watched in awe as the first few racers absolutely screamed by like machines. I will never forget seeing Fabian Cancellera whip by on the steep cobblestone, legs bulging, ferociously beating the climb like a beast. After experiencing this climb myself, I just couldn't believe the pace and the power that I was witnessing. After they had all gone by, we made our way down to the square where a multitude of people watched the finish on a big screen.

It was an extremely eventful two days. When it was all over, I found myself lying in bed, exhausted and tending to my wounds with images of cobblestones and famous riders flying through my head. What an experience. At this point in our European cycling adventure, I simply had no sight of the girl that I had once been. I was completely and 100% in, and ready to take on each challenge as it came.

TIPTOE THROUGH THE TULIPS

'There is more to life than increasing its speed.' –
Mahatma Ghandi – Contributed by Sally-Anne Guertin

Our crazy Belgian adventure had come to an end, and it was time to move on to our next destination. It just so happened that it was tulip time in Holland. Since we were practically right next door, we decided to stop by.

We had an absolutely lovely stay in The Hague, which is full of history and architecture. Since our primary reason for visiting was to see the famous fields of tulips as they blossomed, we needed to figure out the logistics of getting from our hotel to these fields. For a couple of cyclists, what better way to do this than by bike?

This turned out to be more challenging than we expected. We searched and searched for road bikes, but none were to be found. We ended up settling for a couple of city cruiser-style bikes. We chose a cozy little bike shop near the start of our ride from which to pick up our cycles. The lovely gentleman in the shop kindly helped us, making sure we had everything we would need for our journey. He looked at me with horror as I swung my leg over the seat to mount the bike he gave me to test it out for size. "No no!" he declared, "That is not how a lady gets onto a bicycle. Here, let me show you."

I could see the look of pure entertainment on James's face as he was probably thinking something like, "Lady? You don't know my wife!" There are times in life when you simply choose to be polite, though, so this is what I did: I watched the elderly man as he showed me how to sit down on the seat, and then gracefully swing both of my legs together towards the front of the bike. I thanked him for the advice. I can honestly say that once we were out of the shop, I was nothing close to graceful on that city cruiser, but the gentleman didn't need to know that.

To see the tulips, we would have to bike 50 km each way for a round trip of 100 km. Without any major climbing, this would not be a big deal on a road bike, but since we were on city cruisers, which really were only intended for easy city commuting, this turned out to be a somewhat challenging ride. We were here to see the tulips, though, so off we went!

A good portion of the ride was along a well-kept bike path. Considering the type of cycle we were using, we kept up a good pace. We didn't want this ride to drag on all day. As we cruised along the path, occasionally a rider on a real road bike would pass by. I would look longingly at them while wishing I could be flying along as well. Then I would go back to concentrating on keeping the cruiser moving along as best I could.

It was not the most comfortable setup for trying to keep up a good pace, and of course there hadn't exactly been a custom fitting. Cruisers are kind of one size fits all. You can't adjust every little angle and switch out parts. You simply had to go with what you had. My knees were hurting and I felt like my whole body was involved in every pedal stroke. I tried to look on the bright side. It was a lovely day, we were outside riding along the coast, and we were on our way to see the tulips.

Soon enough, we started to see them: Rows upon rows upon rows of perfectly-manicured tulips lined up along never-ending fields bursting with bright colours. It was amazing. It truly was like nothing I had ever seen. I completely understood why so many people came to Holland at this very time of year to see this specific sight. It was breathtaking. We cruised around slowly, taking it all in.

Once we had had our fill of flowers, we started to head back. We still had a good 50 km to go on these heavy cycles. Back down the path we cruised, picking up as much speed as we could. My knees creaked away, my back groaned, and my whole body became extremely fatigued from the position I had to maintain during every bit of exertion, but I had learned long ago that when the options are limited to stopping on the side of the road or continuing to push forward, you keep moving.

Onwards we went. I stood up on every little hill, trying to keep what momentum I had on the rises. The ride began to feel very long. I just kept willing myself to stay as close to James as I could. Bit by bit, we made progress. When we finally hit the home stretch, I was so relieved.

We returned the bikes, and then limped along to find some sustenance. We ended up in a little Italian restaurant where we replenished ourselves on thin crust pizzas and numbed our pain with some wine. It was a very quiet evening in our hotel room, eating leftover pizza and resting our weary bodies. This hadn't exactly been part of our training plan, but with limited bike options we had made it work and I was proud of us for that. What an adventure it had been. I think that I will always remember those tulips, primarily because of the grueling journey we undertook to see them!

ROMANCE, WINE, ART AND MY 'GIRLY' SIDE

'Romance is everything'. – Gertrude Stein

From Holland, we spend several hours on a train to arrive in Paris. I didn't know if it would all just be silly, cheesy, and touristy, but I wanted to see the city for myself. We began the trek to our hotel with backpacks in tow. Hot, tired, and hungry, we arrived in our little room to see exactly what we had expected: the bare minimum accommodation for a premium price. But, hey, we were in Paris!

We ditched our bags and went to hunt for food. After hastily downing a sandwich, we began a very long walk. I had fired off a list of things I wanted to see to James. My dear husband as usual took the lead and off we went to try and fit everything in. First, we made our way down to the water and walked along the bridges. The streets along the canals were replete with vendors selling a huge assortment of items. Everything was on display, including cheap plastic Eiffel Towers, buttons, posters, and old paperback books. At first glance, it all appeared to be junk, but if you took a moment to look you would likely uncover a gem or two. I spotted posters advertising concerts from the 60s and 70s for Zeppelin, Nirvana and others. Some vendors were selling their own drawings and paintings of the beautiful sites in the city, and some were pretty good. It was all so quaint, so romantic, that I felt like I had gone back in time.

We walked past a bridge covered in locks, each with a lovely note proclaiming the infinite love of a couple. It turns out that so many people do this that they have to be cut off every month! As we walked across the bridge, romantic accordion music floated through the air. Aaaaah... Paris.

Next, I got my first real look at the Louvre. I couldn't believe the size! I pondered how long it would take me to see everything inside, but eventually decided that this would be an adventure for another day. We walked from the Louvre through a massive park full of trees, flowers, fountains and even the occasional cafe. I was surprised by how much green space was in the heart of Paris and how extravagant the parks were.

Eventually we came to the Champs Elysees where we could see the Arc de Triomphe in the distance. We imagined what it must look like up close, filled with pro cyclists during the last stage of the Tour de France. James darted into the street during gaps in traffic in an attempt to get the perfect picture of the tall structure. Fortunately, he didn't get hit by a car!

After exploring the fascinating Arc de Triomphe, we continued on all the way to the Eiffel Tower, seeing the Grand Palais and the Petit Palais along the way. Depending on which street we were on, sometimes the tower would leave our view. I recall James saying to me, "How do you lose a tower!" He had a point!

We did eventually find our way to the wondrous tower that we had seen so many pictures of. It was beautiful! We got into the lineup to enter, and soon found ourselves climbing the 422 stairs to the 2nd floor. It was a bit of a game for me to try and keep up with James as he wove around people who were complaining with every step and taking water breaks. I was more than happy to make an adventure out of these stairs rather than joining the complainers. After all, this would likely be my only chance to climb this most famous tower, and I was sure that a little extra work on the legs could only help my performance on the bike.

The view the whole way up was wonderful. We could only make it so far by foot. Sweaty and out of breath, we entered a long winding queue to the lift that would take us the rest of the way to the top. I was the last person to squish into the lift, so I was right against the glass doors and felt my tummy taking a few turns as we went higher, and higher, and higher, and I watched the city disappear below me. We were able to find a quiet spot amongst the commotion at the top, and we watched as the sun went down and the city lit up one little light at a time. It was one of the most romantic moments you could imagine. Surrounded by people, we had carved out a little space where we could truly appreciate the moment. Sometimes it is simply what you make it.

We descended just in time to see the entire tower light up. It was better than the postcard. The reward at the end completely outweighed the several-hour journey to get to the top, and looking back I can say that the journey itself had been an adventure. As we walked back to the hotel, we kept looking back to see the beautiful tower all lit up in the night. At one point the lights turned white and flashed on and off, turning the whole tower into a disco ball! We ended the evening with dinner in a cozy little cafe. Exhausted, we had no trouble sleeping despite the old mattress that literally sunk to the ground with the combined weight of our bodies.

The next day, my sweet husband got me up and going to get to the Louvre. Enjoying our croissants and cappuccinos to go, we found our way to the glass pyramid entrance only to discover that it was closed on the one day of the week we had planned on exploring it. My heart sank. Fortunately, James came up with plan B.

We ended up doing another walking tour of the city on the other side of the Seine, which we had not yet explored. We went into Notre Dame. What magnificence! We then had a lovely lunch of mussels, salmon, pasta, and ice cream. We sat in a little restaurant on the quaint street in the Latin Quarter and drank wine. We talked the afternoon away. In a place like this, you feel like you have nothing but time. Aaaah… Paris.

We then walked the Luxembourg garden surrounding the Palais de Luxembourg. We sat at a pond and watched a lone duckling frolicking in the water while children sailed small boats across a nearby fountain. We watched a group of old French men playing a serious game of bocce with metal balls. We strolled and we took it all in. Gradually, we made our way to the Pantheon. This hadn't been on my original list of things to see, but turned out to be one of the most magnificent. Behind the doors was a blend of history and science within a quiet tomb hidden from the world. The crypt holds the remains of Voltaire and Rousseau among many others, and we had the chance to watch Focault's pendulum swing. We ended the day with a French fondue and more wine. Even an old married couple like us can fall in love all over again in such a romantic place. Aaaaah… Paris.

The next day, we attempted once again to take in the Louvre. Munching on another round of croissants and cappuccinos, we made our way in pursuit of the glass pyramid. We waited in the long line, but it moved quickly and the next thing we knew, we were in. The Louvre is not for the faint of heart. It is a massive collection of paintings, drawings, prints, sculptures, and a plethora of Egyptian, Greek and other Middle Eastern artifacts that date far back in time and have each been individually found and restored with care. The architecture of the building itself is breathtaking, and walking into each room is a unique experience. We spent most of the day taking in as much as we could. We covered a good portion, but there was no way to see it all! We were getting a little tired of the more crowded areas, so we wandered into a quieter spot in the bottom level. It was magical. We found ourselves in an indoor garden filled with lush, green flowing streams and life-sized sculptures. It was like escaping into another world. We took in the surroundings, and peace filled our souls.

We spent the afternoon watching Philipe Gilbert win the Flèche Wallonne, an easy choice since in Paris all of the TVs play the cycling races. We later reconnected with the same fellow who had hiked with us in Ireland. Over happy hour drinks and a lovely dinner, we chatted excitedly about everything we had seen in Ireland and all that there was to see in Paris. It truly amazed me the type of connections that were so easily made amongst fellow travelers, and those who were like-minded in experiencing new cultures. At the end of the evening, we once again walked through the beautiful city that was all lit up at night.

On our last day in Paris, I was really starting to get tired of wearing the same outfit every day. I felt like a ragamuffin. I will admit that even I, the girl who is most comfortable in sweaty cycling gear or my favorite old jeans and a pair of boots, was wishing that I could feel like a chic girl just for a bit. Backpacking with limited attire does take a toll after a while. It didn't help my mindset that the women in Europe, and especially those in Paris, were very well dressed.

Unsurprisingly, I found myself in a cute little clothing store beside our hotel picking out a couple of items that were girly and yet suited my style. What better way to remember Paris? Now that we were out of shampoo and body lotion, I had room to cram them into my backpack! To this day, the little green dress with a flowered fringe fills me with happiness and reminds me of my time in romantic Paris.

Goodbye Paris, je t'aime!

Journals from Tuscany

*'We are going to ride at a gentlemanly pace today.' -
Contributed by Reinier Paauwe*

Surrounded by Beauty

It was still dark out when we pulled ourselves out of the crevice
that the musty, flat old mattress had formed. We walked around
on the sticky rug and finished packing up. After five fabulous
days, we were leaving the romance of Paris behind. The hotel
had been less than spectacular, but in order to be within walking
distance of the heart of the city and not spend our entire
travelling budget, we had had to settle for a shoddy room. It had
definitely been worth it.

We shrugged our backpacks on and made our way down the
stairs. The lobby was deserted, so we left our room key at the
front desk and attempted to leave. Unfortunately for us, the
front door to the hotel was locked and there wasn't anyone at the
front desk or anywhere in sight. We examined the door and
surrounding area for some sort of button or way to release the
lock, but to our dismay, it was a traditional lock and key system.

We had an early flight to catch, so we didn't have time to wait
until someone appeared to let us out. We had to take matters
into our own hands. We began searching around and found a
phone, which we used to call the front desk. Several phones
began ringing simultaneously, including a mobile phone sitting
on the desk. Our guess was that the person manning the desk
was supposed to have the mobile phone with them, which they
most obviously did not.

Our Canadian way of doing things kicked in, and we cautiously
looked around while being careful not to cross any boundaries.
As time quickly passed with no way out becoming apparent,
however, our concern for boundaries disintegrated rapidly. It

started with us searching behind the desk with some trepidation for a key. The clock kept ticking and our panic continued to rise, and soon we were opening drawers and cabinets and frantically rifling through everything we could see for the key to the exit. We began assertively entering back rooms, and I even ventured down into a basement passageway looking for some sort of exit.

At one point, James began pounding on the bell perched on the front desk, probably as much out of frustration as in an attempt to wake the desk man, if there was one. Then, suddenly, the desk man appeared. I don't know where he came from, but he was our ticket out. We both turned and gave him a bewildered look, and exclaimed that we needed to leave!

We were so far behind schedule at this point that we had to abandon our original plan of taking the affordable metro. Instead, we searched the quiet streets for a taxi. Fortunately, we were able to find one and convey our sense of urgency. A hasty cab ride later, and we were at the airport. We checked in and boarded the flight without a hitch.

I was tired, but very excited to be returning to one of our favourite places in the world: Italy. Our flight would take us to Milan, and from there we would drive from the airport to the Tuscan countryside. After the excitement of the morning, the flight was relaxing. What lay in store for us upon arrival was not.

We arrived in Milan and picked up our car from the rental agency without any problems. It was exactly what we had ordered, small and automatic so that I could drive and James could navigate. So far, so good.

The next part of our plan was simple: We would drive to Tuscany. The execution of this simple plan turned out to be shockingly complicated. The problem turned out to be the roundabouts that spring up quickly one after the other. At each one we found ourselves presented with what seemed like millions of signs, each pointing in a different direction, and each with a long Italian name. Even with a full map, we were quickly lost.

The map itself was extremely complex and overcrowded with names, so one wrong decision at a surprise roundabout, one wrong turn, and we quickly lost track of where we were. There I was, rambling off names and making split second decisions to avoid backing up the heavy traffic behind me while having no real idea of where I was actually going. Meanwhile, James was trying to instantly decipher each turn we took and desperately searching for the towns that I named on the ridiculously complicated map.

We probably wasted a good hour and a half. In retrospect this was only a fraction of the time we lost the first time we drove in Italy, but that didn't make this situation any less frustrating. What was absolutely amazing, however, was that after a few changes in direction as we eliminated possibilities, we magically found ourselves on what appeared to be the road that we wanted. As time went on, we realized with certainty that we were on the correct highway! All we needed to do was stay on this road until we passed Florence and arrived in the Tuscan countryside.

We had our direction figured out, but we had a much longer drive ahead of us than we had anticipated. Even though we were on the fast paced autostrade with minimum speed limits for each lane, the drive stretched out well past the three hours we had anticipated. The traffic was crazy, with some spots actually coming to a combination of a halt and a crawl for long periods of time.

The day wore on, but we finally arrived on the outskirts of the Tuscan countryside. James declared that it was just as amazing as the first time he had seen it years ago. I was tempted to look around, but I had to keep my eyes on the road. My concentration was already shot since I was exhausted and my eyes hurt from looking at the road for so long.

Once we reached the winding hills of Tuscany, the driving became fun and the traffic tapered off. We arrived in the town of Radda and stopped. It felt so good to get out of the car, breathe in the fresh air, and stretch our cramped muscles. We walked along the hilly, cobbled streets of the little town and found a tourist information office. The friendly woman behind the counter listed off our options in the area for the evening. One place immediately caught our attention. This accommodation was up on a hill with a working farm and its own restaurant. It turned out it was reasonably priced and we would have a choice of two rooms. That sounded perfect to two weary travelers.

We chose a room with an amazing view of the vineyards and the Tuscan hills and made our dinner reservation by having an informal discussion between us and a man behind the wine counter who spoke only Italian. Then we purchased a couple of bottles of the Chianti Classico from the local vineyard. The friendly man opened one of the bottles and sent us on our way with two wine glasses.

We sat at a picnic bench with a full view of the vineyards and Tuscan hills. With all of the adventure of travelling behind us for the day, I finally relaxed and took in my surroundings. No words could describe it. I exclaimed to James that he was right: It was absolutely breathtaking, and just as beautiful as the first time we had seen it!

We drank the chianti, took in the view, and sank deeper into our surroundings. It felt absolutely surreal to be back in such a beautiful place. It was simply amazing how all of the tension and strain of the journey vanished into thin air as our relaxing afternoon stretched on. Once we finished the wine, we strolled around the lovely grounds, and then rested in our cozy room until dinner time.

Upon entering the ristorante, we quickly realized that the whole business was indeed run by a small group. The same man from behind the wine counter had transformed into our waiter by the simple addition of an apron over his working clothes. We chose the chef's menu and another bottle of the local Classico. What came out of the kitchen was one of the most amazing bowls of traditional Tuscan soup I've ever had, followed by one of the most delectable pieces of fish that I had ever eaten. The service was spectacular. The chef even came out to provide us with a taste of the soup before we made our final decision about what to order. What an evening. Words are simply not enough to capture the beauty and the ambiance of the evening. I quickly and completely fell in love with Tuscany all over again.

LOGISTICS - TUSCAN STYLE

Our second day in Tuscany was a day of dealing with logistics in traditional Tuscan style! At first things seem complicated, but they always have a magical way of working out. The first order of business was to connect with the owner of the villa that we would be renting for the next few weeks. With no Internet access and only a vague idea of where the villa we would be staying at was located, we settled ourselves in front of the unconfirmed, potential meeting point of a restaurant in one of the tiny towns and then waited uncertainly.

When I heard someone stirring in the restaurant, I decided to take my chances and poke my head in. The very friendly, English speaking owner was more than happy to help us out. He promptly called the villa owner and confirmed the meeting point. It was in the stars for us to be here! Our wait was very eventful as we watched a stream of people come and go, delivering all sorts of delectable items to this intriguing restaurant. The fresh produce truck made me want to come back and eat here. The owner of Black Stallion, a winery from back home in Canada, indulged us in an animated conversation. What a small world!

Finally our guides arrived, and off we went following them down winding, unkempt and adventurous roads. The villa was absolutely spectacular! Only one other family would be joining us in this lovely place that could hold eight. We would practically have the beautifully manicured grounds and pool to ourselves!

The next order of business was to find bikes. We ended up in Greve, where we entered the bike shop with cautious optimism. We were really hoping to find good bikes here so we could avoid a complicated driving trip to Florence. The man running the store was eager to help us. He sized us up and pulled down race bikes that would fit my tiny size and others that would accommodate James' tall stature. He worked extremely hard for the next hour to get the bikes completely ready for us, and to deck our rental car out with a bike rack. He even waved off his riding friends when they came for him, and worked past the closing hour. What service!

The last order of business was food. We narrowly missed the closing time for a market, but there would be plenty of time for that. We settled on the grocery store, which in Tuscany isn't that different from the chaotic market. Back at the villa, all stocked up with everything we would need to start our training in the Tuscan countryside, James suited up and went out for a spin. I was tired from all of the day's excitement, and eager to simply relax amidst my luxurious surroundings. I enjoyed a glass of wine paired with olives and cheese, and marvelled at the spectacular view of the Tuscan countryside out the window. For dinner I prepared a tomato sauce from scratch so that we could enjoy bowls of pasta and glasses of wine as James told me how happy he was with the bike and the rolling Tuscan hills.

The next few days ended up containing some challenging riding with nothing less than spectacular views. The long day of logistics would turn out to be more than worth it as we were in some of the most amazing training grounds that a cyclist could ask for. Ever since my first glimpse years ago, I have known that a piece of my heart belongs in Tuscany. This trip had simply reaffirmed that.

TUSCAN HILLS TURNED TRAINING GROUNDS

Our third day in Tuscany marked the official start of our training. We had all the right food, good bikes, and plenty of hills to climb. The Tuscan hills are not really soft, nor are they rolling. Rather, they are steep, some of them are reasonably long, and they come quickly one after another.

For our first two days of riding, we went out for a couple of hours each day. We had a great setup. We would load the bikes onto the rack on the car, drive the adventurous trek down to the main road, and park just at the bottom. From there we had three choices of which direction to go, each with its own climb. This was ideal, really, because we would start our ride with a climb, thus getting quickly warmed up, and we would end our ride with a descent, thus preventing us from having to save up some energy for the end.

On the third day of riding, we decided to lay it down. We finished the first climb out, and then proceeded towards the town of Greve. We then made our way towards the area where we stayed in during our first visit to Tuscany years ago. I remembered the two ways into this area being quite difficult to ride, which had limited how far we could go during our previous trip. Despite my memories of the area's difficulty, I had actually forgotten just how challenging it was.

We took what we recalled as being the easiest way into the hamlet where the villa that we had previously stayed in was situated. After James declared that the hardest part of the six km climb was the beginning, the middle, and the end, I laughed and away we went. Knowing this was the last major portion of climbing for the day and quite tired of my habit of holding myself back, I took the approach of continuously forcing myself to stand up when my pace got too slow or when I looked up to see a daunting steep section glaring down at me. The no-holds-barred approach helped me to stay closer to the cute cyclist just ahead of me and reinforced an attitude of, "I came here to do this, so now just do it!" It felt great and quite freeing.

Despite my positive attitude, I didn't feel so great near the end of the brutal climb. I told myself that this was the whole point of training, to push beyond your comfort zone and to repeat a new challenge over and over again until it becomes your new normal. Knowing that I would have high expectations for my performance once we moved into the French Alps and Italian Dolomites, this was the approach that I wanted to be committed to. Looking around me as I biked up this steep incline that just wouldn't give, I deeply appreciated that I had the opportunity that I did at this moment, to cycle in one of the most beautiful training grounds rather than within four stifling walls on the stationary trainer to which I was accustomed.

The last bit of the trek home was difficult. We were both depleted physically and mentally. A couple of steep sections of our path left me begging for it to end. Soon enough, though, we were back at the car. Once we returned to the villa, James laid on the couch on his back and seemed unable to move. I was quite hungry, so I went to work in the kitchen. It wasn't long before we were eating leftover pasta and talking about an afternoon nap!

We were quite useless for the rest of the day, so what would you expect that we did the next day? Repeat the previous day's workout, of course! It would be quite exciting to see how we were doing at the end of our three weeks here. Perhaps by then a longer ride through the Tuscan hills wouldn't ruin me for an entire day!

AMP IT UP

Continuing to tackle the Tuscan hills was a good idea in theory, but in practice it wasn't always as easy as it sounded. We had taken a day off the previous day, and I was raring to go! I felt great, or so I thought. We had stocked up at the grocery store, so we had a hearty breakfast. With a day of rest and a solid 10 hours of sleep under my belt, I was as ready as I could be, right?

We started the first climb, and oh baby, I felt those legs. All the climbing had gotten to them. I finished the climb, but knew I was slower than I wanted to be. We carried on. We continued through a couple of towns, and climbed up into Panzano, a village that was close to home and a great place to stop for gelato. Alas, there was no gelato for me today. We had no time to stop.

The plan was to go through Panzano and down the other side where another climb awaited us, but the climbing up to the town was painful. My legs were sore, and I just didn't have much oomph. We had been out for nearly two hours. I was tired and lunch was calling, so we packed it in and headed to the finish.

I felt beaten and disappointed. The Tuscan hills had completely whipped my ass. I wanted to be able to climb like I had two days ago with a relentless attitude and legs to back it up. I thought about how hard this cycling was as I ate my lunch, and I really hoped that my legs would rest up tonight and come through for me tomorrow.

There was still hope that the more I chipped away at this, the more strong rides I would have. It was just so easy to get so excited when I performed well, and to expect a repeat performance the next time I went out. Perhaps one of the hardest parts of training was repeating, repeating, repeating, and expecting the same performance every time. I believe that one of the most important lessons to learn is to focus on the present, the current ride at hand, and to patiently take it one day at a time, accomplish one ride at a time, and simply do the best you can on any given day.

My Tuscan Husband

I had a couple of sick days where I felt like I was in a fog. On those days, I felt like I was missing out on the beauty that was all around me. That's not to say that there weren't upsides to be found on those days, though.

My first sick day ended with the arrival of two beautiful wood fired thin crust pizzas brought home by my husband. As we devoured them, he told me of his adventure walking through the town of Greve and taking it all in. He then told me about driving to Panzano and making a stop at the pizzeria, but leaving without pizza in hand as the look of them just didn't meet his expectations. He started driving back towards the villa and stopped at the pizzeria in the tiny town at the main road. It really was hardly a town, but more of a collection of a few homes and a pizzeria. He described to me how he waited for the pizzas and sipped a beer on the patio, looking out at the Tuscan countryside.

As he enjoyed the moment, some American tourists entered the restaurant and engaged him in conversation. He ended up providing them with all sorts of advice, including which sights to see and which to miss. He even helped them with the menu by providing full descriptions of a truffle and a porcini mushroom! I delighted in the story, and referred to my husband as my little Tuscan.

The next day we went to the large outdoor market in Greve. It was so much fun! All around us were loads of fresh fruit and vegetables that looked luscious, ripe, and colourful. After checking out the entire scene, we waited patiently at the produce stand that we had chosen for its large red peppers and delectable-looking oranges. It took a while as there was no formal system and bunches of little old Tuscan ladies barked out orders to the cheerful servers dishing up fresh produce, checking with each customer to verify quantity and quality.

We were finally noticed, and were handed fresh pea pods larger than we could ever imagine back home to munch on while we awaited our turn. As we delighted in the sweet peas dissolving on our tongues, we enjoyed the scene around us. Eventually it was our turn to shop. We walked away with a large bag of better quality produce than we could find at the grocery store for the unbelievable price of €6. Besides, where else would you get such an experience? We were in awe.

We rounded a corner to find ourselves staring at a plethora of olives, sun dried tomatoes, dried fruits, and a multitude of other delicacies. Not sure what to choose, we stood staring dumbfounded at the millions of choices in front of us. The man behind the counter solved our problem as he handed each of us a variety of olives individually pierced by little toothpicks so that we could try them for ourselves. That helped us to decide, and soon enough we walked away with a bag of large, sumptuous green olives, small black marinated olives, sun dried tomatoes soaked in olive oil, and sweet dried mangos and kiwi. Yum.

From there, we found ourselves browsing the interesting variety of clothing. Since we had been wearing the same small selection of clothes for a couple of months now, we thought it might be time to pick up a couple of new items. James's one pair of shorts had become filthy and almost worn through in the wrong areas, so when we saw some shorts that suited his style, away we went trying to find some that might fit. With no other way to determine how the Italian sizes translated to the sizes we know, he was soon pulling on shorts over the thin bathing trunks that he was wearing in lieu of his fraying shorts. Next thing you know, the Italian man behind the table was next to James pulling out all of the color combinations available in his chosen side. We walked away successful. What a fun day!

Later on, we attempted to BBQ. The device that we had initially thought might be an outdoor BBQ had turned out to be an outdoor oven for pizza and bread. I would love to use one of those one day, but for now we had been hoping for an actual BBQ. Marco, one of the owner's sons, had been gracious enough to accommodate our request. The day after our exchange, he had showed up with boxes and began assembling the BBQs for the different units in the villa. Marco, the groundskeeper, assisted Marco, the son, and away they went! Based on how many Marcos we have met, I am convinced that it is the most common name in Tuscany.

Now, equipped with briquettes, a lighter, and some strange white cubes that we had been instructed to light, we made our way out to the brand new little BBQ that had been assembled especially for us. Unfortunately, it was a bit windy and the white cubes would not stay lit long enough to heat the coals. Fortunately, James stayed true to his persistent nature and eventually got it working. After being told to sit down because he had everything under control, I resorted to sipping wine and admiring James's new shorts as I watched him cook the whole fish he had bought and stir the roasting potatoes, carrots, and red pepper from the market.

On With The Training!

I didn't know it when I sat and drank my coffee while writing and reading the quiet morning away, but it was about to be a perfect day. After breakfast we went for a ride. It was my first after a few sick days in a row, and I was aching to be on my bike. I longed for the fresh air and the adrenaline that rushes through my veins as I approach a steep climb. I am not, and never have been, good at being sick. All I can think of is the life that I am missing as I am bedridden, and here, in the perfect training grounds, all I had been able to do for days was to stare longingly at the little race bike over in the corner and wonder why we couldn't go outside together.

Staying indoors for multiple days in a row had been an exercise in willpower. I have learned, or might be starting to learn, that sometimes I do get sick and that pushing too soon does not make for good results. In fact, it only makes the situation worse. It hadn't been easy, but I had taken a couple of days to rest and respect my body. Could it be that I was actually learning the right balance, even in these perfect training grounds? Perhaps. Now, however, I was feeling healthy and ready to get out there. I could feel the Tuscan hills calling to me.

The weather was beautiful. It was sunny and warm, but not too hot. Off we went, up the climb to Panzano and then on to Greve. From there, we took off on a route designed by James, the cycling navigator.

We were soon on a quiet road surrounded by beautiful landscape. In the past, we had joked that the Tuscans only created a single type of road sign to warn of steep climbs, as all the signs that we had seen so far indicated the same 15% gradient. Today, though, we learned that there are in fact a variety of signs. We saw signs warning of 8, 9, 10, and 11% gradient, each of which was seemingly posted at random. It's like they use whatever sign they have readily available when they encounter a steep section, and then call it good enough!

As we worked our way up some steep sections, I started to lay it down. I stood on the pedals most of the time, pounding out an acceptable cadence. I approached a sign that indicated a 10% gradient ahead. There was no way that the section that the sign referred to was a 10% gradient. It felt like at least 15%, and maybe even in the ballpark of 20%. The only way for me to get any momentum at all was to stand up and push full out, so that's what I did.

After a couple of sick days, my body was not quite where I wanted it to be. I had the legs and the attitude, but soon I felt like I was either going to barf or faint. Probably barf. I pushed through for a bit, but the nausea got worse. I had to stop just before the last tough section. I caught my breath, and then I continued. This time, I made it.

The rest of the ride was wonderful. We had a fairly flat trek back to Greve, then a long but gradual climb that took us to Panzano. My legs were burning, but with lactic acid buildup rather than fatigue. What a feeling. I had pushed my limits, and my body was getting used to this. It felt so good to be out there doing what I had come here to do.

As we cycled through Panzano, we investigated the little booths comprising what appeared to be a small outdoor market. We decided that we needed more wine and cheese for our pasta meal tonight, but that we wanted to come back to make our purchases so that we didn't have to carry wine on the descent back to the car.

We finished our trek to the car and then drove back. James waited in the car with the bikes while I walked over to the booths. The lovely woman behind the wine counter offered me some samples of wine, and of small bits of bread dipped in olive oil. She showed me a picture of their farm where they produce both the wine and the oil. She asked me where I was from, and we exchanged friendly banter as I completed my order.

After purchasing a €10 boxed package that included two wines, I moved on to the cheese table, which was literally a long table covered in cheese. I asked for pecorino, and the woman guided me to that section of the table. She quickly starting cutting pieces of cheese for me to sample, and soon my hands were full. I choose a creamier version for sandwiches and snacks, and a harder, sharper version for our pasta. Communicating quantity is an informal thing at such an outdoor market. In this case, I indicated that I had a total of €10 left and ended up with two nicely-sized pieces for a total of just over €6. I eyed the honey table longingly, but I knew I didn't have enough money. Next time, perhaps.

I rejoined James at the car, and together we returned home to the villa. That evening, I sat and sipped the wine purchased at the market, and looking forward to a lovely evening and a tasty dinner. It had indeed been the perfect day.

The training itself is a journey, and was what really brought us here. The journey, it turns out, isn't only about the bikes. It is, in fact, so much more. Surrounded by the beauty of the Tuscan hills, the warmth of the people, and the experience of a culture so entirely different than our own, it is hard not to learn and grow as a person.

DEPLETION AND PATIENCE

On our third day of consecutive riding in the Tuscan hills, we rode to Gaiole and back. The first day we had tackled steep gradients. The second day we had done a longer route with a 19 km climb. Now, on this third day of riding, the first climb out left me feeling depleted. My legs felt good. Mentally I was pumped up for the ride. My body, however, was simply physically not quite up to snuff from the accumulative effect of the previous days' exercise.

We finished the first climb and followed it with a fairly flat longer stretch. After a while, we stopped for a bit and I wolfed down my banana. Off we went, onwards towards Gaiole. After cruising through town, we faced another good climb to complete the loop back. By this point, I had already dipped into my stash of snacks again to grab a power bar. I was still starving, so we indulged in the remaining apples, bars, and dried fruit that were stuffed into the pockets of my jersey.

I had reached that point where the cumulative effects of riding were completely in play. My body was in a state of constant hunger and an overall fatigue. As we made our way up the last trek of climbing, I felt the gnaw of my hunger and I dreamt of pizza, pasta, and salad with sun dried tomatoes and artichoke hearts. My mind drifted to my fatigue, but then I started to think of how the different parts of me actually felt. My legs felt strong. My mind was focused. I was surrounded by lush trees and my nostrils were filled with their delicious scent. I breathed in the fresh air and let it fill me up entirely. I asked myself, where would you rather be right now? The answer was, nowhere else but here.

The Tuscan hills were the most spectacular training grounds that I could ever imagine. Free from the four walls that usually surrounded me as I puff away and pedal towards a nonexistent destination, here I could enjoy beauty, fresh air, and great climbs. I was riding a bike that was fitted for me, light and fast and one of the coolest racing bikes I had ever had the privilege to ride. My training grounds were in the heart of the countryside surrounded by rows upon rows of vines, trees and hills. My daily replenishment was fresh local produce, whole fish doused in local olive oil and sea salt, and fresh pasta topped with mushroom or tomato sauce made fresh from local ingredients. How could I possibly want to be anywhere else?

I thought of how I used to sit at a desk, longing to be out on my bike. I thought also of how I used to go to the gym day after day to push myself as hard as I could in the hope that when I finally did get out on my bike I would be able to ride well. So, this was it, the moment that I had been thinking about and preparing myself for all this time. This was the culmination of all of my training.

As my thoughts built to this point, I felt myself completely sink into the moment. I was truly here, right now, in this place and at this time. My legs found a rhythm that produced a reasonable speed that I could sustain in my depleted state. As we neared the intersection where we would shift from working our way upward to coasting downwards home, I caught a glimpses of James in the distance. This was great. This was confirmation that I had not let my depletion get the best of me and that I had in fact maintained a good pace. As my riding partner had once said, even a bad day on the bike is better than a day without the bike.

The next day, I knew I needed to rest. Sounds simple enough, but remember that responding to this type of need is not my specialty. There are times when one must buck up and battle through. There are also times when one should listen to what their body is telling them and back off. To distinguish these two scenarios, it is vital to tap into your inner self and become aware of your body and what it is saying. I knew that I needed to stop, and that if I did I could then start another string of riding days. I think I really was learning the right balance.

A Madman Emerging from a Cloud of Dust

We had really settled into our Tuscan lifestyle. The villa we were staying in truly felt like home. I preferred the madness of a market filled with old Tuscan women barking out orders to a well organized grocery store. A cup of coffee simply had to be rich with a frothy top, and be enjoyed on a patio in the center square of a small town. Every day included olive oil pressed from olives grown on local farms, fresh cheese rich with flavour, and the smoothness of a local red chianti tantalizing our taste buds.

Driving to the nearest town was a roller coaster adventure of manoeuvring around tight corners and up steep inclines. The atmosphere was chaotic, passionate and full of warmth. We were surrounded by neatly manicured vineyards and open, green countryside. The evenings were blanketed with a feeling of serenity and peace. This was our world, only for three weeks, but for long enough that I could feel completely submerged and like I never wanted to leave.

We had dived into the cycling aspect of this new world just as deeply as we had sunk into our physical and cultural surroundings. The Tuscan hills had become our training grounds, and we cycled every day that we possibly could. Every ride was an adventure, every ride was a challenge.

We often found ourselves chatting with fellow cyclists and sharing our love and respect for the hills that we were all attempting to conquer. Near the end of one of our rides, we were conversing with a group of fellows who had come over for a multi-day cycling tour. One of the guys asked me if I had ridden in Maui before. I quickly realized that I was wearing the jersey that I had bought from the cycling shop that we had booked our tour through when we took on the volcano. We chatted excitedly about our experiences with the same tour guide, and how much we had loved the coastal roads on the island. There's nothing like such incredible shared histories to bring people together.

The famous Giro d'Italia was in progress during our time in Tuscany, making it easy for us to immerse ourselves in the world of professional cycling. Some of the stages even occurred fairly close to where we were staying, making it exceptionally real to us.

Partway through our wonderful time in Tuscany, we had the opportunity to welcome two amazing people to stay with us. We had met Amy and Mark only a short time ago in Ireland on our bus tour. They were two of the warmest, most sincere, and easygoing people we had ever known. Like us, their plan had been to travel around for a while, and we had kept in touch with them. When we found out that they were going to be in Italy, James suggested that they join us in Tuscany for a few days. To our delight, they were able to fit a visit into their schedule.

When we picked them up at the train station, I was already so in tune with my surroundings that it honestly felt like we were welcoming guests to our home. We whisked them off to our villa in the Tuscan hills, and I could see a very familiar look of rapt excitement in their eyes as they took in the surroundings. I don't think it took them very long to feel like Tuscans. They were an absolute delight to spend time with, and we all enjoyed the local scenery, food, and wine together.

Mark and Amy were with us for about three days, and on the last full day of their stay a big adventure unfolded. We had all awoken from a restful night of deep sleep, had enjoyed a lovely breakfast, and were ready to head out shortly to drive around to some of the local towns.

As we were getting ready to go, I found James sitting contemplatively in our room. I knew something was on his mind, so I prodded at him a little to spill his thoughts. It turned out that he was struggling with the balance of being a good host and not missing out on the opportunity of a lifetime. This was the day of a very interesting stage of the Giro d'Italia, which included a fairly significant stretch of extreme gravel roads and a sharp descent. The cycling pros would be conquering gravel on lightweight carbon frames designed for smooth roads. It would be dangerous, exciting, and like nothing we had ever seen.

We talked about it, and then decided to go downstairs to see if our guests would be open to a new agenda for the day. Mark and Amy had made it clear that they didn't want us to change our plans while they were with us, and Mark seemed to have quite an interest in the cycling races that James had talked so much about. With encouragement both from me and from Mark, we all agreed that we should abandon the sightseeing plan and catch the race stage instead. I don't think any of us really realized how adventurous it was actually going to be.

We packed into the car, and off we went. The stage was already underway as James drove us rally style down the autobahn. Once we were off the freeway, we manoeuvred through small towns until we reached a back road. To our dismay, the access road to the town near the gravel portion of the stage was blocked off for the race. We were going to have to walk.

Before we set off on foot, we decided to hightail it back to the closest town to grab some sandwiches and drinks since we didn't know if there were going to be any restaurants or stores on our path once we got moving. Armed with food and beverages, we sped back to the closed off road and parked in a lineup of cars along the side of the road so that we could start walking.

We were moving at a good pace and at a decent incline, but I could see that James was chomping at the bit to move even faster. I told him to go ahead, and that we would find him later. He took my advice, quickening his stride and leaving me behind to walk with Amy and Mark.

The hike was longer than I would have expected. It was hot, it was dusty, and it wasn't the easiest terrain. Amy and Mark must have been wondering if this was a typical day in the Hiner household, and honestly, it was. I was quite used to James's adventurous style by now, but I am sure that most people are a little surprised the first time they are exposed to it.

Eventually, the three of us reached a town, and Mark and Amy found a nice little spot to sit, enjoy their lunch, and see the cyclists come through. I decided to let them relax while I pressed on. I had James's sandwich and beer in my backpack, and I thought it might be nice for him to have a cold one while enjoying the race.

The road continued upwards and eventually turned to gravel. I picked up my pace, and soon I was sweating substantially. Onwards and upwards I pushed. This was more like a hike than a walk, and I had no way of knowing how long I had already been trekking along. I eventually came upon a bunch of the team support cars perched a short distance down the descending side of the peak. I am sure that they were strategically positioned to deal with any technical difficulties that had resulted from cycling on gravel before the riders embarked on the steep incline. I could see the helicopters that are usually used to film pro races overhead, and I could hear a lot of commotion ahead. I realized that this would have to be my end point as I could not continue on the road since the racers would be coming through soon.

I scaled up a small cliff and sat on the grassy perch. I didn't have long to wait before the commotion grew louder, and soon the few cyclists leading the race appeared. At first the cyclists came in small bunches, but soon more and more of them were arriving in larger and larger packs. I even saw Mark Cavendish!

I watched in bewilderment as they came flying around the corner and began to descend at ridiculous speeds over the loose gravel. Dust flew everywhere, and at one point, one of the support cars pulled out and blocked off part of the road. As the dust cloud grew bigger and bigger, the car was hidden from sight, and some of the riders had to screech to sudden a halt to avoid smashing into it. The whole thing was crazy! The excitement and at times chaos around me were insane.

After the bulk of the riders had gone by, things started to settle down a little. For a while the occasional straggler would appear, but eventually they had all gone by. The other people watching began to disperse, but I continued to sit and enjoy the calm after the storm. I waited for a while, relaxing and hoping that James had found a prime spot.

I was still sitting there lost in thought when someone emerged from the top of the hill. He was walking down the gravel road, completely covered from head to toe in dust. I took another look and thought to myself that I recognized those shorts and that pink Giro d'Italia shirt. I realized that it was James! As he approached me, I could see a huge smile on his dust-covered face. I looked at him, and in my bewilderment at his filthy state I asked him how he could see. He removed his glasses and attempted to clean them off a little. He looked like he had literally emerged from a cloud of dust. It turns out that he had.

I handed him a beer and we got moving. While we walked back down to find our friends he told me of his crazy adventure. I had thought that I had been sitting in a dangerous spot of the race until I heard his story. Concerned that he would miss the part of the race after he left us, he had started running. Yes, James had run uphill, on gravel, for about ten kilometres. He said he was drenched in sweat by the time he reached the top of the climb.

He had found a seat in the inside of a sharp corner, just below the peak where the riders would be starting to descend. With the peloton getting closer by the second, one of the security men had asked James to please stand on the other side of the guard rail. It was a good thing that he had. As the riders had approached the corner, the dust had continuously risen until it grew into a full on cloud. The riders had rounded the corner at such speeds that it was shocking that none of them slid out. A lot of them had had one of their shoes unclipped from the pedal, which was unheard of, but necessary due to the loose gravel. The dust cloud had continued to grow, and visibility had diminished. In my mind's eye, I could just see James standing there in complete bewilderment, heart pounding, camera clicking, being eaten up by the dust cloud. Even in this retelling of his adventure his voice was full of excitement and passion, and I could feel his contentment.

We found our friends in the town where I had left them. We wandered into the local bar, ordered a drink, and caught the end of the cycling stage on the television. The experience couldn't have ended better. We wearily walked back to the car and raced back on the autobahn to the quiet Tuscan hills.

We stopped in the lovely little medieval town of San Gimignano just as the sun was setting. Amy was able to take some lovely photos, and we picked up some mushrooms for the pasta sauce we were going to make for dinner and of course some wine for us. In true Tuscan fashion, we dined late and enjoyed several glasses of wine each.

To this day, I can't imagine what must have been going through Mark and Amy's heads during their stay with us, especially in light of our adventure on their final day. Honestly, we must have looked like crazy people. They were the perfect guests, though, and if there was any part of that day that they didn't enjoy, they didn't even slightly hint at it. Now, that is true grace and style!

THE EGYPTIAN PAINTER

We were nearing the end of our time in Tuscany, so we decided to take a day to explore the medieval town of San Gignamano. It had been highly recommended to us by a lovely Australian couple who were staying in one of the units in the same villa as us. We had cycled to San Gignamano, and our brief glimpse of it had piqued our curiosity. Taking the time to explore it in earnest was an idea we happily embraced.

This time, we decided to drive so that we could properly explore all the little treasures that San Gimignano had to offer. As we walked towards the town center, a collection of art spilling out of a shop caught my eye. There is nothing more wonderful than not having a schedule and being able to meander wherever your heart pulls you. Into the shop I went with James in tow. We were slow to enter as we took in the works surrounding us with each step. A particular piece caught both our eyes. The paintings all appeared to be watercolor, yet this particular piece portrayed such incredible detail that we were in awe.

The man in the small shop was delighted by our interest, and was soon pulling out works in response to the ones that we gravitated towards and holding them up into the light and at various angles so that we could examine them more thoroughly. We asked him if these were his, and he declared that yes, these were his masterpieces. He told us, "I have time!" and continued to remove and insert pieces into the little collage he had formed for us in the prime spot of the shop.

James picked out a collection of three small works aligned horizontally and beautifully mounted and matted. I stared at this perfect little set portraying different seasons, and I felt myself being pulled into the Tuscan countryside and filled with warmth. We both agreed that we wanted to take it home with us. We inquired about shipping and being able to order online, and the artist responded that yes, he can ship anywhere, but that it was better to see the work and pick it out here instead of ordering online.

In light of his advice, we continued our examination. We took our time, carefully scrutinizing many of his works and enjoying the engaging conversation that he offered. Eventually we settled on the beautifully mounted set of three seasons and a second work that depicted a mountain scene. The artist then declared that he would need to call his wife as he did the painting and she handled everything else! He picked up his phone, and from outside we heard a ring.

In the few moments it took for her to appear, he explained that his studio was next door and he lived upstairs. His wife entered. The artist declared to James, "My wife is short like your wife! Like good wine in a small bottle!" As his wife measured and calculated, he told us that he was from Egypt, and that was where he had attended art school. His wife was from Tuscany. They lived here, but spent several months a year in Egypt.

As he talked, he looked directly into my eyes and the warmth of his energy filled the room. He was so centered, so complete. He knew exactly who he was and he was brimming full from the life that he lead. He told us that he doesn't have an abundance of things, but that he has enough, and that his life is balanced. He and his wife have been together for 35 years and have worked together every day, with him painting and his wife doing anything necessary to support his painting. She handles all of the logistics, and she was the one who had matted the painting that we bought. They were an impressive couple!

Eventually, his wife calculated the shipping cost. The artist happily announced that it was pretty much what he had estimated to us initially. We were able to pay for the works with our credit card, but we would need cash for the shipping. Since we didn't have any, we would need to visit a bank machine to complete the transaction. Before we left, we inquired how late he would be open. He declared, "It is simple. I am here. My door is right there. Any time, you come back. If you don't pay, I don't ship!" The last bit was punctuated with some merry laughter.

After a long lunch in the main square, a visit to the gelato shop, and some shopping for an assortment of delectable items including biscotti, dessert wine, and pasta made with truffle, we headed back to the art shop. As we walked in, I declared, "We pay, you ship!" The artist giggled. We finalized our deal, took a picture with the cute little couple, and left the town replete with a second dose of the warmth and content energy that the Egyptian artist seeped.

MOVING ON TO BIGGER PEAKS

It was time to move to the French mountains, and to put our Tuscan training to the test. There was so much I had learned from our weeks in Tuscany. To this day, it remains one of the most perfect training grounds I can imagine. The beauty of the hills and the passion of the people had swept me away into another world. Surrounded by a level of zeal that even surpassed my own, I learned to transform my fire into fuel and to tackle the steep, unforgiving Tuscan hills with zest. My attitude and my legs grew stronger as day after day I got on the little race bike I had rented and simply got out there.

Tuscany taught me patience. When I was sick, I respected my body. Instead of hindering my recovery by pushing on, I made the difficult decision to hold back and give myself time to heal. The result was a shorter recovery period, and more net days on the bike. I also learned to be patient while on the bike. Consecutive training days take a toll. Pushing hard and exceeding my limits is very important, but so is taking a rest day when I know that I have gone as far as I can. This one simple ability, to truly listen to my body and to know when I needed a break, would become a crucial skill as we moved on to the French and Italian mountains.

I had finally learned to let go, to allow myself to completely sink into my surroundings and the moment. There was so much more to life than work and training. Life had become a daily adventure to experience. The craft of cooking and enjoying local, fresh ingredients slowly and while connecting with the people around me had transformed what I used to know as dinner time into a complete experience. Allowing my soul to completely connect with my surroundings, to be in the moment and to stop, entirely stop, and take a look around had opened up entirely new worlds to me.

The day didn't have to be about executing a carefully laid out schedule to accomplish a set of tasks. Yes, that was an important skill back home, one that had helped to get me to the place where I was now. Now that I was here, the ability to completely let go of my structured life and to let my heart guide me had opened up new experiences that could have easily been missed. Allowing myself to be swept away into adventure had exposed me to moments that I never knew existed. I didn't always need to be in control. It was possible for me to let go and simply chase a man in a Giro d'Italia shirt up the side of a mountainside and into a cloud of dust.

These were my thoughts as we moved on to the French mountains. I am not sure that I was aware of it at the time, but I was completely ready for the challenges that lay ahead. A part of my heart would forever remain in the Tuscan hills, but my legs and my dreams would take me to mountain peaks.

GETTING SERIOUS – FRANCE

' *"There is no use trying", said Alice; "one can't believe impossible things." "I dare say you haven't had much practice," said the Queen. "When I was your age, I always did it for half an hour a day. Why, sometimes I've believed as many as six impossible things before breakfast." ' – Lewis Carroll*

THE FRENCH ALPS…MORE COMPLETE!

On this trip I had the opportunity to climb Alpe d'Huez for the second time. It was quite an experience. Seven years after my first ascent, there were some drastic differences. What surprised me more than the differences, though, were the significant similarities between the two ascents.

The first time I had ascended Alpe d'Huez had also been my first time climbing a real mountain on a road bike. At the time, I had had absolutely no idea what I was getting into, and I had not really understood the concept of training. I had just begun to learn how to ride a road bike.

On our first trip, we had stayed at the top of the mountain and descended before trying an ascent. With dramatic switchbacks, gradients of up to 10%, and no guard rails most of the way, the descent had been a psychological monster. My arms had been in pain from braking so much. My confidence had been nonexistent. At the bottom, I had had a good cry and wondered how I was going to make it back to the hotel for the evening. This had been one of my most significant lessons in the power of the mind, and how easy it is to talk yourself into or out of almost anything. After facing the first brutal switchback on the way back up, I had stopped and wondered how I would do all 21. This had continued for a while. Eventually my mind had switched from wondering to just doing.

Since the climb had been a time trial in the Tour de France that year, there had been pros training at the same time that we were climbing. I will never forget the sense of awe that I felt when Ivan Basso, the lead rider of team CSC, passed me. His cadence had been smooth as silk, and his speed had been amazing. He had been worried about performance whereas I, feeling the effort of every single pedal stroke, had merely been worried about making it back to my hotel! As we had dined in the hotel that evening, I had looked out in awe at the 21 switchbacks that my legs had somehow carried me up.

Seven years later, we drove from Tuscany through the Italian Alps and into the French Alps. The beauty of the landscape was breathtaking. We stopped in the town of Borg d'Oisans at the base of Alpe d'Huez. After finding a hotel and bikes, we dined right across the road from where we had had lunch after riding in the area so long ago. It felt like things were coming full circle, like I was back somewhere that I was always meant to return. We had a lovely salad Nicoise, some wine, and a wonderful chat with two chaps from Montreal.

The next morning, we fuelled up on steaming hot quiche and very strong cafe au lait in the prettiest little patisserie as we eyeballed the luscious freshly baked treats on display. We were able to withstand the call of the treats, instead choosing to hop onto our rental bikes and make our way towards the Alpe. We started to climb.

After what seemed like an impossibly long first stretch, I finally passed the sign that indicated switchback number 21. They are numbered from the bottom of the climb starting at 21 and ending at one at the summit. I was surprised by how long and difficult this first stretch had been, and I wondered how, seven years ago with no clue as to what I was getting into, I had showed up and actually made it up this brute.

The climb was tough. The switchbacks were steep and gruelling. Some of them were so long you wondered if you would ever make it to the next numbered sign. Thinking of my fitness and nutrition regimen over the last year, and all that I have learned about cycling, I continued to marvel at how I had made it up the first time we came here. Between the more gruelling sections, I took moments to look around me and was amazed at the beauty everywhere my eyes rested. Those lovely views made every pedal stroke worth it.

As we neared the top, the temperature dropped, and a light snow began to fall. We cycled past the hotel we had stayed at on our first trip, and then on to the very end of the Tour de France stage finish. As we took photos, put on our jackets, and made our chilly descent, I was surprised by how much I had to brake and the resulting pressure on my arms. It turns out that my memories of this descent from all those years ago really hadn't been exaggerated!

Alpe d'Huez: 13.2 km, average gradient 8.1%, maximum gradient 13%, 1071 m ascent

Fortunately, this second time was different than the first in many important ways. I didn't cry. I didn't question whether or not I could make it. I even pushed fairly hard on the first sections and stood on the pedals at the steeper sections. I was, however, quickly reminded by the beginnings of a cramp that I needed to pace myself. None of this came as a surprise. What did surprise me was the significant similarities between the two ascents. It was tough. This mountain demanded respect. A positive mental outlook was mandatory. It was just me and a bike going at a pace that I could maintain and make it to the top. I definitely developed a fresh new respect for that girl who had showed up here seven years ago and taken on a mountain that struck fear within her.

CONTINUING TO CLOSE LOOPS

The day after Alpe d'Huez we took on one of the Tour de France monsters, Croix de Fer. This was to be another homecoming for us. Seven years ago we had also attempted this mountain the day after climbing Alpe d'Huez.

There is nothing easy about Croix de Fer. The first part is a continuous and gruellingly steep ascent. There is just relentless climbing without any switchbacks to offer some relief. After making it through this first section, we found that we were already becoming depleted. We were extremely relieved to find a restaurant open in a little town a little further on, especially since the first time we had tried to do this climb nothing had been open. We simply had not had enough sustenance to get us to the top.

As we devoured plates of pasta and de l'eau de la montagne, a couple of guys from Quebec who were also attempting the climb joined us. When we were replenished, we continued on with them. We climbed the second part of this ascent, also relentless and steep, straight into a head wind. I felt like I was barely moving. I wanted to pull over and lay in the grass. I just couldn't believe how hard it was!

My body was definitely not feeling as strong as it had the day before, but if there was one lesson I had learned well by this point it was that giving up wasn't an option. I just kept focusing keeping my legs going one pedal stroke at a time. I finally caught up to where James was waiting and was delighted with his news that the hard stuff was done and we only had 11 km to go of the 27 km climb. Best of all, the gradients that were still ahead were much less than those that we had already faced!

After a rest and a much needed boost of my mental state, on we went. The gradients were indeed better, and the headwind had let up a bit. We biked for what felt like forever, and despite the improved conditions I started to feel defeated again. Just as I was starting to feel hopeless, I spotted James just up the road! I started to slow down, but he told me to keep going and that we were almost there as he pointed at our destination. I could see it! That was all the motivation I needed to dig in for the final push.

We finally made it, and I felt so happy to be at the top! We were so deep into the mountains. The view was absolutely breathtaking. It was a clear day and the mountaintops were still dusted in snow. What beauty.

The descent was going to be chilly, so we bundled up. I did my best to prepare mentally, knowing that there we a couple of sections of climbing on the way back. I really hoped they weren't too long. As we made our way down, I found it hard to believe how far we had ascended. It was crazy. This was one of those rides that left me absolutely physically and mentally exhausted, but also 100% satisfied and a bit emotional about what we had accomplished, especially since the last time we hadn't made it. This time, thanks to the little restaurant and some positive reinforcement from my cycling partner, we had reached the top.

Later, I sank into the deep soaker tub in our hotel room and relaxed into the hot water and soft bubbles as my whole body went limp with exhaustion. My bath was followed by a fantastic meal and a couple of glasses of wine. We slept like we were in some sort of coma.

On the third day we tackled Les Deux Alpes, a smaller but still respectable climb. I wondered if I would be able to move at all after the exertion of the last two days, but I wound up surprising myself by moving better than I would have thought possible. We had to cycle about 11 km, mostly climbing, to get to the base of the mountain. The ascent itself was nine km of switchbacks.

Once we got going, I was pleased by how well my body responded. My legs weren't just okay, they were good. It was a beautiful sunny day, and I felt very light and positive. The route itself was gorgeous. I found myself taking the advice of a wise woman who sometimes spoke in a Maudlin style, and I took every opportunity to really look around me to appreciate the beauty everywhere. I truly felt that all parts of me, physically, mentally, spiritually, were in harmony. At the top, we had lunch on a patio in the sunshine. What a wonderful day.

Croix de Fer: 27.53 km, average gradient 4.7%, 1292 m ascent

The first few days in Borg d'Oisans were one of my favourite parts of our European cycling adventure. Hard work and patience had truly paid off. Never in a million years had I thought that I would be riding a bike up famous mountains, let alone conquering three of them on consecutive days. Thanks, mom, for having the patience to teach me how to ride a bike so many years ago. Thanks, James, for turning me into a road cyclist.

Finally Learning to Fly!

After completing Alpe d'Huez, Croix de Fer, Les Deux Alpes, and Col du Lautaret, we had one riding day remaining in Borg d'Oisans. We decided to take on Alpe d'Huez one last time. It was quite a warm day, much nicer than the day of our previous climb. We agreed that we would do our best to take the climb all in one shot, time trial style. Off we went.

The first four switchbacks were a challenge, especially that first one as it seems to go on forever. It just wouldn't let up. Keeping in mind that we were simulating a time trial, I was able to push quite hard for almost a third of the way, and then ease up a little to catch my breath for a few precious moments before going full tilt again. Who knew when I would be back here? We certainly don't get to climb these mountains every day.

I continued to push it out, constantly monitoring my cadence and willing myself into a good flow. As I approached the halfway point and didn't see James at all, I realized that the decision was definitely made: We weren't stopping. Once you are past that halfway mark, it just starts to make less and less sense to take a break.

I continued counting down the switchbacks, and once I had only four left, I really laid the hammer down. What reason did I have to hold back now? The remainder of the climb was not long, so I didn't have any reason to save up any energy. Besides, I was quite curious to find out how far ahead James was. By the time I hit the second last switchback I was flying, or at least I felt like I was. I whizzed by a couple cycling casually around the switchback and posing for the camera (there is a guy that perches there all day to take pictures and hand out cards so you can order them online). As I rounded the switchback, he took several action shots, and then placed the card in my jersey pocket and yelled, "Continue!"

A short time later, I rounded the corner and saw the sign with the number one on it. At that point, I absolutely laid it down and put forth everything I had. This was the time to show myself that I do indeed have a set. I was sure that Mark Cavendish had never held back on a sprint to a stage finish, so what was I waiting for? I flew by a patio filled with cyclists claiming to have reached the top, but I knew that I wasn't finished until I saw James. Just as I suspected, he was sitting right by the Tour de France "Arrivée" sign indicating the stage finish. Completely out of breath, I asked about my time, and was informed that it was 1:33. Not bad! It just felt so good not to hold back anything at all.

This was truly one of the most amazing moments of my long cycling journey. It had taken a lot for me to get to this point, but here I was fresh from biking up a famous French mountain without stopping once. I had affected an attitude of continuously willing myself to push harder and harder, holding nothing back as I put it all out there. I had achieved the fitness and the legs to back up my attitude.

This journey wasn't something that simply happened for me. Before climbing my first real mountain on a road bike, I had had no idea what real physical exertion felt like. I hadn't known a thing about training, heart rates, food as fuel, and the physical and mental gusto that it takes to execute an athletic accomplishment of such magnitude.

Once I had committed to cycling, I had spent years and years trying to balance an intense career with meal planning and training routines. Each time I got off track, I regrouped and redirected myself. When I got sick, I was forced to be patient. Day after day after day I had executed whatever piece of training I had planned until it became habit.

During our European adventure, I had learned to get up each day and get out there on the bike and try. All of the pieces had come together and here I was now, once again at the summit where it all began. This time I felt a triumph that I had never guessed would be mine.

That evening we dined at our favourite restaurant in Borg d'Oisans and drank wine under the stars. We bade farewell to the little town that we had called home for a week, and wondered when we would be back again.

Les Deux Alpes: 17.78 km, average gradient 5.3%, 949 m ascent

Col de Lautaret: 27.75 km, average gradient 3.1%, 853 m ascent

A Daunting Climb: Snow, Hail, and Gaping Cliffs

The next day was a day of logistics. We drove to Briancon where we ended up setting up camp for a few days. We checked in to a lovely hotel run by the friendliest people. We delighted in the cozy little log cabin-style room we were given, and in the rather spacious private balcony with a full mountain view that came along with it. After checking in, we walked through the town in search of bikes to rent.

We found the most amazing bike shop. The guy running the place, who was perhaps the owner, spent a good couple of hours making sure that we had everything we needed. He sized me up and decided that I could use his daughter's Trek for my adventures. I had never had such a detailed bike sizing session in my life. Every bit of that bike was adjusted to fit my body perfectly. Logistics complete, we ended the day by fuelling up with wood fired pizza and a good night's sleep.

The next day, we decided to take on Galibier, which has been the highest point of the Tour de France on a number of occasions. After a full week of significant climbs, I felt ready to really tackle this one without any shred of self doubt or worry. I was deep into the mindset of climbing French mountains, and doubt simply had no place in my life anymore.

To get to Galibier, we would first need to make the gradual 24 km ascent up Lautaret. At that point we would be at the start of the 8 km Galibier stretch, which had a bit more of a challenging gradient. We made reasonable time to Lautaret without breaks. It was a long stretch, but it felt good. I just sank into the ride and got into a really good flow despite the irritating head wind.

When we did take a break, it was just to have a quick Orangina and to fill our water bottles before heading towards the summit. The roads in this part of our trek were a bit sketchy, quite narrow in spots and uncomfortable without guard rails. I tried to focus on the road ahead rather than looking over the edge of the daunting cliff beside me. The terrain was also intimidating; it was quite surreal to be so high up and completely exposed on the side of this mountain. Snow surrounded me and the chilly air nipped at me.

My legs were a bit tired, and they were definitely feeling the steeper gradients. I kept telling myself to just keep going, just keep going. I needed to keep my nerves in check and stay focused. I counted down the kilometres, and next thing I knew, I only had two left to go.

At this point it started raining with hail sprinkled in. I got to a point where there was a barrier ahead, and it was unclear upon first glance if I would be able to get through. I found shelter in a lonely little shop perched on the mountainside and took stock of the situation. James was nowhere to be found. I looked ahead, and was able to determine that a cyclist could go around the barrier. It had really started to rain and hail quite hard. I looked up at the daunting last kilometre and knew that James was up there.

This was decision time. I knew it would take me a while to make this last stretch, and that I would end up drenched. I knew from experience how cold it was to descend a brute like this even when I was dry. I knew that James would likely take a snapshot, then get the hell down from there. I took another look up, and then decided that I should stay put. I didn't want either of us to get wetter and colder than necessary.

Just as I expected, a few minutes later I saw him descending. Soaking wet, he joined me under the shelter where we waited for the rain to let up. The road was sketchy enough when it was dry, and we didn't need to increase our chances of sliding off the side of the cliff on the way down.

Once the rain slowed to a drizzle, we had to get going down as it was going to take time to battle the cold, wet, and slippery conditions. I had dealt with this type of situation before on Furka Pass, an experience that served me well now. This time, I simply gathered my nerve and followed James slowly down the scary, winding descent.

I lost most of the feeling in my fingers and toes on the way down, but I didn't really have time to think about it as I concentrated on the slippery road and sharp turns. Once we made it down to the longer stretches of road that lay in the direct sun, the warmth fueled us and allowed us to pick up the pace. This part of the ride was truly glorious. I basked in hot sunshine and the feeling of freedom after the physical and mental feat that I had just accomplished. I had worked hard and kept my nerve on that entire climb. Breaking free of worry, doubt, and nervousness, even for one significant climb, felt amazing.

I indulged in a fantastic nap in the late afternoon after our return to the hotel. When I woke up, James was nowhere to be found. Since we were in a town with one main street and one bar, I was pretty sure he was either walking around or sitting and enjoying a well-earned beer. I got ready for dinner, and then chilled out for a while.

I was just thinking about meandering down the main street to find James when he burst through the door. He told me to come! I followed him to the bar where he introduced me to his new friends, a group of three cyclists from London. What a hoot! It is so easy to meet people in places like this where everyone goes to the local spot for an evening aperitif. The time passed, and we chatted and laughed and drank delicious Belgian beer.

After a surprisingly large number of beverages had been consumed, our three new friends decided to cycle the short distance to their hotel and get cleaned up for dinner. I was amazed that they could ride at all. James and I continued with the beers while we waited for them to return. We chatted about our ride up Galibier as we listened to the sounds of Guns and Roses coming from inside the bar. When our friends returned, more beers were consumed and then we eventually made our way to a pizzeria to enjoy more delicious thin crust wood fired pizza. We were so wound up by then that we must have been a sight in this little town.

The next day, we were regretting the number of beverages consumed the night before. It would have been easy to take a day off, but we knew that we had one day left here and that there was still one more French mountain to climb. We got moving.

The goal was to summit Col d'Izoard. It was a good climb, that's for sure. Despite my slow, hungover state, the scenery was unbelievable. As we made our way up, we approached a little town nestled into the mountainside that I swear could have been part of a postcard. Little cottages were perched perfectly on the green hills surrounding the little town, with a glistening stream running through it.

We continued on, and soon found ourselves on a series of switchbacks within a small forest. It was lovely. It was also getting quite difficult in my weakened state from too much Belgian beer. I willed my legs to continue. I had gotten myself here, and now I needed to get myself to the top.

After leaving the forest, I found myself looking up at more switchbacks. Now that I was above the treeline, snowy peaks glared down at me. The gradients were significant and I was running out of water. At least there was a solution for that problem: the nice thing about this time of year in the French mountains is that all of the snow is melting, which creates many opportunities to enjoy the runoff of l'eau de la montagne!

That cold refreshing water was exactly what I needed to continue on. I felt replenished, and I was sure I could make it to the top of this beast. My confidence faded a bit after another few pedal strokes, but I willed myself on and was so happy when I saw James looking down over the last switchback! Victory, again. Next time, less beer.

Lautaret: 27.75 km, average gradient 3.1%, 853 m ascent

Galibier: 8.52 km, average gradient 6.9%, maximum gradient 10%, 585 m ascent

ON TO THE CLIMAX

It seemed unbelievable to me that we had conquered so many big French mountains in such a short time. Returning to Alpe d'Huez had showed me that what I used to have to break down into little pieces in order to digest, I could now swallow up in a single attempt. Moving right on to Croix de Fer the very next day and then achieving a successful outcome had showed me that consecutive climbing days were now possible for me. Continuing on for a third day with Les Deux Alpes had been proof that I could simply climb the French mountains day after day.

The cherry on top had been the time trial up Alpe d'Huez. How was it that the girl who barely made it to the top of this beast so many years ago could now cycle to the summit as fast as possible, as if in some sort of race? It seemed that all the years of training and learning, succeeding and failing, but continuing to redirect and to dig deep, had completely paid off. Of course I was intimidated by these mountains, and of course doubt and worry found their way into my thoughts. This time, though, drive and belief had won! I will never forget what it felt like to fly up the last switchback of Alpe d'Huez without a doubt in my mind.

With the French chapter of our European adventure now at a close, we were to move onto the final and most challenging piece: The Dolomite mountains of northern Italy awaited us. As with the French Alps, there was unfinished business for me in these Italian beasts. As we started heading towards Italy, I didn't overthink it. I simply allowed myself to move into the next transition.

Getting Serious – Italy

'Aut inveniam viam aut faciam (I shall either find a way or make one).' – Hannibal Barca – Contributed by Calvin Chow

A Barren Brute

My stomach churned, mixing together the sensations of nausea, nervousness, and adrenaline into a perfect storm that left me feeling like pulling over and puking, and yet strangely elated at the same time. It was the result of simultaneous excitement and raw fear, the true sign that I was out of my comfort zone. Oddly, this was a feeling that had become addictive for me. The more I put myself into these types of situations, the more normal it was beginning to feel.

This time, I found myself heading to the base of the barren, monstrous Gavia. The last time I had been here, the only thing I had felt was the churning of my nerves. Years ago I had slowly struggled my way up this mountain while constantly combating my fears. This time I recognized the sick feeling. I embraced it, and I felt it evolve into excitement.

Like a raging bull locked in a pen, I raised my hoof and pulled it back through the dirt to indicate my eagerness to be released. I flared my nostrils, thick mucus seeped out to signify my ferociousness. I eased into a reasonably aggressive, yet comfortable flow. Two cyclists were riding ahead with heavy packs and mountain bikes, and I felt my adrenaline soar as my natural competitiveness kicked in. Don't take it personally, boys. I weigh less than you, my Madone 3.1 is lighter than your heavy bikes, and if I didn't pass you, then it would be my fault for not trying hard enough. I whizzed by, pigtails flapping in the wind.

I had the attitude, the legs, and the fire for this mountain today, but alas, today would not be the day that I would achieve my second summit up this beast. Not far into the ride, I caught up to James. He was pulled over to the side, waiting for me, which was really unusual. He was always the one to charge to the top of a mountain without a second thought. He was always the one to wait patiently for me, to encourage me, and to convince me that I, too, could make it to summit after summit.

He was not well and wasn't going to be able to make the ascent. I wasn't going to climb this mountain on my own without him, so we made our way back to town. It turned out that both of us would experience some illness over the next couple of days. We took some time off to rest, and spent a wonderful restoration day in the healing pools in Bormio. We soaked in the water, feeling it pumping health into our bodies. While we soaked we gazed up at the mountains surrounding us, waiting for us to climb them.

We were finally able to take on Gavia a few days later. Once again, I was amazed by my ability to ascend this absolute brute years back. The climb up Gavia is not for the faint of heart. Its unrelenting, steep switchbacks just keep on coming, turn after turn after turn. The mountainside is barren and rough, leaving you with a feeling like you are all alone in the middle of nowhere. It is a physical and psychological beast.

The first time I did this climb, I think I was simply awestruck by my surroundings to the point where all I could do was focus on one pedal stroke at a time. This time, I found myself standing up on the pedals, pushing out the steeper sections, and welcoming my heart as it tried to pound its way through my chest. I felt like I belonged here on this carbon fibre bike on the side of this mountain, surrounded by rock and snow as I pushed my limits. There was no sign of the girl that I once had been.

At the summit, we took our picture and then made our chilly descent. It was not warm. We did not have much extra clothing with us to put on. We made the rookie mistake of not bringing full gloves. We had to stop several times on the way down to try and force some feeling back into our fingers so that we could actually brake and not fly off the mountainside.

It was cold and it was tough, but the only solution was to continue on towards our cozy little hotel. The relief of pulling up to the hotel was wonderful. After such exertion, a warm shower and a comfortable sweater are the most amazing things ever. We rested, and we planned out our next adventure.

Gavia (from Bormio): 25.6 km, average gradient 5.5%, 1404 m ascent

ME AND MORTIROLO

Mortirolo is a mountain in the Italian Dolomites that is also known as a famous climb of the professional cycling race known as the Giro d'Italia and the women's version, the Giro Donne. There are many sections of this climb that are 15% gradient or higher, with a maximum gradient of a whopping 24%. Of the 12 km that comprise the climb we planned, the middle six stay at an average gradient of about 13% with plenty of 20% and above.

At these gradients, I have to put my entire being into the effort of climbing. It is a true challenge. Climbing Mortirolo from the difficult side allows the cyclist to pass by the memorial in honour of Marco Pantani, who holds the record time for this ascent of 42 minutes. This climb is considered to be one of the most difficult in the world by many of the pros, and is easily hard enough to make a grown man cry. Now I know why.

I became aware of this climb years ago during our first Italian cycling tour. I watched as my husband's battle with the mountain unfolded, although I never made the attempt myself since I was completely depleted from the plethora of climbs already conquered by the time this one entered my life.

Things were different this time around. Now, deep into our European cycling adventure, I finally found myself overcoming years of inconsistency in my ability to commit to my cycling passion. I had been able to execute a long cycling season including a trip to Napa Valley in the spring, biking to work all summer and into the fall, and completing a tour in San Diego in the fall. I had committed to a very regimented gym routine that had gradually ramped up as the off season went on. I had augmented this routine with sessions with an amazing personal trainer who pushed my limits, built my confidence, and knew just how to deal with all of my attitude. I had backed all of this up with a balanced nutritional approach to fuel my body for all the hard work I was putting it through.

In addition to my training efforts, I had now spent the past several months cycling in Europe. During this time, I had graduated from training rides in Mallorca to interval-style climbing on the hills of Tuscany. From there, I had gone on to tackle the longer climbs of the French Alps. Now I was finally ready to face the steep monsters of the Italian Dolomites.

I looked forward to returning to the little town of Bormio nestled in the Italian Dolomites, and I toyed with the idea of attempting Mortirolo. The more I thought about it, the more I realized that this was the time to do it. As the week in Bormio went on, Mortirolo became a concrete part of our agenda.

The hotel we were staying in was full of cyclists, all attempting to conquer the same climbs that we were taking on. There was so much talk in the lounge each evening about what everybody would be attempting the next day. On the eve of our attempt, my head was buzzing with all sorts of thoughts amidst these conversations. We had spent this particular evening chatting with three guys who were also going to attempt Mortirolo the next day. There was plentiful talk about the difficult gradients and the narrow road, and general comments about how hard it would be. Our new friends were even watching a video that took you to the top one painful switchback a time.

Their comments all mixed together in my mind. I had heard so much about this mountain, and I was genuinely afraid of experiencing it in the morning. I was unspeakably nervous, but I knew that I wouldn't be satisfied until I had seen it for myself.

I am not sure how well I slept as my mind worked and worked, trying to convince me that I would make it. Many years ago, James had completed the climb up Mortirolo and had declared that it was the most unpleasant thing he had ever done and that he would not do it again. Despite his long ago assertion, he got up the next morning and lead me out on his bike to the base of the climb. It took us about an hour to get there, and the whole way I felt combined nerves and excitement churning my stomach.

When we reached the bottom of the ascent, we stopped and had a snack. I was so nervous that I wanted to barf. I am so glad that James put his coach hat on and coaxed me into eating that banana anyway.

We started to climb. The first difficult section reared its head within the first three km. The long, steep road glared down at me dauntingly. I rose to my feet and pushed out each pedal stroke. My breath was heavy, my heart felt like it was going to pound out of my chest, and my whole being was consumed by the effort. I knew that I could not stop until I got to the next turn where the road would be flatter, as stopping on such a steep incline would not end well. I could see James waiting just ahead, so I took a deep breath and willed myself on.

Once I was stopped, I declared how hard this was and I questioned why I even wanted to do this. I honestly think that if James had not been there, I may have turned back. Fortunately, I had his support and company to keep me motivated. At this point, he was completely in coach mode. He told me that I was talking myself out of this. He told me that all I had to do was calm down, not stop on really steep parts to prevent falling and the inability to get going again, and take breaks at the flatter ends of each switchback.

We continued. I repeated his pep talk over and over in my mind. I stopped whenever I reached a flatter corner and my heart was pushing its way out of my chest, which happened a lot. Piece by piece, James and I chipped away at the beast. I soon found myself all in and only looking forward. There was no time now for questions or nerves.

The next thing I knew, my coach was telling me that we only had two and a half kilometers left of the brutal six km stretch of road in the middle of the climb. Then there was only one km remaining. When I reached the water fountain that I had seen pictures of, I recalled the words that I had heard James say. He had told me that when you reach the water fountain, you know you will be ok. I cycled past the Pantani memorial, and tears welled in my eyes with the power of the moment. Just a few more kilometres to go, with only an average of about eight to nine percent! I never thought that nine percent would feel so easy.

When I saw James, my husband, my coach, waiting ahead at the top, I felt overwhelmed. He cycled towards me, and we crossed the finish line together. We chatted excitedly with the other triumphant cyclists, and we even got our picture taken together at the summit sign.

Sounds of thunder interrupted our impromptu party, and we all quickly prepared for the descent. It was a long, tough journey home. The trek was a good 30 km, mostly upwards, and left me completely depleted and desperately wanting it to be over. Despite my fatigue, however, I felt so triumphant that I simply dug deep and put my head down.

Back in our hotel room, the beer and ham sandwich that I gobbled down tasted like the most glorious things I had ever consumed. As I soaked in a hot bubble bath, the fatigue fully set into my body. I felt like a bit of a gimp as I hobbled around that evening. We celebrated our accomplishments with a bottle of champagne over dinner, and a frosty limoncello in the cozy lobby afterwards. I felt exhausted, beat up, happy, and very grateful. What a journey.

The next day, we drove to the top of Stelvio on our way to our next destination. I found a cycling jersey bearing the names Gavia, Stelvio, and Mortirolo. I felt that I now had the right to wear such a jersey, and thus made the purchase. Then we indulged in one of the famous sausages at the little carts at the top of this amazing mountain.

Mortirolo (from Mazzo): 12.4 km, average gradient 10.5%,
1300 m ascent

After a long day of driving, we spent a lovely evening in the coastal town of Riccione. Here, I relearned the true meaning of celebration. The full realization of what I had achieved completely sank in throughout the course of the day. That evening, we sipped wine and limoncello for hours on a patio, people watching and enjoying the fresh sea air. I found myself a sugar cone topped with a largely disproportionate amount of cioccolata (chocolate) gelato, and we animatedly challenged each other over multiple courses of a Fast and Furious arcade racing game. We ended the evening with the most glorious sleep ever, with our hotel balcony doors wide open so the fresh sea air could pour in and the gentle sound of crashing waves could lull us into a deep slumber.

OVER AND OUT

*'Sometimes you already are what you are striving to be'. -
Source unknown*

She was a little ways ahead of me, wearing a sporty red kit and some shiny carbon. She looked strong. She rounded the corner, stood up on her pedals, and pounded her way up the short, steep climb.

As I approached the corner just behind her, I looked ahead at her and then focused inwards. I stood up and refused to cower away from the steepness ahead of me. I ground out every pedal stroke. My heart was pounding hard against my chest.

She was still there, still ahead but no further than she had been. The gap between us had not opened. This girl, she must be better than I am. She looked so strong.

The steepness subsided, but the hill wasn't over. She sat up. I did not. I started to close the gap. Could this be true? Was I going to pass her? You bet. I wasn't letting up until I reached the top. This girl, she must be something that I could never be. Beating her was going to be a challenge.

I put my all into speeding up, drawing alongside her. Then I was ahead, and as I passed her I realized: I am her.

Acknowledgements

A big thank you to my editor, Elyssa Gutbrod. She transformed my words into a work of art while allowing my voice to shine through.

A sincere thank you to all the people who inspired and supported me on my journey. You will find yourselves embedded within the chapters of my story.

A warm thank you to all of the people who contributed inspirational quotes.

Thank you mom for your sincere excitement and joy when you saw the first proof of this book, and for all the help editing the pictures.

CPSIA information can be obtained
at www.ICGtesting.com
Printed in the USA
FFOW02n2047300417
35106FF